SPURGEON
ON THE BLOOD
OF CHRIST

SPURGEON
ON THE BLOOD
OF CHRIST

CHARLES H. SPURGEON

Compiled and Edited by Beverlee J. Chadwick

BRIDGE
LOGOS

Alachua, Florida 32615

Bridge-Logos

Alachua, FL 32615 USA

Spurgeon on the Blood of Christ
Charles H. Spurgeon
Compiled and Edited by Beverlee J. Chadwick

Printed in the United States of America.

Library of Congress Catalog Card Number: 2015937461
International Standard Book Number 978-1-61036-148-4

VP 04-13-15

TABLE OF CONTENTS

Preface 1

A Brief Biography of
Reverend Charles Haddon Spurgeon. 3

PART ONE—THE SACRIFICE 35

Christ—Our Substitute. 37

Christ Our Passover 57

The Exodus 79

The Only Atoning Priest. 99

PART TWO—THE BLOOD 121

The Blood 123

The Blood-Shedding 143

The Voice of the Blood of Christ 159

The Precious Blood of Christ 181

The Blood of Sprinkling—Part One of Two 205

The Blood of Sprinkling—Part Two of Two 227

PART TWO—THE BLOOD WASHED 249

Walking in the Light and Washed in the Blood 251

The Three Witnesses. 273

The Meat and Drink of the New Nature 297

Depths and Heights Intended For Reading 321

Truly Eating the Flesh of Jesus. 337

The Double Forget-Me-Not 359

Study Guide 381

PREFACE

CHARLES SPURGEON presented many sermons on the blood of Christ Jesus. He looked at the preciousness of the blood from many aspects and for us to obtain any conception of the unspeakable preciousness and value to God—and its efficacy on our behalf—we must read and meditate on these aspects presented in these writings by asking the Holy Spirit to enlighten our understanding and show us how each vital aspect of the shed blood applies to us and our eternal salvation through Christ Jesus our Lord and Savior.

Spurgeon's whole ministry was based on 1 Corinthians 2:2, *"Jesus Christ and him crucified."* The great truths in the Word of God from which he never deviated, defined everything for him and greatly benefited those hearing his preaching and reading his inspired and timeless books. Regarding sermons, Spurgeon said: "Our sermons should be our mental lifeblood—the outflow of our intellectual and spiritual vigor; or, to change the figure, they should be diamonds well cut and well set, precious intrinsically and bearing the marks of labor. God forbid that we should offer to the Lord that which costs us nothing."

In this book Spurgeon presents the aspects of the sacrifice of Christ's blood including: reconciliation, cleansing, sanctification, baptism, justification, redemption, peace, communion, and much more. Jesus said in Matthew 26:28 *"This is my blood of the New Testament"* and it was founded and ratified in the blood of Christ. In Hebrews 13:20, the Apostle Paul says, Jesus' blood is *"the blood of the everlasting covenant."*

The precious gift of Jesus Christ, His sacrifice, and His holy blood opened the portal of redemption and reconciliation for every true believer to have a Father-to-child and child-to-Father

1

relationship with our holy God. You will gain knowledge, spiritual understanding, and a deeper love for God, Christ Jesus and the Holy Spirit as you read these sermons on the blood of Jesus prayerfully presented to us from the Word of God and the Spirit-inspired mind and pen of Charles H. Spurgeon, the Prince of Preachers.

All glory and praise to God,
Beverlee J. Chadwick, Senior Editor
Bridge-Logos, Inc.

A Brief Biography
of
Reverend Charles
Haddon Spurgeon

CHARLES HADDON SPURGEON was born on June 19, 1834, in Kelvedon, Essex, England, 40 miles northeast of London. Early in his life it was obvious he was destined to be a preacher like his father and grandfather who were both independent ministers. Charles Spurgeon's conversion took place on January 6, 1850. He was fifteen years old at the time and here in his own words is how it happened.

"I sometimes think I might have been in darkness and despair now, had it not been for the goodness of God in sending a snowstorm one Sunday morning, when I was going to a place of worship. When I could go no further, I turned down a court and came to a little Primitive Methodist Chapel. There might be a dozen or fifteen people in that chapel. The minister did not come that morning: snowed in, I suppose. A poor man, a shoemaker, a tailor, or something of that sort, went up into the pulpit to preach. He was obliged to stick to his text, for the simple reason he had nothing else to say. The text was, *'Look unto me, and be ye saved, all the ends of the earth'* [Isaiah 45:22]. He did not even pronounce the words rightly, but that did not matter.

"There was, I thought, a glimpse of hope for me in the text. He began thus: 'My dear friends, this is a very simple text indeed. It says, "Look." Now that does not take a deal of effort. It ain't lifting your foot or your finger; it is just "look." Well, a man need not go to college to learn to look. You may be the biggest fool, and yet you can look. A man

3

need not be worth a thousand a year to look. Anyone can look; a child can look. But this is what the text says. Then it says, "Look unto me." 'Ay,' said he, in broad Essex, 'many of ye are looking to yourselves. No use looking there. You'll never find comfort in yourselves.' Then the good man followed up his text in this way: 'Look unto Me: I am sweating great drops of blood. Look unto Me; I am hanging on the Cross. Look: I am dead and buried. Look unto Me; I rise again. Look unto Me; I ascend; I am sitting at the Father's right hand. O, look to Me! Look to Me!' When he had got about that length, and managed to spin out ten minutes, he was at the length of his tether.

"Then he looked at me under the gallery, and I daresay with so few present, he knew me to be a stranger. He then said, 'Young man, you look very miserable.' Well, I did; but I had not been accustomed to having remarks made on my personal appearance from the pulpit before. However, it was a good blow struck. He continued: 'And you will always be miserable—miserable in life and miserable in death—if you do not obey my text. But if you obey now, this moment, you will be saved.'

"Then he shouted, as only a Primitive Methodist can, 'Young man, look to Jesus Christ.' Then and there the cloud was gone, the darkness had rolled away, and in that moment I saw the sun. I had been waiting to do fifty things, but when I heard the word look, I could have almost looked my eyes away. I could have risen that instant and sung with the most enthusiastic of them of the precious blood of Christ, and the simple faith that looks alone to Him. I thought I could dance all the way home and I now understand what John Bunyan meant when he declared he wanted to tell the crows on the plowed land all about his conversion. He was too full to hold it in. He must tell somebody. There was no doubt about his conversion; it went through every part of his being.

"As Richard Knill [a missionary] said, 'At such a time of the day, clang went every harp in Heaven, for Richard Knill was born again'; it was even so with me."

Spurgeon later said if there had been a pile of blazing faggots [bundles of sticks] next to the church door, he could have stood in the midst of them without chains, happy to give his flesh and blood and bones to be burned, if only such action might have testified of the love he felt for Jesus. "Between half past ten, when I entered that chapel, and half past twelve, when I returned home, what a change had taken place in me!"

Spurgeon, who was soon to become known as "the boy preacher," was admitted to the church at Newmarket on April 4, 1850. At that time, he had not yet received the Lord's Supper, because though he had never heard of Baptists until he was fourteen, he had become convinced, by the Church of England catechism and by study of the New Testament, that believers in Christ should be baptized in His name after they received Him, and so he naturally desired baptism before his first communion.

He could not find a Baptist minister anywhere nearer than Isleham, where a Reverend W. W. Cantlow, who was a former missionary in Jamaica, ministered. Having decided to go there to be baptized, Charles first wrote to his parents to ask permission. They readily consented, although his father warned him that he must not trust in his baptism, and his mother reminded him that though she often prayed that her son would be a Christian, she had never asked that he would be a Baptist. Spurgeon playfully responded that the Lord had dealt with her in His usual bounty, and had given her exceedingly, abundantly, above all that she had asked.

It was on his mother's birthday, May 3, 1850, that Spurgeon "put on Christ," just short of his sixteenth birthday. He rose early in the morning, spent two hours in prayer and dedication, and walked eight miles to Isleham Ferry, on the river Lark, which is a beautiful stream that divides Suffolk from Cambridgeshire. Though there were not as many people at the baptism as there normally were on a Sunday baptism, there were a sufficient number watching to make Spurgeon, who had never seen a baptism before, a bit nervous. Here is his description of the scene.

"The wind blew down the river with a cutting blast as my turn came to wade into the flood; but after I had walked a few steps, and noted the people on the ferryboat, and in boats, and on either shore, I felt as if Heaven and Earth and hell might all gaze upon me, for I was not ashamed, then and there, to declare myself a follower of the Lamb. My timidity was washed away; it floated down the river into the sea, and must have been devoured by the fishes, for I have never felt anything of the kind since. Baptism also loosed my tongue, and from that day it has never been quiet."

That evening a prayer meeting was held in the Isleham vestry, at which time the newly baptized Spurgeon prayed openly. The people wondered and wept for joy as they listened to the lad. In the morning he went back to Newmarket, and the next Sunday he had communion for the first time, and was appointed a Sunday school teacher.

Some years later he wrote, "I did not fulfill the outward ordinance to join a party and to become a Baptist, but to be a Christian after the apostolic fashion; for they, when they believed were baptized. It is not a question whether John Bunyan was baptized, but the same question can never be raised concerning me. I, who scarcely belong to any sect, am nevertheless by no means willing to have it doubted in time to come whether or not I followed the conviction of my heart."

Later that year he moved to Cambridge. In the winter of 1850-1851, when he was just sixteen, he preached his first sermon in a cottage at Teversham, Cambridge. He hadn't planned on preaching there; in fact, he hadn't known he was going to, but he was tricked into it by a Mr. James Vinter in Cambridge, who was president of the Preachers' Association. Bishop Vinter, as he was generally known, called on Spurgeon one morning just as school was dismissed, and told him "to go over to Teversham the next evening, for a young man was to preach there who was not much used to services, and very likely would be glad of company."

Bishop Vinter apparently knew Spurgeon well, for a direct request for him to preach probably would have been refused. But Vinter knew that the young man had in him those qualities that make great preachers, and he only had to get started. Considering Vinter's reason for the ruse, it was excusable—it was also successful. Spurgeon and the other young man Vinter had mentioned started off in the early evening along the Newmarket Road to Teversham. After walking some distance in silence, Spurgeon expressed the hope that his companion, who was a bit older, would sense the presence of God when he preached. Horrified, the older man said he had never preached, could not preach, and would not preach. The older man said there would be no sermon at all unless Spurgeon preached. Spurgeon hesitated at first, saying he did not know what he could preach. The older man replied that if Spurgeon would just give one of his Sunday school teachings it should do quite well. Spurgeon then agreed to preach, and reproached himself for his hesitation: "Surely I can tell a few poor cottagers of the sweetness and love of Jesus, since I feel them in my own soul." Now having settled the matter, it was as if the Lord himself walked with them as He did with the two men on the road to Emmaus.

Spurgeon's text that memorable evening *was "Unto you therefore which believe he is precious"* [1 Peter 2:7]. Then he expounded the praises of his Lord for nearly an hour, while those gathered in that thatched cottage listened attentively, enthralled with the eloquence of the young lad. When he finished, he was happy with the fact that he had been able to complete his sermon, which showed how little he thought of his preaching ability. Spurgeon then picked up a hymnbook to close out the service with praise and worship songs. Before he could starting singing, however, an aged woman called out, "Bless your dear heart, how old are you?" Perhaps a bit prideful, or embarrassed to tell how young he was, Spurgeon replied, "You must wait until the service is over before making any such inquiries. Let us now sing."

During the friendly conversation that followed the singing, the elderly woman asked Spurgeon again, "How old are you?"

To this Spurgeon replied, "I am under sixty."

"Yes," said the elderly woman, "and under sixteen."

"Never mind," Spurgeon said, "think of the Lord Jesus Christ and His preciousness." Then upon the urging of several of the church members, he promised he would come back—if Bishop Vinter thought he was fit to preach again.

From that small but notable beginning, Charles Spurgeon's fame as a preacher spread around the countryside, and he was invited to preach in Teversham both on Sundays and weekdays. Over the years in his writings and sermons, Spurgeon described his daily routine in those days. He would rise early in the morning for prayer and reading the Bible, and then he would attend to school duties until about five in the evening. Almost every evening he would visit the villages near Cambridge to tell the people what he had learned during the day. He found that those things took solid hold of him when he proclaimed them to others. He also said he made many blunders in those days, but he usually had a friendly audience and there were no reporters at that time writing down his every word.

Spurgeon promised to preach at the small Baptist church

in October of 1851 in Waterbeach, six miles from Cambridge. The chapel at Waterbeach was a primitive building with a thatched roof, which was common in those days. Spurgeon promised to preach for a few Sundays, but continued for more than two years. It was here that he published his first literary work: a gospel tract written in 1853. When Spurgeon took up the pulpit at Waterbeach, the village was notorious for its godlessness, public drunkenness and profanity, like many of the towns where Charles Finney preached during the Great American Awakening. And like those towns, Waterbeach was soon to come under the power of the gospel, for God had sent His chosen messenger there. Here is Spurgeon's account of the changes that took place.

"In a short time the little thatched chapel was crammed, the biggest vagabonds of the village were weeping floods of tears, and those who had been the curse of the parish became its blessing. I can say with joy and happiness that almost from one end of the village to the other, at the hour of eventide, one might have heard the voice of song coming from every rooftree, and echoing from almost every heart."

Spurgeon's first convert in Waterbeach was a laborer's wife, and he said he prized that soul more than the thousands that came afterward. She received Christ at the Sunday service, and early the next morning the seventeen-year-old Spurgeon hurried down to see his first spiritual child. "If anybody had said to me, 'Somebody has left you twenty thousand pounds,' I would not have given a snap of my fingers for it compared with the joy I felt when I was told that God had saved a soul through my ministry. I felt like a boy who had earned his first guinea, or like a diver who had been down to the depth of the sea, and brought up a rare pearl."

Spurgeon's style and ability were considered to be far above the average from the beginning of his ministry. Of these early days, his brother James wrote, "When I drove my brother about the country to preach, I thought then, as I have thought ever since, what an extraordinary preacher he was. What wonderful unction and power I remember in some of those early speeches! The effect upon the people listening to him I have never known exceeded in after years. He seemed to have leaped full-grown into the pulpit. The breadth and brilliance of those early sermons, and the power that God's Holy Spirit evidently gave to him, made them perfectly marvelous. When he went to Waterbeach his letters came home, and were read as family documents, discussed, prayed over and wondered at. We were not surprised, however, for we all believed that it was in him."

It's a measure of how much Spurgeon ministered in the country where God had placed him that by the time he was called to London he had preached six hundred and seventy sermons.

While the young Spurgeon was busy in Waterbeach and content to stay there, the New Park Street Baptist Church in London was looking for a pastor who could revive its fallen condition. It was an influential church because of having probably the largest chapel of any Baptist church building—it could seat nearly 1200 people, and was one of only six churches that had a listed membership of over three hundred. For a number of years, however, the church had been unable to find pastors of any distinction and the active membership had dwindled to less than two hundred. At this time the pastorate had been vacant for three months, and then they discovered nineteen-year-old Charles Spurgeon.

It happened unexpectedly. George Gould, a deacon of the church at Loughton, Essex, was in Cambridge and attended the anniversary meeting of the Cambridge Sunday School Union. Charles Spurgeon was one of the speakers. During their speeches, the two older speakers scorned Spurgeon's youth. Spurgeon asked if he could reply. Both his speech and his reply so impressed Gould that when he returned to London one of the New Park Street deacons, Thomas Olney, complained to him that they had been unable to find a suitable pastor, Gould suggested young Spurgeon. The suggestion was ignored the first time it was made, but when it was made again at a later date, Olney spoke to another New Park Street deacon and they agreed "to try the experiment" and wrote to Waterbeach, which was the only address they had, and invited Spurgeon to preach one Sunday.

When the invitation reached Spurgeon on the last Sunday of 1853, he was certain it was a mistake and passed the letter to Robert Coe, one of his church deacons. Coe said he was certain it *wasn't* a mistake, and that what he had long dreaded had happened. But he was surprised at the invitation coming so soon and coming from London, which was "a great step from this little place." Spurgeon still wasn't convinced, but on November 28, he wrote a cautious answer to the invitation, and said that he was willing to go to London for a Sunday, but suggested that the invitation was probably a mistake since he was only nineteen, and was quite unknown outside of the Waterbeach area. A second letter from London, however, eased his mind and he arranged to preach at New Park Street on December 18, 1853.

When the reluctant Spurgeon reached London he was greeted with a total lack of hospitality. Rather than house him in the home of one of the affluent members, as was often the custom with visiting clergy, they sent him to a boarding house in Queen's Square, Bloomsbury, where he was given a bedroom barely large enough to hold a bed. The clothing he wore clearly showed his country breeding and upon hearing he was going to preach at New Park Street, the other boarders told him tall tales of London's wonderful preachers. By the time Spurgeon went to his small bedroom to sleep, he was thoroughly discouraged, which, along with the unaccustomed street noise, kept him awake most of the night.

When he went to New Park Street the next morning and saw the imposing building, he was amazed at his own recklessness at thinking he could preach there. If he hadn't been certain of his calling, he probably would have returned immediately to Waterbeach. But once in front of the sparse congregation that attended that morning—only about eighty people, he regained his normal confidence and delivered his sermon from James 1:17: *"Every good gift and every perfect gift is from above, and cometh down from the Father of lights, with whom is no variableness, neither shadow of turning."* His message so affected the congregation that after the meeting one of the deacons said that if Spurgeon was only with them for three months the church would be filled. News of the splendid young preacher from Waterbeach spread by word-of-mouth all Sunday afternoon, and that evening the congregation had more than tripled what it was in the morning. Among them was the young lady who was later to become Spurgeon's wife. His text that evening was from Revelation 14:5b: *"They are without fault before the throne of God."*

The people were so excited at the end the service that they would not leave until the deacons had convinced Spurgeon to come again, and before he left the building he agreed to return. Here is his account of that service. "The Lord helped me very graciously. I had a happy Sabbath in the pulpit, and spent the interval with warm-hearted friends; and when at night I trudged back to the Queen's Square narrow lodging, I was not alone, and I no longer looked on Londoners as flinty-hearted barbarians. My tone was altered, and I wanted no pity of anyone; I did not care a penny for the young gentlemen lodgers and their miraculous ministers, nor for the grind of the cabs, nor for anything else under the sun. The lion had been looked at all around, and his majesty did not appear to be a tenth as majestic as when I had only heard his roar miles away."

No other preacher who had spoken at New Park Street during the three months when the pastorate was vacant had been invited a second time, but Spurgeon was invited back on the first, third, and fifth Sundays of January, 1854. His ministry was so successful that on January 25, the Wednesday before the last Sunday, he was invited to occupy the pulpit for six months, with a view to becoming their new pastor.

Spurgeon was in Cambridge when the invitation from the church reached him, and he immediately wrote back stating that he dared not accept an unqualified invitation for such a long time. "My objection is not to the length of the time of probation, but it ill becomes a youth to promise to preach to a London congregation so long until he knows them and they know him. I would engage to supply for three months of that time, and then, should the congregation fail or the church disagree, I would reserve to myself the liberty, without breach of engagement, to retire, and you on your part would have the right to dismiss me without seeming to treat me ill. . . . Enthusiasm and popularity are often like the crackling of thorns, and soon expire. I do not wish to be a hindrance if I cannot be a help."

The suggested probation was cut short, however, when fifty of the men members signed a request to the deacons that a special meeting be called. The meeting was held on April 19, and a resolution was passed in which they expressed with thankfulness the esteem in which their new preacher was held and the extraordinary increase in attendance at all the church meetings. Thus they "consider it prudent to secure as early as possible his permanent settlement among us."

On April 28, just over four months after he arrived in London, the nineteen-year-old Spurgeon replied, "There is but one answer to so loving and candid an invitation. I accept it."

Then he asked for their prayers, "Remember my youth and inexperience, and I pray that these may not hinder my usefulness. I trust also the remembrance of these will lead you to forgive mistakes I may make, or unguarded words that I may utter."

Spurgeon was a man of great courage, especially when it came to spiritual matters and defense of the Bible. He once said, "I have hardly ever known what the fear of man means." Along with this, God increasingly added courage to his faith, until there was literally nothing that could stop him from doing the work to which God had called him.

In his exposition of the ninety-first Psalm in *The Treasury of David,* perhaps one of this greatest works, he wrote this: "In the year 1854, when I had scarcely been in London twelve months, the neighborhood in which I lived was visited by Asiatic cholera, and my congregation suffered from its inroads. Family after family summoned me to the bedside of the smitten, and almost every day I was called to visit the grave. I gave myself up with youthful ardor to the visitation of the sick, and was sent for from all quarters of the district by persons of all ranks and religions. I became weary in body and sick at heart. My friends seemed falling one by one, and I felt or fancied that I was sickening like those around me. A little more work and weeping would have laid me low among the rest; I felt that my burden was heavier than I could bear, and I was ready to sink under it. As God would have it, I was returning mournfully from a funeral, when my curiosity led me to read a paper that was wafered [taped] up in a shoemaker's shop in the Dover Road. It did not look like a trade announcement, nor was it, for it bore in a good bold handwriting these words: *"Because thou hast made the LORD, which is my refuge, even the most High, thy habitation; there shall no evil befall thee, neither shall any plague come nigh thy dwelling"* (Psalm 91:9-10).

The effect on my heart was immediate. Faith appropriated the passage as her own. I felt secure, refreshed, girded with immortality. I went on with my visitation of the dying in a calm and peaceful spirit; I felt no fear of evil and I suffered no harm. The providence which moved the tradesman to place those verses on the window I gratefully acknowledge, and in the remembrance of its marvelous power I adore the Lord my God."

Though only about eighty people attended Spurgeon's first service at New Park Street, it soon became impossible to crowd into the building all the people who wanted to hear and see "the boy preacher," and the services moved to increasingly larger buildings. Soon the decision was made to enlarge the New Park Street Chapel, and the services were moved to a public building, Exeter Hall. Although using a public place for churches services is common practice today, it was virtually unheard of in Spurgeon's day. However, even though Exeter Hall held several thousand more than the Park Street Chapel, it also wasn't large enough to contain the increasing crowds flocking to his meetings.

The work on the chapel took place from February 11 to May 27, 1855, and during this time Spurgeon became increasingly busy. Besides all his other ministerial duties and his writing, he was preaching as much as thirteen times a week. Soon his voice was overtaxed and the services in Exeter Hall were too much for him (keep in mind that there were no sound systems in those days and the preacher had to speak loudly enough for all in even the largest hall to hear him).

About his voice, his wife later wrote: "Sometimes his voice would almost break and fail as he pleaded with sinners to come to Christ, or magnified the Lord in His sovereignty and righteousness. A glass of chili vinegar always stood on a shelf under the desk before him, and I knew what to expect when he had recourse to that remedy. I remember with strange vividness the Sunday evening when he preached from the text, *"His name shall endure for ever"* [Psalm 72:17]. It was a subject in which he reveled, it was his chief delight to exalt his glorious Savior, and he seemed in that discourse to be pouring out his very soul and life in homage and adoration before his gracious King. However, I really thought he was going to die there, in the face of all those people. At the end he made a mighty effort to recover his voice; but utterance well nigh failed, and only in broken accents could the pathetic peroration [conclusion of the sermon] be heard—'Let my name perish, but let Christ's name last forever! Jesus! Jesus! JESUS! Crown Him Lord of all! You will not hear me say anything else. These are my last words in Exeter Hall for this time. Jesus! Jesus! JESUS! Crown Him Lord of all!' and then he fell back almost fainting in the chair behind him."

Their return to the enlarged New Park Street Chapel on May 31 was disappointing for it was discovered that the money spent on it was almost wasted. Several hundred more could get into the chapel. However, the crowds were larger than before and thousands were disappointed. They remained there for about a year before it became necessary to rent Exeter Hall again.

In the meantime, like George Whitefield, Spurgeon preached in the open air whenever the opportunity was offered, once in a field to a crowd of almost twenty thousand. Writing on June 3 of the same year to the soon-to-be Mrs. Spurgeon, Spurgeon said: "Yesterday I climbed to the summit of a minister's glory. My congregation was enormous; I think ten thousand, but certainly twice as many as at Exeter Hall. The Lord was with me, and the profoundest silence was observed; but oh, the close—never did mortal man receive a more enthusiastic oration! I wonder I am alive! After the service five or six gentlemen endeavored to clear a passage, but I was borne along, amid cheers, and prayers, and shouts, for about a quarter of an hour—it really seemed more like a week! I was hurried round and round the field without hope of escape until, suddenly seeing a nice open carriage, with two occupants, standing near; I sprang in, and begged them to drive away. This they most kindly did, and I stood up, waving my hat, and crying, 'The blessing of God be with you!' while from thousands of heads the hats were lifted and cheer after cheer was given. Surely amid these plaudits I can hear the low rumbling of an advancing storm of reproaches; but even this I can bear for the Master's sake."

As if on cue, the storms rumbled and rolled in. Spurgeon soon had almost as many detractors as he did admirers. On one occasion when his carriage was driven through a crowd in London, he was heartily hooted and booed. All throughout his ministry a portion of the press was scornfully critical of him. Spurgeon once said, "A true Christian is one who fears God, and is hated by the *Saturday Review*." But no matter how highly and often he was criticized, he never changed one dot of what he believed to be the truth of God. His Pauline Calvinism, his sturdy Puritanism, his old-fashioned apostolic gospel, remained unchanged to the end.

A criticism that followed him all his life was that he was conceited. His biographer, W. Y. Fullerton, wrote about this: "As to the question of conceit, in later years he gave a sufficient answer. 'A friend of mine was calling upon him some time ago,' wrote one after his death, 'and happened to say, "Do you know, Mr. Spurgeon, some people think you are conceited?"' The great preacher smiled indulgently, and after a pause said, 'Do you see those bookshelves? They contain hundreds, nay, thousands of my sermons translated into every language under Heaven. Well, now, add to this that ever since I was twenty years old there never has been built a place large enough to hold the numbers of people who wished to hear me preach, and, upon my honor, when I think of it, I wonder I am not more conceited than I am.' Upon which the writer remarks, 'That is the kind of bonhomie [geniality] that disarms criticism.'"

Spurgeon became known through much of London, but not all its inhabitants had heard of him. Strangely, what quickly made him known in every part of the city was an accident. The owners of Exeter Hall said they could no longer rent the hall to one congregation, so plans were immediately formulated to build a structure larger than the Hall that would hold the thousands the Hall could not accommodate. In the meantime, some temporary building was needed. Fortunately, the Surrey Music Hall, which could hold ten to twelve thousand people, became available. The news that Spurgeon was to preach in the Music Hall spread like wildfire, and on Sunday evening, October 19, 1956, the hall was jammed with ten thousand people and another ten thousand in the gardens surrounding the hall. The building was so crowded that the service began before its appointed time. A prayer was offered, then a hymn with the customary running commentary, then another hymn. Prayer before the sermon was being offered when suddenly a loud cry of "Fire!" rang throughout the hall. There was instant panic and bedlam. In the ensuing rush for the door, a stairway gave way and toppled people to the floor; others were knocked down and trampled underfoot. Seven were killed and twenty-eight were taken to the hospital seriously injured. There was, however, no fire; it was a false alarm, given perhaps out of malice against Spurgeon.

In the midst of it all, Spurgeon was unaware of the extent of the disaster, and did not know there had been any fatal injuries. He attempted to quiet the people, and at the urging of repeated cries endeavored to preach. He told the crowd the text he had intended to use was the thirty-third verse of the third chapter of Proverbs, *"The curse of the LORD is in the house of the wicked: but he blesseth the habitation of the just,"* and asked the people to remain quiet or retire gradually if they felt they must leave. But there were more disturbances, and the service had to be discontinued. Spurgeon was so distressed by it all; he had to be carried from the pulpit.

The next day every newspaper in London carried vivid descriptions of the disaster and the deaths and injuries and vilified Spurgeon for holding services in a public Music Hall. One leading newspaper said, "This hiring of places of amusement for Sunday preaching is a novelty, and a powerful one. It looks as if religion were at its last shift [a qualitative change]. It is a confession of weakness, rather than a sign of strength. It is not wrestling with Satan in his strongholds—to use the old earnest Puritan language—but entering into a very cowardly truce and alliance with the world." Within days every part of London was talking about the young preacher, and when he resumed preaching, after spending several days deeply depressed and discouraged, the crowds were larger than ever. Hoping to turn people against Spurgeon, the newspapers had done just the opposite, and made him the best known preacher in all of London. What the enemy had intended for evil, God had turned to good.

Through all the years of his ministry, Spurgeon's popularity increased until he was known all over the civilized world. His sermons were reproduced by the millions in virtually every language. Even today they are read more than any other sermons ever printed.

On March 25, 1861, Spurgeon preached his first sermon in his newest and largest building, the Metropolitan Tabernacle at Elephant and Castle, Southwark. The building would seat four thousand six hundred people, but often another thousand, and often more, found some place to sit or stand. One of the deacons once claimed that on a special occasion they had crammed eight thousand people into it. "We counted eight thousand out of her" he said. "I don't know where she put 'em, but we did."

D. L. Moody had not yet arrived on the London scene, but Spurgeon invited him to preach at the tabernacle, to which Moody replied, "In regard to coming to your tabernacle, I consider it a great honor to be invited; and, in fact, I should consider it an honor to black your boots, but to preach to your people would be out of the question. If they will not turn to God under your preaching, neither will they be persuaded though one rose from the dead." Moody did later preach for Spurgeon, and in writing to thank him, Spurgeon said, "I wish you could give us every night you can for the next sixty days. There are so few men who can draw on a weeknight."

That was the wonder of it, Spurgeon built a tabernacle seating between five and six thousand persons, able to contain over seven thousand, and for thirty-eight years he maintained that congregation there and elsewhere in London. Other great preachers, like Wesley and Whitefield, gathered as great crowds, but they traveled to various places to do so. Spurgeon remained rooted to London.

At a prayer meeting on May 26, 1890, Spurgeon looked around the Metropolitan Tabernacle and exclaimed, "How many thousands have been converted here! There has not been a single day but what I have heard of two, three or four having been converted; and that not for one, two, or three years, but for the last ten years!" It is an interesting note that additions to the church year by year were double the additions to New Park Street in the same periods of time, which shows that the number of new converts bears a relationship to the size of the congregation. With few exceptions, that great building was crowded every Sunday morning and evening for thirty years, and the attendance at the Thursday night meeting was usually even larger.

Spurgeon once said, "Somebody asked me how I got my congregation. I never got it at all. I did not think it was my duty to do so. I only had to preach the gospel. Why, my congregation got my congregation. I had eighty, or scarcely a hundred, when I preached first. The next time I had two hundred. Everyone who heard me was saying to his neighbor, 'You must go and hear this young man!' Next meeting we had four hundred, and in six weeks, eight hundred. That was the way in which my people got my congregation. Now the people are admitted by tickets. That does very well; a member can give his ticket to another person and say, 'I will stand in the aisle'; or 'I will get in with the crowd.' Some persons, you know, will not go if they can get in easily, but they will go if you tell them they cannot get in without a ticket. That is the way congregations ought to bring a congregation about a minister. A minister preaches all the better if he has a large congregation."

On October 26, 1891, Reverend Spurgeon, though he was feeling increasingly ill and weak from a combination of rheumatism, gout, and Bright's disease [chronic inflammation in the kidneys], which he had suffered from for many years, started out on a journey to Menton, France, where he often went to rest and recuperate. When he and Mrs. Spurgeon reached the Hotel Beau-Rivage, where they were staying, he enjoyed three months of "earthly paradise" without difficulty, and despite his weakness. By the middle of January, however, he began to weaken rapidly, though he conducted brief services in his room on January 10 and 17. These services were the last of his earthly work for his Lord. He died at the age of 58 on January 31, 1892. His wife and two sons outlived him, as did his father, who died at the age of almost ninety-two.

The news of his home-going flashed around the world. One London newspaper had the terse headline, "Death of Spurgeon." That day it was difficult to obtain a newspaper anywhere in England, the demand was so great. Spurgeon's coffin was brought back from Menton, France, and arrived at Victoria Station, London, on Monday, February 9, 1892. It was met by a small group of friends and taken to the Pastor's College, where it remained for the rest of the day. That night it was carried into the Metropolitan Tabernacle, and over sixty thousand people passed by it to pay their homage. Four funeral services were held on Wednesday to accommodate the crowds. Ira D. Sankey, Moody's associate, was there and sang twice. Evan Herber Evans, a Welsh Nonconformist minister, spoke briefly and concluding said, "But there is one Charles Haddon Spurgeon whom we cannot bury; there is not earth enough in Norwood to bury him—the Spurgeon of history. The good works that he has done will live. You cannot bury them."

The funeral was on Thursday, and one newspaper said you could search all of London and not find three women who were not wearing black. At the graveside, Archibald G. Brown, a close friend and one of Spurgeon's most distinguished associates, gave a eulogy that some have said will be remembered forever.

"Beloved President, faithful Pastor, Prince of Preachers, brother beloved, dear Spurgeon—we bid thee not 'Farewell,' but only for a little while 'Goodnight.' Thou shalt rise soon at the first dawn of the Resurrection day of the redeemed. Yet is the 'goodnight' not ours to bid, but thine; it is we who linger in the darkness; thou art in God's holy light. Our night shall soon be passed, and with it all our weeping. Then, with thine, our songs shall greet the morning of a day that knows no cloud nor close; for there is no night there.

"Hard worker in the field, thy toil is ended. Straight has been the furrow thou hast ploughed. No looking back has marred thy course. Harvests have followed thy patient sowing, and heaven is already rich with thine ingathered sheaves, and shall still be enriched through the years yet lying in eternity.

"Champion of God, thy battle, long and nobly fought, is over; thy sword, which clave to thy hand, has dropped at last: a palm branch takes it place. No longer does the helmet press thy brow, oft weary with its surging thoughts of battle; a victor's wreath from the great Commander's hand has already proved thy full reward.

"Here, for a little while, shall rest thy precious dust. Then shall thy Well-beloved come; and at His voice thou shalt spring from thy couch of earth, fashioned like unto His body, into glory. Then spirit, soul, and body shall magnify the Lord's redemption. Until then, beloved, sleep. We praise God for thee, and by the blood of the everlasting covenant, hope and expect to praise God with thee. Amen."

Spurgeon's coffin was then lowered into the ground. On it was a Bible open to the text that led Spurgeon to the Lord and Savior he had served faithfully for more than forty years, *"Look unto me, and be ye saved, all the ends of the earth: for I am God, and there is none else"* [Isaiah 45:22].

Quotations and Comments on the Blood

by Charles Spurgeon and other Ministers

The First Shedding of Blood

Scripture: Genesis 3:21

Unto Adam also and to his wife did the Lord God make coats of skins, and clothed them.

Quotations and Comments:

"These coats of skin had a significancy. The beasts whose skins they were, must be slain; slain before their eyes to shew them what death is. And probably 'tis supposed they were slain for sacrifice, to typify the great sacrifice which in the latter end of the world should be offered once for all. Thus the first thing that died was a sacrifice or Christ in a figure."—John Wesley

"And Adam called his wife's name Eve; because she was the mother of all living. Unto Adam also and to his wife did the LORD God make coats of skins, and clothed them. Some creature had to die in order to provide them with garments . . . and you know who it is that died in order that we might be robed in His spotless righteousness. The Lamb of God has made for us a garment which covers our nakedness so that we are not afraid to stand even before the bar of God."—Charles Spurgeon

"These coats of skin had a significancy. The beasts whose

skins they were must be slain, slain before their eyes, to show them what death is, and (as it is Ecclesiastes 3:18) that they may see that they themselves were beasts, mortal and dying. It is supposed that they were slain, not for food, but for sacrifice, to typify the great sacrifice, which, in the latter end of the world, should be *offered once for all. Thus the first thing that died was a sacrifice, or Christ in a figure, who is therefore said to be the Lamb slain from the foundation of the world. These sacrifices were divided between God and man,* in token of reconciliation: the flesh was offered to God, a whole burnt-offering; the skins were given to man for clothing, signifying that, Jesus Christ having offered himself to God a sacrifice of a sweet-smelling savor, we are to clothe ourselves with his righteousness as with a garment, that the shame of our nakedness may not appear. Adam and Eve made for themselves aprons of fig-leaves, a covering too narrow for them to wrap themselves in, Isaiah 28:20. Such are all the rags of our own righteousness. But God made them coats of skins; large, and strong, and durable, and fit for them; such is the righteousness of Christ. Therefore put on the Lord Jesus Christ."—Matthew Henry

THE SECOND SHEDDING OF BLOOD
SCRIPTURE: GENESIS 4:8-10

And Cain talked with Abel his brother: and it came to pass, when they were in the field, that Cain rose up against Abel his brother, and slew him. And the Lord said unto Cain, Where is Abel thy brother? And he said, I know not: Am I my brother's keeper? And he said, What hast thou done? the voice of thy brother's blood crieth unto me from the ground.

THE THIRD AND FINAL SHEDDING OF BLOOD

SCRIPTURE: MATTHEW 27:22-25

Pilate saith unto them, What shall I do then with Jesus which is called Christ? They all say unto him, Let him be crucified. And the governor said, Why, what evil hath he done? But they cried out the more, saying, Let him be crucified. When Pilate saw that he could prevail nothing, but that rather a tumult was made, he took water, and washed his hands before the multitude, saying, I am innocent of the blood of this just person: see ye to it. Then answered all the people, and said, His blood be on us, and on our children.

QUOTATIONS AND COMMENTS:

"Although believers by nature, are far from God, and children of wrath, even as others, yet it is amazing to think how nigh they are brought to him again by the blood of Jesus Christ."—George Whitefield

"Only the blood of Jesus can cleanse us, yet if we withhold ourselves from that blood, we will be unclean forever."—A. W. Tozer

"I may doubt my washing, but not when I believe in the cleansing virtue of the precious blood! It may be difficult to believe in my salvation, but not to believe in my Savior!"—Charles Spurgeon, 1891

"This is the chief aim of the enemy's assaults—to get rid of Christ, to get rid of the Atonement, to get rid of His suffering in the place of men! They say they can embrace the rest of the Gospel, but what, 'rest,' is there? What is there left? A bloodless, Christless Gospel is neither fit for the land nor for the dunghill—it neither honors God nor converts the sons of men."—Charles Spurgeon, 1894

"My meditation *of Him* shall be sweet. Of Him—that is, of the Well-Beloved of the Father, of the Well-Beloved of the Church, of the Well-Beloved of my own soul—of Him who loved me, in whose blood I have washed my robes and made them white. It is meditation *of Him* that is sweet—not merely of doctrine about Him, but of Him, of himself—my meditation of Him. Not merely of His offices, and His work, and all that concerns Him, but of His own dear Self! There lies the sweetness and the closer we come to His blessed Person, the more truly have we approached the very center of bliss!"—Charles Spurgeon, 1895

"We need to have a Church in which all the members do something, in which all do all they can, in which all are always doing all they can—for this is what our Lord deserves to have from a living, loving people bought with His precious blood! If He has saved me, I will serve Him forever and ever. And whatever lies in my power to do for His Glory that shall be my delight to do, and to do at once!" —Charles Spurgeon, 1892

"If the atoning sufferings of Christ are left out of a ministry, that ministry is worthless. "The blood is the life thereof," is as true about sermons as it is about animals and sacrifices. A bloodless gospel, a gospel without the atonement, is a gospel of devils, and not the gospel of God." —Charles Spurgeon

"My soul, admire the boundless love of God to thee and others of the human race. Worms are bought with the blood of the Son of the Highest! Dust and ashes redeemed with a price far above silver and gold!"—Charles Spurgeon

"Blood, always precious, is priceless when it streams from Immanuel's side."—Charles Spurgeon

"Behold His brow! O heavens! Drops of blood are streaming down His face, and from His body; every pore is open, and it sweats! But not the sweat of men that toil for bread; it is the sweat of one that toils for Heaven—He 'sweats great drops of blood!'"—Charles Spurgeon

"'There is no remission [of sin] without the shedding of blood,' says the text, in positive and plain words; and yet men will be trying to get remission in fifty other ways, until their special pleading becomes as irksome to us as it is useless for them."—Charles Spurgeon

"He took the payment and bore it to God,—took His wounds, His rent body, His flowing blood, up to His Father's very eyes, and there He spread His wounded hands and pleaded for His people. Now here is a proof that the Christian cannot be condemned, because the blood is on the mercy seat. It is not poured out on the ground; it is on the mercy seat, it is on the throne; it speaks in the very ears of God, and it must of a surety prevail."—Charles Spurgeon

"Place innocence, and merit, and dignity, and position, and the God-head itself, in the scale, and then conceive what must be the inestimable value of the blood which Jesus Christ poured forth."—Charles Spurgeon

"Did it never strike you how the whole tabernacle must have been smeared with blood everywhere? Blood was on every side. The priest himself, when at his work, with garments on which showed every stain, must have looked as though all besmeared with gore. You could not look at his hands or at his vestments without seeing everywhere blood; indeed, when consecrated, he had blood on his ear, blood on his foot, blood on his hands; he could not be made a priest without it. The apostle says, "Almost everything under the law was sprinkled with blood." It was blood, blood everywhere. Now, this could have been very far from a pleasant sight, except to the spiritual man who, as he looked at it, said, 'What a holy God is the God of Israel! How He hates sin! See, He will only permit sinners to approach Him by the way of blood!'"—Charles Spurgeon

"The Lord did not study attractive aesthetics, He did not prepare a tabernacle that should delight men's tastes; it was rich indeed, but so blood-stained as to be by no means beautiful. No staining of glass to charm the eye, but instead thereof the innards of slaughtered bullocks. Such sights would disgust the delicate tastes of the fops of this present age. Blood, blood on every side; death, fire, smoke, and ashes, varied with the bellows of dying beasts, and the active exertions of men whose white garments were all crimson with the blood of victims. How clearly did the worshippers see the sternness and severity of the justice of God against human sin, and the intensity of the agony of the great Son of God who was in the fullness of time by His own death to put away all the sins and transgressions of His people!"—Charles Spurgeon

"The blood of Christ is still on the earth, for when Jesus bled it fell upon the ground and was never gathered up." —Charles Spurgeon

"A bloodless gospel is a lifeless gospel; if the atonement be denied or frittered away, or put into a secondary place, or obscured, in that proportion the life has gone out of the religion which is professed."—Charles Spurgeon

"Why was the fountain filled with blood if you need no washing? Is Christ a superfluity? Oh, it cannot be." —Charles Spurgeon

"Now, if the precious blood of Jesus only put away the sin which we perceived in detail, its efficacy would be limited by the enlightenment of our conscience, and therefore some grievous sin might be overlooked and prove our ruin: but inasmuch as this blood puts away all sins, it removes those which we do not discover as those over which we mourn." —Charles Spurgeon

"You must never look at Christ's sacrifice in a carnal way, as though the mere drops of literal blood, as a material substance, could have virtue in them for the purging of sin. Do not know Christ after the flesh: be no longer children, but understand spiritual things. It is true that our Lord had a material body and poured forth material blood; but the essence of His sacrifice lay in His will, intent, motive, and spirit. I once heard a dissertation upon what became of those drops of blood which fell to the ground on Calvary, and I felt that it was foolish talk."—Charles Spurgeon

"Those drops of blood that fell on Calvary were never gathered up; and they have left the broad crimson mark of the redeeming Lord upon this globe of ours, and therefore His it must be."—Charles Spurgeon

"Brethren, when we climb to Heaven itself, and pass the gate of pearl, and wend our way through the innumerable hosts of angels, and come even to the throne of God, and see the spirits of the just made perfect, and hear their holy hymn, we shall not have gone beyond the influence of the blood of sprinkling; nay, we shall see it there more truly present than in any other place beside. "What!" say you, 'the blood of Jesus in heaven?' Yes.'"—Charles Spurgeon

"As no atom of matter ever perishes, that matter remains on Earth even now. His body has gone into glory, but the blood and water are left behind. I see much more in this fact than I will now attempt to tell. O world, the Christ has marked thee with His blood and He means to have thee!" —Charles Spurgeon

"Albeit that the guilty are taken up to dwell with God, and our poor prayers are accepted of God, neither we nor our prayers carry any defilement into the holy place, because the atoning blood is there beforehand."—Charles Spurgeon

"Not, my brethren, that Christ's blood was less than infinite in its value,—less than infinite it could never be. The question is not concerning the value of it, but the purpose of it."—Charles Spurgeon

"There are some preachers who cannot or do not preach about the blood of Jesus Christ, and I have one thing to say to you concerning them,—Never go to hear them! Never listen to them! A ministry that has not the blood in it is lifeless, "for the blood is the life thereof;" and a dead ministry is no good to anybody."—Charles Spurgeon

"Jesus Christ himself cannot save us, apart from His blood. It is a supposition which only folly has ever made, but we must refute even the hypothesis of folly, when it affirms that the example of Christ can put away sin, that the holy life of Jesus Christ has put the race on such a good footing with God that now He can forgive its faults and its transgression. Not so; not the holiness of Jesus, not the life of Jesus, not the death of Jesus, but the blood of Jesus only; for "Without shedding of blood there is no remission."—Charles Spurgeon

"The Blood deals with what we have done, whereas the Cross deals with what we are. The Blood disposes of our sins, while the Cross strikes at the root of our capacity for sin."—Watchman Nee

""Out, damned spot!" That is the true cry of human nature. That stain cannot be removed without blood, and that which is infinitely more, and deeper, and profounder, and more terrible than blood, of which blood is but the symbol—the suffering of Deity."—G. Campbell Morgan

"Our method of proclaiming salvation is this: to point out to every heart the loving Lamb, who died for us, and although He was the Son of God, offered Himself for our sins . . . by the preaching of His blood, and of His love unto death, even the death of the Cross."—Count Zinzendorf

"It is not thy hold on Christ that saves thee; it is Christ. It is not thy joy in Christ that saves thee; it is Christ. It is not even thy faith in Christ, though that be [is] the instrument; it is Christ's blood and merit."—Charles Spurgeon

"God does not leave you wondering whether you are

saved or not. He tells you outright that you are His and that nothing can ever separate you from the love of Christ. Not even sin because His blood is greater than your sin!" —Joseph Prince

"...Jesus Christ, the Lamb of God slain from the foundation of the World, and the High Priest of our confession. Now not the blood of bulls and goats slain on the brazen altar, but the blood of the Son of God slain on the Cross of Calvary. Now not the ever-dying, ever-changing priesthood after the order of Aaron, but the eternal, never-changing priesthood after the order of Melchizedek. Now not the daily ministering and continual offering of animal sacrifices that can never take away sin, but the one sin sacrifice of Christ for sins forever: *"For by one offering [of himself] he hath perfected for ever them that are sanctified"* [Hebrews 10:11-14].

Jesus Christ was both the sacrifice of the New Covenant and the High Priest who ministered His own blood upon the true Mercy Seat in the heavenly Tabernacle. Taking His blood into the true Tabernacle in Heaven, Jesus offered it to God for the propitiation of your sins and mine. He returned to Heaven to be the High Priest of the New Covenant and ever intercede with God on our behalf [Hebrews 7:25]. From there, the light of His divine resurrected life shines in us and through us as beacons of hope in a dark sea of sin. —Excerpts from *Christ Is God's Everything For You* —Harold J. Chadwick

PART ONE
THE SACRIFICE

CHAPTER 1
CHRIST—OUR SUBSTITUTE

A SERMON
(No. 310)

Delivered on Sabbath Evening, April 15th, 1860, by the

REVEREND CHARLES H. SPURGEON,

at New Park Street, Southwark, London, England.

"For he hath made him to be sin for us, who knew no sin; that we might be made the righteousness of God in him." —2 Corinthians 5:21.

SOMETIME AGO an excellent lady sought an interview with me, with the object of enlisting my sympathy upon the question of "Anti-Capital Punishment." I heard the excellent reasons she urged against hanging men who had committed murder, and though they did not convince me, I did not seek to answer them. She proposed that when a man committed murder, he should be confined for life. My remark was, that a great many men who had been confined half their lives were not a bit the better for it, and as for her belief that they would necessarily be brought to repentance, I was afraid it was but a dream.

"Ah," she said, good soul as she was, "that is because we have been all wrong about punishments. We punish people because we think they deserve to be punished. Now, we ought to show them," she said, "that we love them and that we only punish them to make them better." "Indeed, madam," I said, "I have heard that theory a great many times, and I have seen much fine writing upon the matter, but I am no believer in it. The design of punishment should be amendment, but the ground of punishment lies in the positive guilt of the offender. I believe that when a man does wrong, he ought to be punished for it, and that there is a guilt in sin which justly merits punishment." "Oh no;" she replied. She could not see that. She agreed that sin was a very wrong thing, but punishment was not a proper idea.

She thought that people were treated too cruelly in prison, and that they ought to be taught that we love them. She said, "If they were treated kindly in prison, and tenderly dealt with, they would grow so much better, she was sure." With a view of interpreting her own theory, I said, "I suppose, then, you would give criminals all sorts of indulgences in prison. Some aimless vagabond who has committed burglary dozens of times—I suppose you would let him sit in an easy chair in the evening before a nice fire, and mix him a glass of spirits and water, and give him his pipe, and make him happy, to show him how much we love him." "Well, no," she said, "I would not give him the spirits, but, all the rest would do him good."

I thought that was a delightful picture certainly. It seemed to me to be the most prolific method of cultivating rogues which ingenuity could invent. I imagine that you could grow any number of thieves in that way; for it would be a special means of propagating all manner of roguery and wickedness. These very delightful theories to such a simple mind as mine were the source of much amusement, the idea of coddling villains, and treating their crimes as if they were the tumbles and falls of children, made me laugh heartily. I fancied I saw the government resigning its functions to these excellent persons, and the grand results of their marvelously kind experiments. The sword of the magistrate transformed into a spoon for gruel, and the jail becoming a sweet retreat for injured reputations.

Little, however, did I think I should live to see this kind of stuff taught in pulpits; I had no idea that there would come out persons and a teaching that would bring down God's moral government from the solemn aspect in which Scripture reveals it, to a namby-pamby sentimentalism that adores a deity destitute of every masculine virtue. But we never know today what may occur tomorrow. We have lived to see a certain sort of men—thank God they are not Baptists, though I am sorry to say there are a great many Baptists who are beginning to follow in their trail—who seek to teach now-a-days, that God is a universal Father, and that our ideas of His dealing with the impenitent as a Judge and not as a Father, are remnants of antiquated error.

Sin, according to these men, is a disorder rather than an offence, an error rather than a crime. Love is the only attribute they can discern, and the full-orbed Deity they have not known. Some of these men push their way so far into the bogs and mire of falsehood that they inform us that eternal punishment is ridiculed as a dream.

In fact, books now appear that teach us that there is no such thing as the *vicarious sacrifice* of our Lord Jesus Christ. They use the word *atonement* it is true, but in regard to its meaning, they have removed the ancient landmark. They acknowledge that the Father has shown His great love to poor sinful man by sending His Son, but:

Not that God was inflexibly just in the exhibition of His mercy.

Not that He punished Christ on the behalf of His people, Nor that indeed God ever will punish anybody in His wrath.

Or that there is such a thing as justice apart from discipline.

Even *sin* and *hell* are but old words employed henceforth in a new and altered sense. Those are old-fashioned notions, and we poor souls who go on talking about election and imputed righteousness, are behind our time. Yes, and the gentlemen who bring out books on this subject, applaud Mr. Maurice[1], and Professor Scott[2], and the like, but are too cowardly to follow them, and boldly propound these sentiments. These are the new men whom God has sent down from Heaven, to tell us that the Apostle Paul was all wrong—

1. That our faith is vain, that we have been quite mistaken.
2. That there was no need for propitiating blood to wash away our sins.
3. That the fact was, our sins needed discipline, but penal vengeance and righteous wrath are quite out of the question.

When I thus speak, I am free to confess that such ideas are not boldly taught by a certain individual whose volume excites these remarks, but as he promotes the books of those who grossly pervert the truth, I am compelled to believe that he endorses such theology.

Well, brethren, I am happy to say that sort of stuff has not gained entrance into this pulpit. I dare say the worms will eat the wood before there will be anything of that sort sounded in this place. Furthermore, may these bones be picked by vultures, and this flesh be rent asunder by lions, and may every nerve in this body suffer pangs and tortures, before these lips shall ever give utterance to any such doctrines or sentiments. We are content to remain among the vulgar souls who believe the old doctrines of grace. We are willing still to be behind in the great march of intellect, and stand by that unmoving Cross, which, like the pole star, never advances, because it never stirs, but always abides in its place, the guide of the soul to Heaven, the one foundation other than which no man can lay, and without building upon which, no man

---

1. J. Frederick Denison Maurice, Professor of Religion with liberalist viewpoints and author of *Theological Essays*.
2. William Scott, English clergyman.

shall ever see the face of God and live.

Thus much have I said upon a matter that is just now exciting controversy. It has been my high privilege to be associated with six of our ablest brethren in the ministry, in a letter of protest against the countenance which a certain newspaper seemed willing to lend to this modern heresy. We trust it may be the means, in the hands of God, of helping to check that downward march—that wandering from truth which seems by some singular infatuation, to have unsettled the minds of some brethren in our denomination.

Now I come to address you upon the topic which is most continually assailed by those who preach another gospel "which is not another—but there are some that trouble you, and would pervert the Gospel of Christ," namely, the doctrine of the substitution of Christ on our behalf, His actual atonement for our sins, and our positive and actual justification through His sufferings and righteousness. It seems to me that until language can mean the very reverse of what it says, until by some strange logic, God's Word can be contradicted and can be made to belief itself, the doctrine of *substitution* can never be rooted out of the words that I have selected for my text *"He hath made him to be sin for us, who knew no sin, that we might be made the righteousness of God in him."* [See 2 Corinthians 5:21.]

> **First,** *the sinlessness of the substitute.*
> **Second,** *the reality of the imputation of sin to Him.*
> **Third,** *the glorious reality of the imputation of righteousness to us.*

I. THE SINLESSNESS OF THE SUBSTITUTE

The doctrine of Holy Scripture is this, that inasmuch as man could not keep God's Law, and having fallen in Adam, Christ came and fulfilled the law on the behalf of His people. And inasmuch as man had already broken the divine Law and incurred the penalty of the wrath of God, Christ came and suffered in the room, place, and stead of His elect ones, so that by His enduring the full vials of wrath, they might be emptied out and not a drop might ever fall upon the heads of His blood-bought people.

Now, you will readily perceive that if one is to be a substitute for another before God, either to work out a righteousness or to suffer a penalty, that substitute must himself be free from sin. If he has sin of his own, all that he can suffer will be the due reward of his own iniquity. If he has himself transgressed, he cannot suffer for another, because all his sufferings are already due on his own personal account. On the other hand, it is quite clear that none but a perfect man could ever work out a spotless righteousness for us, and keep the Law in our stead. For if he has dishonored the commandment in his thought, there must be a corresponding flaw in his service. If the warp and woof be speckled, how shall he bring forth the robe of milk-white purity, and wrap it about our loins? He must be a spotless one who shall become the representative of his people, either to give them a passive or active righteousness, to either offer a satisfaction as the penalty of their sins, or a righteousness as the fulfillment of God's demand.

It is satisfactory for us to know, and to believe beyond a doubt, that our Lord Jesus was without sin. Of course, in His divine nature He could not know iniquity; and as for His human nature, it never knew the original taint of depravity.

42

He was of the seed of the woman, but not of the tainted and infected seed of Adam. The virgin was overshadowed by the Holy Ghost, therefore, no corruption entered into His nativity. That *holy thing* which was born of her was neither conceived in sin nor shaped in iniquity. He was brought into this world immaculate. He was immaculately conceived and immaculately born.

The black blood we have inherited from Adam never dwelt in Him. His heart was upright within Him; His soul was without any bias to evil; His imagination had never been darkened. He had no infatuated mind. There was no tendency whatever in Him other than to do that which was good, holy, and honorable. And as He did not share in the original depravity, so He did not share in the imputed sin of Adam which we have inherited—not, I mean, in himself personally, though He took the consequences of that, as He stood as our representative.

The sin of Adam had never passed over the head of the second Adam. All that were in the loins of Adam sinned in him when he touched the fruit; but Jesus was not in the loins of Adam. Though He might be conceived of as being in the womb of the woman—"*a new thing which the Lord created in the earth,*" [Jeremiah 31:22]—He lay not in Adam when he sinned, and consequently no guilt from Adam, either of depravity of nature, or of distance from God, ever fell upon Jesus as the result of anything that Adam did. I mean upon Jesus as considered *in himself* though He certainly took the sin of Adam as He was the representative of His people.

Again, as in His nature He was free from the corruption and condemnation of the sin of Adam, so also in His life, no sin ever corrupted His way. His eye never flashed with unhallowed anger; His lip never uttered a treacherous or deceitful word; and His heart never harbored an evil imagination. Never did He wander after lust; no covetousness ever so much as glanced into His soul. He was *"holy, harmless, undefiled, separate from sinners"* [Hebrews 7:26]. From the beginning of His life to the end, you cannot put your finger even upon a mistake, much less upon a willful error.

So perfect was He, that no virtue seems to preponderate, or by an opposing quality give a bias to the scale of absolute rectitude. John is distinguished for his love, Peter for his courage; but Jesus Christ is distinguished for neither one above the other, because He possesses all in such sublime unison, such heavenly harmony, that no one virtue stands out above the rest. He is meek, but He is courageous. He is loving, but He is decided; He is bold as a lion, yet He is quiet and peaceful as a lamb. He was like that fine flour which was offered before God in the burnt offering; a flour without grit, so smooth, that when you rubbed it, it was soft and pure, no particles could be discerned: so was His character fully ground, fully compounded.

There was not one feature in His moral countenance which had undue preponderance above the other; but He was replete in everything that was virtuous and good. He was tempted, it is true, but He never sinned. The whirlwind came from the wilderness, and smote upon the four corners of that house, but it fell not, for it was founded upon a rock. The rains descended, Heaven afflicted Him; the winds blew, the mysterious agency of hell assailed Him; the floods came, all Earth was in arms against Him, but yet He stood firm in the midst of all.

Never once did He even seem to bend before the tempest; but buffeted the fury of the blast, bearing all the temptations that could ever happen to man, which summed themselves up and consummated their fury on Him. He stood to the end without a single flaw in His life or a stain upon His spotless robe. Let us rejoice in this, my beloved brothers and sisters, that we have such a substitute—one who is fit and proper to stand in our place, and to suffer in our stead, seeing He has no need to offer a sacrifice for himself; no need to cry for himself, "Father, I have sinned;" no need to bend the knee of the penitent and confess His own iniquities, for He is without spot or blemish, the perfect Lamb of God's Passover.

I would have you carefully notice the particular expression of the text, for it struck me as being very beautiful and significant—*"who knew no sin."* It does not merely say *did* none, but *knew* none. Sin was no acquaintance of His; He was acquainted with grief, but no acquaintance of sin. He had to walk in the midst of its most frequented haunts, but He did not *know it;* He was a stranger to it. He never gave it the wink or nod of familiar recognition. Of course He knew what sin was, for He was very God, but with sin He had no communion, no fellowship, and no brotherhood. He was a perfect stranger in the presence of sin; He was a foreigner; He was not an inhabitant of that land where sin is acknowledged. He passed through the wilderness of suffering, but into the wilderness of sin He could never go. "He *knew* no sin;" mark that expression and treasure it up, and when you are thinking of your substitute, and see Him hang bleeding upon the Cross, think that you see written in those lines of blood written along His blessed body, "He knew no sin." Mingled with the redness of his blood—that Rose of Sharon; behold the purity of His nature, the Lily of the Valley—*"He knew no sin."* Let us pass on to notice the second and most important point. The actual substitution of Christ, and the real imputation of sin to Him.

II. THE REALITY OF THE IMPUTATION OF SIN TO HIM

Here be careful to observe who transferred the sin. God the Father laid on Jesus the iniquities of us all. Man could not make Christ sin. Man could not transfer his guilt to another. It is not for us to say whether Christ could or could not have made himself sin for us; but it is certain He did not take this priesthood upon himself, but he was called of God, as was Aaron. The Redeemer's vicarious position is warranted, or rather ordained by divine authority. *"He hath made him to be sin for us."* I must now beg you to notice how very explicit the term is.

Some of our expositors will have it that the word here used must mean "sin-offering." "He made him to be a sin-offering for us." I thought it well to look to my Greek Testament to see whether it could be so. Of course we all know that the word here translated "sin," is very often translated "sin-offering," but it is always useful, when you have a disputed passage, to look it through, and see whether in this case the word would bear such a meaning. These commentators say it means a sin-offering,—well, I will read it: *"He hath made him to be a sin-offering for us who knew no sin-offering."* Does that not strike you as being ridiculous? But they are precisely the same words; and if it is fair to translate it "sin-offering" in one place, it must, in all reason, be fair to translate it so in the other.

The fact is, while in some passages it may be rendered "sin-offering," in this passage it cannot be so, *because it would be to run counter to all honesty to translate the same word in the same sentence two different ways.* No; we must take them as they stand. "He hath made him to be sin for us," not merely an offering, *but sin for us.*

My predecessor, Dr. Gill[3], edited the works of Tobias Crisp[4], but Tobias Crisp went further than Dr. Gill or any of us can approve; for in one place Crisp calls Christ *a sinner,*

---

3. Dr. John Gill, English clergyman.
4. English clergyman and antinomian.

though he does not mean that He ever sinned himself. He actually calls Christ a transgressor, and justifies himself by that passage, *"He was numbered with the transgressors"* [Mark 15:28]. Martin Luther is reputed to have broadly said that, although Jesus Christ was sinless, yet He was the greatest sinner that ever lived, because all the sins of His people lay upon Him.

Now, such expressions I think to be unguarded, if not profane. Certainly Christian men should take care that they do not use language that by the ignorant and uninstructed may be translated to mean what they never intended to teach. The fact is, brethren, that in no sense whatever—take that as I say it—in no sense whatever can Jesus Christ ever be conceived of as having been guilty. *"He knew no sin."* Not only was He not guilty of any sin which He committed himself, but He was not guilty of our sins. No guilt can possibly attach to a man who has not been guilty. He must have had complicity in the deed itself, or else no *guilt* can possibly be laid on him. Jesus Christ stands in the midst of all the divine thunders, and suffers all the punishment, but not a drop of sin ever stained Him. In no sense is He ever a guilty man, but He is always an accepted and a holy one.

Then what is the meaning of that very forcible expression from my text? We must interpret scriptural modes of expression by the verbiage of the speakers. We know that our Master once said himself, *"This cup is the new covenant in my blood;"* He did not mean that the cup was the covenant. [1 Corinthians 11:24, NKJV] He said, *"Take, eat; this is my body"* —not one of us conceives that the bread is the literal flesh and blood of Christ. We take that bread as if it was the body, and it actually represents it.

Now, we are to read a passage like this, according to the analogy of faith. Jesus Christ was made sin for us by His Father, that is, He was treated as if He had himself been sin. He was not sin; He was not sinful; He was not guilty; but, He was treated by His Father, as if He had not only been sinful, but as if He had been *sin itself*. That is a strong expression used here. Not only has He made Christ to be the substitute for sin, but to be sin. God looked on Christ as if Christ had been sin; not as if He had taken up the sins of His people, or as if they were laid on Him, though that were true, but as if He himself had positively been that noxious, God-hating, soul-damning thing, called sin.

When the Judge of all the Earth said, "Where is Sin?" Christ presented himself. He stood before His Father as if He had been the accumulation of all human guilt; as if He himself were that thing which God cannot endure, and must drive from His presence forever. Now note how this making of Jesus to be sin was enacted to the fullest extent. The righteous Lord looked on Christ as being sin, and therefore Christ must be taken without [5] the camp. Sin cannot be borne in God's Zion, nor allowed to dwell in God's Jerusalem; it must be taken without the camp, for it is a leprous thing, and must be put away. Sin must forever be cast out from fellowship, from love, and from pity.

Take Him away; take Him away, O, crowd! Hurry Him through the streets and bear Him to Calvary. Take Him without the camp—as was the beast which was offered for sin without the camp, so must Christ be who was made sin for us. God now looks on Him as being sin, and sin must bear punishment. Christ is punished. The most fearful of deaths is exacted at His hand, and God has no pity for Him. How could He have pity on sin? God hates it. No tongue can tell, no soul can divine the terrible hatred of God to that which is evil, and He treats Christ as if He were sin.

---

5. Outside

Christ prays, but Heaven shuts out His prayer; He cries for water, but Heaven and Earth refuse to wet His lips except with vinegar. He turns His eyes to Heaven, He sees nothing there. How could He? God cannot look on sin, and sin can have no claim on God: *"My God, my God,"* He cries, *"why hast thou forsaken me?"* [Matthew 27:46] O solemn necessity, how could God do anything with sin but forsake it? How could iniquity have fellowship with God? Shall divine smiles rest on sin? No, no, it must not be.

Therefore, He who is made sin must endure desertion and terror. God cannot touch Him, cannot dwell with Him, and cannot come near Him. He is abhorred, cast away; *"it hath pleased the Father to bruise him; he hath put him to grief"* [Isaiah 53:10]. At last He dies. God will not keep Him in life—how could He? Is it not the right thing in the world that sin should be buried? "Bury it out of my sight, hide this corruption." Therefore, as if He were sin, Jesus is put out of the sight of God and man as an obnoxious thing.

I do not know whether I have clearly uttered what I want to state, but what a grim picture that is, to conceive of sin gathered up into one mass—murder, lust, rape, adultery, and all manner of crime, all piled together in one hideous heap. We ourselves, brethren, impure though we are, could not bear this; how much less could God with His pure and holy eyes bear with that mass of sin. Yet, it is so, and God looked upon Christ as if He were that mass of sin. He was not sin, but God looked upon Him as made sin for us. He stands in our place, assumes our guilt, takes on himself our iniquity, and God treats Him as if He had been sin.

Now, my dear brothers and sisters, let us just lift up our hearts with gratitude for a few moments. Here we are tonight; we know that we are guilty, but our sins have all been punished years ago. Before my soul believed in Christ, the punishment of my sin had all been endured. We are not to think that Christ's blood derives its efficacy from our faith. Fact precedes faith. Christ has redeemed us; faith discovers this; but it was a fact of that finished sacrifice. Though still defiled by sin, yet who can lay anything to the charge of the man whose guilt is gone, lifted bodily from off him, and put upon Christ? How can any punishment fall on that man who ceases to possess sins, because his sin has over eighteen hundred years ago been cast upon Christ, and Christ has suffered in his place and stead?

Oh, glorious triumph of faith to be able to say, whenever I feel the guilt of sin or whenever conscience pricks me, "Yes, it is true, but my Lord is answerable for it all, for He has taken it all upon himself, and suffered in my room, and place, and stead." How precious when I see my debts, to be able to say, "Yes, but the blood of Christ, God's dear Son, has cleansed me from all sin!" How precious, not only to see my sin dying when I believe, but to know that it was dead, it was gone, it ceased to be more than eighteen hundred years ago. All the sins that you and I have ever committed, or ever shall commit, if we are heirs of mercy, and children of God, are all dead things.

> "Our Jesus nailed them to his cross,
> And sung the triumph when he rose."6

These cannot rise in judgment to condemn us; they have all been slain, shrouded, buried; they are removed from us as far as the east is from the west, because *"He hath made him to be sin for us, who knew no sin"* [2 Corinthians 5:21].

---

6. Hymn by Isaac Watts titled, "Stand Up My Soul".

III. THE GLORIOUS REALITY OF THE IMPUTATION OF RIGHTEOUSNESS TO US

You see this reality from the amazing doctrine that Christ is made sin for us. But now notice the concluding thought, upon which I must dwell a moment, but it must be very briefly for two reasons, my time has gone, and my strength has gone too. *"That we might be made the righteousness of God in Him."* Now, here I beg you to notice, that it does not simply say that we might be made *righteous,* but *"that we might be made the righteousness of God in him;"* as if righteousness, that lovely, glorious, God-honoring, God-delighting thing—as if we were actually made *that.*

God looks on His people as being abstract righteousness, not only righteous, but righteousness. To be righteous is as if a man would have a box covered with gold, the box would then be golden; but to be righteous*ness* is to have a box of solid gold. To be a righteous man is to have righteousness cast over me; but to be made righteousness, *that is to be made solid essential righteousness in the sight of God.* Well now, this is a glorious fact and a most wonderful privilege, that we poor sinners are made *"the righteousness of God in him."*

God sees no sin in any one of His people, no iniquity in Jacob, when He looks upon them in Christ. In themselves, He sees nothing but filth and abomination, in Christ, nothing but purity and righteousness. Is it not, and must it not ever be one of the most delightful privileges to the Christian to know that altogether apart from anything that we have ever done, or can do, God looks upon His people as being righteous, even more, as being righteousness? Despite all of the sins they have ever committed, they are accepted in Him as if they had been Christ, while Christ was punished for them as if He had been sin.

When I stand in my own place, I am lost and ruined; my place is the place where Judas stood, the place where the devil lies in everlasting shame. But when I stand in Christ's place—and I fail to stand where faith has put me until I stand there—when I stand in Christ's place, the Father's everlastingly beloved One, the Father's accepted One, Him whom the Father delights to honor—when I stand there, I stand where faith has a right to put me, and I am in the most joyous spot that a creature of God can occupy.

Oh, Christian, get up, get up into the high mountain, and stand where your Savior stands, for that is your place. Lie not on the dunghill of fallen humanity, that is not your place now; Christ has once taken it on your behalf. *"He made him to be sin for us."* Your place is up there, above the starry hosts, *where* "he hath raised us up together, and made us sit together in heavenly places in him" [Ephesians 2:6]. Not there, at the day of judgment, where the wicked shriek for shelter, and beg for the hills to cover them, but there, where Jesus sits upon His throne—there is your place my soul.

He will make you to sit upon His throne, even as He has overcome, and has sat down with His Father upon His throne. Oh! That I could mount to the heights of this argument tonight; it needs a seraphic[7] preacher to picture the saint in Christ, robed in Christ's righteousness, wearing Christ's nature, bearing Christ's palm of victory, sitting on Christ's throne, and wearing Christ's crown. And yet this is our privilege! He wore my crown, the crown of thorns; I wear His crown, the crown of glory. He wore my dress, or rather, He wore my nakedness when He died upon the Cross; I wear His robes, the royal robes of the King of kings. He bore my shame; I bear His honor. He endured my sufferings to

---

7. Angelic

52

this end that my joy may be full, and that His joy may be fulfilled in me. He laid in the grave that I might rise from the dead and that I may dwell in Him, and all this He comes again to give me, to make it sure to me and to all that love His appearing, to show that all His people shall enter into their inheritance.

Now, my brothers and sisters, Mr. Maurice[8], McLeod, Campbell, and their great admirer, Mr. Brown, may go on with their preaching as long as they like, but they will never make a convert of a man who knows what the vitality of religion is; for he who knows what substitution means, he who knows what it is to stand where Christ stands, will never care to occupy the ground on which Mr. Maurice stands. He who has been made to sit together with Christ and to enjoy the real preciousness of a transfer of Christ's righteousness to him and his sin to Christ, that man has eaten the bread of Heaven, and will never renounce it for husks. No, my brethren, we could lay down our lives for this truth rather than give it up. No, we cannot by any means turn aside from this glorious stability of faith, and for this good reason, that there is nothing for us in the doctrine which these men teach. It may suit intellectual gentlefolk, I dare say it does; but it will not suit us. We are poor sinners and nothing at all, and if Christ is not our all in all, there is nothing for us.

I have often thought the best answer for all these new ideas is, that the true gospel was always preached to the poor;— *"The poor have the gospel preached to them"* [Matthew 11:5]—I am sure that the poor will never learn *the gospel* of these new divines, for they cannot make head or tail of it, nor the rich either; for after you have read through one of their volumes, you will not have the least idea of what

---

8. J. Frederick Denison Maurice, a liberalist and English clergyman.

the book is about until you have read it through eight or nine times. However, you will then begin to think you are a very stupid being for ever having read such inflated heresy, for it sours your temper and makes you feel angry, to see the precious truths of God trodden under foot.

Some of us must stand out against these attacks on truth, although we do not love controversy we do rejoice in the liberty of our fellow-men, and would have them proclaim their convictions; but if they touch these precious things, they touch the apple of our eye. We can allow a thousand opinions in the world, but that which infringes upon the precious doctrine of a covenant salvation, through the imputed righteousness of our Lord Jesus Christ,—against that we must, and will, enter our hearty and solemn protest, as long as God spares us.

Take away those glorious doctrines from us and where are we brethren? We may as well lay us down and die for nothing remains that is worth living for. We have come to the valley of the shadow of death, when we find these doctrines to be untrue. If these things which I speak to you tonight are not the verities of Christ; if they are not true, then there is no comfort left for any poor man under God's Heaven, and it would have been better for us never to have been born. I may say what Jonathan Edwards says at the end of his book, "If any man could disprove the doctrines of the gospel, he should then sit down and weep to think they were not true, for," says he, "it would be the most dreadful calamity that could happen to the world, to have a glimpse of such truths, and then for them to melt away in the thin air of fiction, as having no substantiality in them."

Stand up for the truth of Christ; I would not have you to be bigoted, but I would have you to be decided. Do not give countenance to any of this trash and error that is going around but stand firm. Do not be turned away from your steadfastness by any pretence of intellectuality and high philosophy, but *"earnestly contend for the faith once delivered to the saints"*, and hold fast the form of sound words which you have heard of us, and have been taught, even as ye have read in this sacred Book, which is the way of everlasting life. [See Jude 1:3.]

Therefore, beloved, without gathering up my strength for the fray, or attempting to analyze the subtleties of those who would pervert the simple gospel, I speak out my mind and utter the kindnesses of my heart among you. You, whom the Holy Ghost has given me oversight, will have no harm to your faith by what the grievous wolves may design if you keep within the fold. Break not the sacred bounds wherein God has enclosed His Church. He has encircled us in the arms of covenant love. He has united us in indissoluble bonds to the Lord Jesus. He has fortified us with the assurance that the Holy Spirit shall guide us into all truth. God grant that those beyond the pale of visible fellowship with us in this eternal gospel may see their danger and escape from the fowler's snare!

CHAPTER 2
CHRIST OUR PASSOVER
A SERMON
(No. 54)

Delivered on Sabbath Evening, December 2, 1855, by the

REVEREND C. H. SPURGEON,
at New Park Street Chapel, Southwark, England

"For even Christ our passover is sacrificed for us."
—1 Corinthians 5:7b

THE MORE YOU READ THE BIBLE, and the more you meditate upon it, the more you will be astonished at it. One, who is but a casual reader of the Bible, does not know the height, the depth, the length and breadth of the mighty meanings contained in its pages. There are certain times when I discover a new vein of thought, and I put my hand to my head and say in astonishment, "Oh, it is wonderful I never saw this before in the Scriptures."

You will find the Scriptures enlarge as you enter them; the more you study them the less you will appear to know of them, for they widen out as we approach them. You will especially find this the case with the typical parts of God's Word. Most of the historical books were intended to be types either of dispensations, or experiences, or offices of Jesus Christ. Study the Bible with this as a key, and you will not blame Herbert[9] when he calls it "not only the book of God, but the God of books." One of the most interesting points of the Scriptures is their constant tendency to display Christ; and perhaps one of the most beautiful figures under

---

9. George Herbert, 1593-1633, poet and rector of Fugglestone in Bemerton, Wiltshire, England

which Jesus Christ is ever exhibited in sacred writ, is the Passover Paschal Lamb. It is Christ of whom we are about to speak tonight.

The Israelites were in Egypt, in extreme bondage; the severity of their slavery had continually increased until it was so oppressive that their incessant groans went up to Heaven. God who avenges His own elect, though they cry day and night unto Him, at last, determined that He would direct a fearful blow against Egypt's king and Egypt's nation, and deliver His own people. We can picture the anxieties and the anticipations of the Israelites, but we can scarcely sympathize with them, unless we as Christians have had the same deliverance from spiritual Egypt.

Let us, brethren, go back to the day in our experience, when we abode in the land of Egypt, working in the brickkilns of sin, toiling to make ourselves better, and finding it to be of no avail. Let us recall that memorable night, the beginning of months, the commencement of a new life in our spirit, and the beginning of an altogether new era in our soul. The Word of God struck the blow at our sin; He gave us Jesus Christ our sacrifice; and in that night we went out of Egypt. Though we have passed through the wilderness since then, and have fought the Amalekites, trodden on the fiery serpent, scorched by the heat, and frozen by the snows, but we have never since that time gone back to Egypt. Our hearts may sometimes have desired the leeks, onions, and fleshpots of Egypt but we have never been brought into slavery since then.

Come; let us keep the Passover this night, and think of the night when the Lord delivered us out of Egypt. Let us behold our Savior Jesus as the Paschal Lamb on which we feed; let us not only look at Him as such, but let us sit down tonight at His table, let us eat of His flesh and drink of His blood; for His flesh is meat indeed, and His blood is drink indeed. In holy solemnity let our hearts approach that ancient supper; let us go back to Egypt's darkness, and by holy contemplation behold, instead of the destroying angel, the angel of the covenant, at the head of the feast,—"... *the Lamb of God which taketh away the sin of the world"* [John 1:29].

I shall not have time tonight to enter into the whole history and mystery of the Passover; you will not understand me to be preaching tonight concerning *the whole of it;* but a few prominent points therein as a part of them. It would require a dozen sermons to do so; in fact a book as large as Caryl[10] upon Job—if we could find a divine equally prolix[11] and equally sensible. But we shall first of all look at the Lord Jesus Christ, and show how He corresponds with the Paschal Lamb, and endeavor to bring you to the two points—of having His blood sprinkled on you, and having fed on Him.

I. FIRST, JESUS CHRIST IS TYPIFIED HERE UNDER THE PASCHAL LAMB

Should there be one of the seed of Abraham here who has never seen Christ to be the Messiah, I beg his special attention to that which I am to advance, when I speak of the Lord Jesus as none other than the Lamb of God slain for the deliverance of His chosen people. Follow me with your Bibles, and open first at the 12th chapter of Exodus.

We commence, first of all, with the victim—*the lamb.* How fine a picture of Christ. No other creature could so well have typified Him who was holy, harmless, undefiled, and separate from sinners. Being also the emblem of sacrifice, it most sweetly portrayed our Lord and Savior Jesus Christ. Search natural history through, and though you will find

---

10. Joseph Caryl, 1602-1673, English clergyman and author of an *Exposition on the Book of Job.*
11. Prolific

other emblems which set forth different characteristics of His nature, and admirably display Him to our souls, yet there is none which seems as appropriate to the person of our beloved Lord as that of the Lamb. A child would at once perceive the likeness between a lamb and Jesus Christ, so gentle and innocent, so mild and harmless, neither hurting others, nor seeming to have the power to resent an injury.

"A humble man before his foes, a weary man and full of woes."

What tortures the sheepish race has received from us! Though innocent, they are continually slaughtered for our food! Their skin is dragged from their backs; their wool is shorn to give us a garment. And so the Lord Jesus Christ, our glorious Master, gives us His garments that we may be clothed with them. He is torn asunder for us; His very blood is poured out for our sins; harmless and holy, a glorious sacrifice for the sins of all His children. Thus the Paschal Lamb might well convey to the pious Hebrew the person of a suffering, silent, patient, harmless Messiah.

Look further down. It was a lamb *without blemish*. A blemished lamb, if it had the smallest speck of disease, the least wound, would not have been allowed for a Passover. The priest would not have suffered[12] it to be slaughtered, nor would God have accepted the sacrifice at his hands. It must be a lamb without blemish. And was not Jesus Christ even such from His birth? Unblemished, born of the pure virgin Mary, begotten of the Holy Ghost, without a taint of sin; His soul was pure, and spotless as the driven snow, white, clear, perfect; and His life was the same. In Him was no sin. He took our infirmities and bore our sorrows on the Cross. He was in all points tempted as we are, but there was that sweet exception, "...*yet without sin*." [Hebrews 4:15].

---

12. Allowed

A lamb without blemish. You who have known the Lord, who have tasted of His grace, who have held fellowship with Him, do not your hearts acknowledge that He is a lamb without blemish? Can you find any fault with your Savior? Have you aught[13] to lay to his charge? Has His truthfulness departed? Have His words been broken? Have His promises failed? Has He forgotten His engagements? And, in any respect, can you find in Him any blemish? Ah, no! He is the unblemished lamb, the pure, the spotless, the immaculate, "the Lamb of God which taketh away the sin of the world;" and in Him there is no sin.

Go on further down the chapter. "Your lamb shall be without blemish, *a male of the first year.*" I need not stop to consider the reason why the male was chosen; we only note that it was to be a male of the first year. Then it was in its prime, its strength was unexhausted, and its power was just ripened into maturity and perfection, God would not have an untimely fruit. God would not have that offered which had not come to maturity. And so our Lord Jesus Christ had just come to the ripeness of manhood when He was offered. At 34 years of age He was sacrificed for our sins; He was then hale and strong, although His body may have been emaciated by suffering, and His face more marred than that of any other man, yet He was then in the perfection of manhood. [See Isaiah 52:14.]

I think I see Him then. His goodly beard flowing down upon His breast; I see Him with His eyes full of genius, His form erect, His mien[14] majestic, His energy entire, His whole frame in full development,—a real man, a magnificent man—fairer than the sons of men; a Lamb not only without blemish, but with all His powers fully brought out. Such was

13. Nothing
14. Manner

Jesus Christ—a Lamb of the first year—not a boy, not a lad, not a young man, but a full man, that He might give His soul unto us. He did not give himself to die for us when He was a youth, for He would not then have given all He was to be. He did not give himself to die for us when He was in old age, for then He would have given himself when He was in decay; but just in His maturity, in His very prime—then Jesus Christ our Passover was sacrificed for us.

And, moreover, at the time of His death, Christ was full of life, for we are informed by one of the evangelists that *"he cried with a loud voice and gave up the ghost"* [Mark 15:37]. This is a sign that Jesus did not die through weakness, or through decay of nature. His soul was strong within Him; He was still the Lamb of the first year. He was still mighty; He could, if He pleased, even on the Cross, have unlocked His hands from their iron bolts; and descending from the tree of infamy, He could have driven His astonished foes before Him, like deer scattered by a lion, yet He meekly yielded obedience unto death.

My soul; can you not see your Jesus here, the unblemished Lamb of the first year, strong and mighty? O my heart does not the thought rise up—if Jesus consecrated himself to me when He was in all His strength and vigor, should not I in youth dedicate myself to Him? And if I am in manhood, am I not doubly bound to give my strength to Him? And if I am in old age, I should still seek while the little time remains, to consecrate that little time to Him? If He gave His all to me, which was much, should I not give my little all to Him? Should I not feel bound to consecrate myself entirely to His service, to lay body, soul, and spirit, time, talents, all upon His altar?

And though I am not an unblemished lamb, yet I am happy that as the leavened cake was accepted with the sacrifice, though never burned with it—I, though a leavened cake, may be offered on the altar with my Lord and Savior, the Lord's burnt offering, and so, though impure, and full of leaven, I may be accepted in the Beloved, an offering of a sweet savor, acceptable unto the Lord my God. Here is Jesus, beloved, a Lamb without blemish, a Lamb of the first year!

The subject now expands and the interest deepens. Let me have your very serious consideration to the next point, which has much gratified me in its discovery and will instruct you in the relationship. In the 6th verse of the 12th chapter of Exodus we are told that this lamb which would be offered at the Passover was to be *selected* four days before its sacrifice, and to be kept apart:—

> "In the tenth day of this month they shall take to them every man a lamb, according to the house of their fathers, a lamb for an house: and if the household be too little for the lamb, let him and his neighbour next unto his house take it according to the number of the souls; every man according to his eating shall make your count for the lamb."

The 6th verse says, *"And ye shall keep it until the fourteenth day of the same month."* For four days this lamb, chosen to be offered, was taken away from the rest of the flock and kept alone by itself, for two reasons: partly that by its constant bleating they might be put in remembrance of the solemn feast which was to be celebrated; and moreover, that during the four days they might be quite assured that it had no blemish, for during that time it was subject to constant inspection, in order that they might be certain that it had no hurt or injury that would render it unacceptable to the Lord.

And now, brethren, a remarkable fact flashes before you—just as this lamb was separated four days, the ancient allegories used to say that Christ was separated four years. Four years after He left his father's house He went into the wilderness, and was tempted of the devil. Four years after His baptism He was sacrificed for us. But there is another, better than that:—about four days before His crucifixion, Jesus Christ rode in triumph through the streets of Jerusalem. He was thus openly set apart as being distinct from mankind. He, on the donkey, rode up to the temple, that all might see Him to be Judah's Lamb, chosen of God, and ordained from the foundation of the world. What is still more remarkable during those four days you will see, if you turn to the Evangelists that as much is recorded of what He did and said as through all the prior part of His life.

During those four days:

- He upbraided the fig tree, and straightway it withered.
- It was then that He drove the buyers and sellers from the temple.
- It was then that He rebuked the priests and elders, by telling them the similitude of the two sons, one of whom said he would go, and did not, and the other who said he would not go, and went.
- It was then that He narrated the parable of the husbandmen, who slew those who were sent to them.
- Afterwards He gave the parable of the marriage of the king's son.
- Then comes His parable concerning the man who went unto the feast, not having on a wedding garment.
- And then also, the parable concerning the ten virgins, five of whom were very wise, and five of whom were foolish.
- Then comes the chapter of very striking denunciations against the Pharisees:—"*Woe unto you O ye blind Pharisees! cleanse first that which is within the cup and platter.*" [Matthew 23:25]
- And then also comes that long chapter of prophecy concerning what would happen at the siege of

Jerusalem, and an account of the dissolution of the world: *"Learn a parable of the fig-tree: when his branch is yet tender and putteth forth leaves, ye know that summer is nigh."* [Mark 13:28]

But I will not trouble you by telling you here that at the same time He gave them that splendid description of the Day of Judgment, when the sheep shall be divided from the goats. [See Matthew 25:32-33.] In fact, the most splendid utterances of Jesus were recorded as having taken place within these four days. Just as the lamb separated from its fellows, did bleat more than ever during the four days, so did Jesus during those four days speak more; and if you want to find a choice saying of Jesus, turn to the account of the last four days' ministry to find it. There you will find that chapter, *"Let not your hearts be troubled...;"* [John 14:1] there also, His great prayer, *"Father, I will...;"* [John 17:24] and so on. The greatest things He did, He did in the last four days when He was set apart.

And there is one more thing to which I beg your particular attention, and that is, that during those four days I told you that the lamb was subject to the closest scrutiny, so, also, during those four days, it is singular to relate, that Jesus Christ was examined by all classes of persons. It was during those four days that the lawyer asked Him which was the greatest commandment. And He said, *Thou shalt love the Lord thy God with all thy heart and with all thy soul, and with all thy might; and thou shalt love thy neighbour as thyself* [Matthew 22:36-40]. It was then that the Herodians came and questioned Him about the tribute money; it was then that the Pharisees tempted Him; it was then, also, the Sadducees tried Him upon the subject of the resurrection.

He was tried by all classes and grades—Herodians, Pharisees, Sadducees, lawyers, and the common people. It was during these four days that He was examined: but how did He come forth? An immaculate Lamb! *"The officers answered, Never man spake like this man"* [John 7:46]. His foes found none who could even bear false witness against Him, such as agreed together; and Pilate declared, *"I find no fault in him"* [John 19:4]. He would not have been fit for the Paschal Lamb had a single blemish been discovered, but *"I find no fault in him,"* was the utterance of the great chief magistrate, who thereby declared that the Lamb might be eaten at God's Passover, the symbol and the means of the deliverance of God's people.

O beloved! You have only to study the Scriptures to find out wondrous things in them; you have only to search deeply, and you stand amazed at their richness. You will find God's Word to be a very precious word; the more you live by it and study it, the more will it be endeared to your minds.

But the next thing we must mark is *the place where this lamb was to be killed,* which peculiarly sets forth that it must be Jesus Christ. The first Passover was held in Egypt, the second Passover was held in the wilderness; but we do not read that there were more than these two Passovers celebrated until the Israelites came to Canaan. And then, if you turn to a passage in Deuteronomy, the 16th chapter, you will find that God no longer allowed them to slay the Lamb in their own houses but appointed a place for its celebration. In the wilderness, they brought their offerings to the tabernacle where the lamb was slaughtered; but at its first appointment in Egypt, of course they had no special place to which they took the lamb to be sacrificed.

Afterwards, we read in the 16th chapter of Deuteronomy, verses 5 and 6,

> "Thou mayest not sacrifice the Passover within any of thy gates, which the Lord thy God giveth thee; but at the place which the Lord thy God shall

choose to place his name in, there thou shalt sacrifice the Passover at even at the going down of the sun, at the season that thou camest forth out of Egypt. "

It was in Jerusalem that men ought to worship, for salvation was of the Jews; there was God's palace, there His altar smoked, and there only might the Paschal Lamb be killed. So our blessed Lord was led to Jerusalem. The infuriated throng dragged Him along the city streets. In Jerusalem our Lamb was sacrificed for us; it was at the precise spot where God had ordained that it should be. Oh consider this! if that mob who gathered around Him in Nazareth had been able to push Him headlong down the hill, then Christ could not have died at Jerusalem; but as He said, *"a prophet cannot perish out of Jerusalem,"* [Luke 13:33] so was it true that the King of all prophets could not do otherwise,—the prophecies concerning Him would not have been fulfilled. "Thou shalt kill the lamb in the place the Lord thy God shall appoint." He was sacrificed in the very place. Thus, again you have an incidental proof that Jesus Christ was the Paschal Lamb for his people.

The next point is *the manner of His death*. I think the manner in which the lamb was to be offered so peculiarly sets forth the crucifixion of Christ, that no other kind of death could by any means have answered all the particulars set down here. First, the lamb was to be slaughtered, and its blood caught in a basin. Usually blood was caught in a golden basin. Then, as soon as it was taken, the priest standing by the altar on which the fat was burning threw the blood on the fire or cast it at the foot of the altar. You may guess what a scene it was. Ten thousand lambs sacrificed, and the blood poured out in a purple river. Next, the lamb was to be roasted; but it was not to have a bone of its body broken. Therefore, I say there is nothing but crucifixion which can answer all these three things. Crucifixion has in it the shedding of blood—the hands and feet were pierced. It has in it the idea of roasting, for roasting signifies a long torment, and as the lamb was for a long time before the fire, so Christ, in crucifixion, was for a long time exposed to a broiling sun, and all the other pains which crucifixion engenders. Moreover not a bone was broken; which could not have been the case with any other punishment. Suppose it had been possible to put Christ to death in any other way. Sometimes the Romans put criminals to death by decapitation; but by such a death the neck is broken. Many martyrs were put to death by having a sword pierced through them; but, while that would have been a bloody death, and not a bone broken necessarily, the torment would not have been long enough to have been pictured by the roasting.

So that, take whatever punishment you will—take hanging, which sometimes the Romans practiced in the form of strangling, that mode of punishment does not involve shedding of blood, and consequently the requirements would not have been answered. And I do think that any intelligent Jew reading through this account of the Passover, and then looking at the crucifixion, must be struck by the fact that the penalty and death of the Cross by which Christ suffered, must have taken in all these three things. There was blood-shedding; the long continued suffering—the roasting of torture; and then added to that, singularly enough, by God's providence not a bone was broken, but the body was taken down from the Cross intact.

Some may say that burning might have answered the matter; but there would not have been a shedding of blood in that case and the bones would have been virtually broken in the fire. Moreover, the body would not have been preserved entire. Crucifixion was the only death which could answer all of these three requirements. And my faith receives great strength from the fact, that I see my Savior not only as a fulfillment of the type, but the only one. My heart rejoices to look on Him whom I have pierced, and see His blood, as the lamb's blood, sprinkled on my lintel and my doorpost, and see His bones unbroken, and to believe that not a bone of His spiritual body shall be broken hereafter; and rejoice, also, to see Him roasted in the fire, because thereby I see that He satisfied God for that roasting which I ought to have suffered in the torment of hell forever and ever.

Christian! I wish that I had words to depict in better language; but, as it is, I give you the undigested thoughts, which you may take home and live upon during the week; for you will find this Paschal Lamb to be an hourly feast, as well as supper, and you may feed upon it continually, until you come to the mount of God, where you shall see Him as He is, and worship Him in the Lamb in the midst thereof.

II. HOW WE DERIVE BENEFIT FROM THE BLOOD OF CHRIST

Christ our Passover is slain for us. The Jew could not say that; he could say, *a* lamb, but *"the Lamb,"* even "Christ our Passover," had not yet become a victim. And here are some of my hearers within these walls tonight who cannot say "Christ our Passover is slain for us." But glory be to God some of us can! There are not just a few here who have laid their hands upon the glorious Scapegoat; and now they can put their hands upon the Lamb also, and they can say, "Yes; it is true, He is not only slain, but Christ our Passover is slain for us." We derive benefit from the death of Christ in two modes: first, by having His blood sprinkled on us for our *redemption*; second, by our eating His flesh for food, *regeneration and sanctification*.

The first aspect in which a sinner views Jesus is that of a

lamb slain, whose blood is sprinkled on the doorpost and on the lintel. Note the fact, that the blood was never sprinkled on the threshold. It was sprinkled on the lintel, the top of the door, on the side post, *but never on the threshold,* for woe unto him who tramples underfoot the blood of the Son of God! [See Hebrews 10:29.] Even the priest of Dagon[15] trod not on the threshold of his god; much less will the Christian trample underfoot the blood of the Paschal Lamb. But His blood must be on our right hand to be our constant guard, and on our left to be our continual support.

We want to have Jesus Christ sprinkled on us. As I told you before, it is not alone the blood of Christ poured out on Calvary that saves a sinner; it is the blood of Christ sprinkled on the heart. Let us turn to the land of Zoan.[16] Do you not think you behold the scene tonight! It is evening. The Egyptians are going homeward—little thinking of what is coming. But just as soon as the sun is set, a lamb is brought into every house. The Egyptian strangers passing by, say, "These Hebrews are about to keep a feast tonight," and they retire to their houses utterly careless about it. The father of the Hebrew house takes his lamb, and examining it once more with anxious curiosity, looks it over from head to foot, to see if it has a blemish. He finds none. "My son," he says to one of them, "bring hither the basin." It is held. He stabs the lamb, and the blood flows into the basin.

Next, see the Hebrew husband as he commands his matronly wife to roast the lamb before the fire! "Take heed," he says, "that not a bone be broken." Do you see her intense anxiety, as she puts it down to roast, lest a bone should be broken? Now, says the father, "Bring a bunch of hyssop." A

---

15. A false god of the Philistines.
16. City built on a branch of the Nile in Egypt said to be where Pharaoh held court at the time of his dealings with Moses and Aaron.

child brings it. The father dips it into the blood. "Come here, my children, wife and all, and see what I am about to do." He takes the hyssop in his hands, dips it in the blood, and sprinkles it across the lintel and the door-post. His children say, "What do you mean by this ordinance?" He answers,

> "This night the Lord God will pass through to smite the Egyptians, and when He sees the blood upon the lintel and on the two side posts, the Lord will pass over the door, and will not suffer the destroyer to come into the houses to smite you." [Exodus 12:23]

The thing is done; the lamb is cooked; the guests are set down to it; the father of the family has supplicated a blessing; they are sitting down to feast upon it. And mark how the old man carefully divides joint from joint, lest a bone should be broken; and he is particular that the smallest child of the family should have some of it to eat, for so the Lord has commanded. Do you not think you see him as he tells them "it is a solemn night—make haste—in another hour we shall all go out of Egypt?" He looks at his hands, they are rough with labor, and clapping them, he cries, "I am not to be a slave any longer."

His eldest son, perhaps, has been smarting under the lash, and he says, "Son, you have had the taskmaster's lash upon you this afternoon; but it is the last time you shall feel it." He looks at them all, with tears in his eyes—"This is the night the Lord God will deliver you." Do you see them with their hats on their heads, with their loins girt, and their staves in their hands? It is the dead of the night. Suddenly they hear a shriek! The father says, "Keep within doors, my children; you will know what it is in a moment." Now another shriek—another shriek—shriek succeeds shriek: they hear perpetual wailing and lamentation. "Remain within;" says he, "the angel of death is flying abroad." A solemn silence is in the room, and they can almost hear the wings of the angel flap in the air as he passes their blood-marked door. "Be calm," says the sire, "that blood will save you."

The shrieking increases. "Eat quickly, my children," he says again, and in a moment the Egyptians coming, say, "Get yourselves hence! Get yourselves hence! We are not here for the jewels that you have borrowed. You have brought death into our houses." "Oh!" says a mother, "Go! For God's sake! Go. My eldest son lies dead!" "Go!" says a father, "Go! And peace go with you. It was an ill day when your people came into Egypt, and our king began to slay your firstborn, for God is punishing us for our cruelty." Ah! See them leaving the land; the shrieks are still heard; the Egyptian people are running to and fro seeking and finding their dead. As they go out, a son of Pharaoh is taken away without being embalmed, to be buried in one of the pyramids. Presently they see one of their taskmaster's sons taken away.

A happy night for them—when they escape! And do you see, my hearers, a glorious parallel? They had to sprinkle the blood, and also to eat the lamb. Ah! My soul, have you ever had the blood sprinkled on you? Can you say that Jesus Christ is yours? It is not enough to say "He loved the world, and gave His Son," you must say, "He loved *me* . . . and gave himself for *me.*" There is another hour coming, dear friends, when we shall all stand before God's judgment; and then God will say, "Angel of death, you once smote Egypt's first born; you know your prey. Unsheathe your sword." I behold the great gathering; you and I are standing amongst them. It is a solemn moment. All men stand in suspense. There is neither hum nor murmur. The very stars cease to shine lest the light should disturb the air by its motion. All is still. God says, "Have you sealed those that are mine?" "I have," says Gabriel; "they are sealed by blood every one of them." Then He says next, "Sweep with your sword of slaughter! Sweep the Earth! And send the unclothed, the unpurchased, and the unwashed ones to the pit." Oh! How shall we feel beloved, when for a moment we see that angel flap his wings? He is just about to fly. "But," will the doubt cross our minds "perhaps he will come to me?" Oh! No; we shall stand and look the angel full in his face.

> "Bold shall I stand in that great day!
> For who aught to my charge shall lay?
> While through thy blood absolved I am
> From sin's tremendous curse and shame."[17]

If we have the blood on us, we shall see the angel coming, we shall smile at him; we shall dare to come even to God's face and say, "Great God! I'm clean! Through Jesus' blood, I'm clean!"

But if, my hearer, your unwashed spirit shall stand unshriven[18] before its maker, if your guilty soul shall appear with all its black spots upon it, not sprinkled with the purple tide, how will you speak when you see the flash from the scabbard of the angel's sword; swift for death, and winged for destruction, as it is raised to split you apart? I think I see you standing there now. The angel is swiftly sweeping away thousands. Look! There is one of your drinking companions. There is the one with whom you danced and swore. There is another, who after attending the same chapel with you, was a despiser of religion. Now death comes nearer to you. Just as when the reaper sweeps the field and the next ear trembles because its turn shall come next, I see a brother and a sister swept into the pit. Have I no blood upon me? Then, O rocks! Be kind to me and hide me. You have no benevolence in your arms. Mountains! Let me find in your

---

17. Hymn by Count Zinzendorf, in 1739.
18. Not absolved of sin. Unforgiven.

caverns some little shelter. But it is all in vain, for vengeance shall cleave the mountains and split the rocks open to find me out. Have I no blood? Have I no hope? Ah! No! He smites me. Eternal damnation is my horrible portion. The depth of the darkness of Egypt for you, and the horrible torments of the pit from which none can escape! Ah! My dear hearers, if I could preach as I wish, I would speak to you without my lips and with my heart. I would bid you seek that sprinkled blood, and urge you by the love of your own soul, by everything that is sacred and eternal, to labor to get this blood of Jesus sprinkled on your souls. It is the blood sprinkled that saves a sinner.

But when the Christian gets the blood sprinkled, that is not all he wants. *He wants something to feed upon.* And, O sweet thought! Jesus Christ is not only a Savior for sinners, but He is food for them after they are saved. The Paschal Lamb by faith we eat. We live on it. You may tell, my hearers, whether you have the blood sprinkled on the door by this: do you eat the Lamb? Suppose for a moment that one of the old Jews had said in his heart, "I do not see the use of this feasting. It is quite right to sprinkle the blood on the lintel or else the door will not be known; but what good is all this inside?

"We will have the lamb prepared, and we will not break his bones; but we will not eat of it." And suppose he went and stored the lamb away. What would have been the consequence? Why, the angel of death would have smitten him as well as the rest, even if the blood had been upon him. And if, moreover, that old Jew had said, "there, we will have a little piece of it; but we will have something else to eat, we will have some unleavened bread; we will not turn the leaven out of our houses, but we will have some leavened bread." If they had not consumed the lamb, but had reserved some of it, then the sword of the angel would have found the heart out as well as that of any other man.

Oh! Dear hearer, you may think you have the blood sprinkled, you may think you are just; but if you do not live *on* Christ as well as *by* Christ, you will never be saved by the Paschal Lamb. "Ah!" say some, "we know nothing of this." Of course you don't. When Jesus Christ said, "except ye eat my flesh, and drink my blood, ye have no life in you," [John 6:53] there were some that said, "This is a hard saying, who can hear it?" and many from that time went back—and walked no more with Him. They could not understand Him; but, Christian, do you not understand it? Is not Jesus Christ your daily food? And even with the bitter herbs, is He not sweet food?

Some of you, my friends, who are true Christians, live too much on your changing frames and feelings, on your experiences and evidences. Now, that is all wrong. That is just as if a worshipper had gone to the tabernacle and began eating one of the coats that were worn by the priest. When a man lives on Christ's righteousness, it is the same as eating Christ's dress. When a man lives on his frames and feelings, that is as much as if the child of God should live on some tokens that he received in the sanctuary that never were meant for food, but only to comfort him a little. What the Christian lives on is not Christ's righteousness, but Christ; he does not live on Christ's pardon, but on Christ; and on Christ he lives daily, on nearness to Christ.

Oh! I do love preaching Christ. It is not the doctrine of justification that does my heart good, it is Christ, the justifier; it is not pardon that so much makes the Christian's heart rejoice, it is Christ the pardoner; it is not election that I love half so much as my being chosen in Christ before the worlds began. Oh yes! it is not final perseverance that I love so much as the thought that in Christ my life is hid, and that since He gives unto His sheep eternal life, they shall never perish, neither shall any man pluck them out of His hand. Take care, Christian, to eat the Paschal Lamb and nothing else. I tell you man, if you eat that alone, it will be like bread to you—your soul's best food. If you live on something else but the Savior, you are like one who seeks to live on some weed that grows in the desert, instead of eating the manna that comes down from Heaven. Jesus is the manna. *In* Jesus as well as *by* Jesus we live. Now, dear friends, in coming to this table, we will keep the Paschal Supper. Once more, by faith, we will eat the Lamb, by holy trust we will come to a crucified Savior, and feed on His blood, and righteousness, and atonement.

And now, in concluding, let me ask you, are you hoping to be saved my friends? One says, "Well, I don't hardly know; I hope to saved, but I do not know how." Do you know, you imagine I tell you a fiction, when I tell you that people are hoping to be saved by works, but it is not so, it is a reality. In traveling through the country I meet with all sorts of characters, but most frequently with self-righteous persons. How often I meet with a man who thinks himself quite godly because he attends the church once on a Sunday, and who thinks himself quite righteous because he belongs to the Establishment; as a churchman said to me the other day, "I am a rigid churchman." "I am glad of that," I said to him, "because then you are a Calvinist, if you hold the 'Articles[19].'" He replied "I don't know about the 'Articles,' I go more by the 'Rubric.'[20]" And so I thought he was more of a formalist than a Christian.

There are many persons like that in the world. Another says, "I believe I shall be saved. I don't owe anybody anything; I have never been bankrupt; I pay everybody twenty

---

19. A distinct often numbered section of a writing.
20. A rule of conduct for a liturgical service.

shillings in the pound; I never get drunk; and if I wrong anybody at any time, I try to make up for it by giving a pound a year to such-and-such a society; I am as religious as most people; and I believe I shall be saved." That will not do. It is as if some old Jew had said, "We don't want the blood on the lintel, we have got a mahogany lintel; we don't want the blood on the doorpost, we have a mahogany doorpost." Ah! Whatever it was, the angel would have smitten it if it had not had the blood upon it. You may be as righteous as you like: if you have not the blood sprinkled, all the goodness of your doorposts and lintels will be of no avail whatever.

"Yes," says another, "I am not trusting exactly there. I believe it is my duty to be as good as I can; but then I think Jesus Christ's mercy will make up the rest. I try to be as righteous as circumstances allow; and I believe that whatever deficiencies there may be, Christ will make them up." That is as if a Jew had said, "Child, bring me the blood," and then, when that was brought, he had said, "bring me a ewer[21] of water;" and then he had taken it and mixed it together, and sprinkled the doorpost with it. Why, the angel would have smitten him as well as anyone else, for it is *blood, blood, blood, blood* that saves! It is not blood mixed with the water of our poor works; it is *blood, blood, blood, blood* and nothing else.

And the only way of salvation is by blood. For, without the shedding of blood there is no remission of sin. Have the precious blood sprinkled upon you, my hearers; trust in the precious blood; let your hope be in a salvation sealed with an atonement of Christ's precious blood, and you are saved. But having no blood, or having blood mixed with anything else, you are damned as you are alive—for the angel shall slay you, however good and righteous you may

---

21. A type of pitcher or jug shaped like a vase and used in the past for holding water.

be. Go home, then, and think of this: "Christ our Passover is sacrificed for us."

CHAPTER 3
THE EXODUS

A SERMON
(No. 55)

Delivered on Sabbath Morning, December 9, 1855, by

REVEREND CHARLES H. SPURGEON,
at New Park Street Chapel, Southwark, England

*"And it came to pass at the end of the four hundred
and thirty years, even the selfsame day it came to pass,
that all the hosts of the Lord went out from the land of
Egypt."—Exodus 12:41.*

I T IS OUR FIRM CONVICTION and increasing belief,
that the historical books of Scripture were intended to
teach us by types and figures spiritual things. We believe
that every portion of Scripture history is not only a faithful
transcript of what actually did happen, but also a shadow
of what happens spiritually in the dealings of God with His
people, or in the dispensations of His grace towards the
world at large. We do not look upon the historical books
of Scripture as being mere rolls of history, such as profane
authors might have written, but we regard them as being the
most true and infallible records of the past, and also the most
bright and glorious foreshadowings of the future, or else the
most wondrous metaphors and marvelous illustrations of
things which are verily received among us, and most truly
felt in the Christian heart.

We may be wrong—however, we believe we are not; at
any rate, the very error has given us instruction, and our
mistake has afforded us comfort. We look upon the Book of
Exodus as being a book of types of the deliverances which

God will give to His elect people: not only as a history of what He has done, in bringing them out of Egypt by smiting the firstborn, leading them through the Red Sea, and guiding them through the wilderness, but also as a picture of His faithful dealings with all His people, whom by the blood of Christ He separates from the Egyptians, and by His strong and mighty hand takes out of the house of their bondage and out of the land of their slavery.

Last Sabbath evening we had the type of the Passover—the Paschal Lamb; and we showed you then, how the sprinkled blood, and the eaten lamb, were types of the blood applied for our justification, and of the flesh received by inward communion with Christ Jesus, the soul living and feeding upon Him. We now take the Exodus, or the going of the children of Israel out of Egypt, as being a type and picture of the going out of all the vessels of mercy from the house of their bondage, and the deliverance of all the lawful captives from the chains of their cruel taskmasters, by sovereign and omnipotent grace, through the Passover of our Lord Jesus Christ.

The land of Egypt is a picture of the house of bondage into which all God's covenant people will, sooner or later, be brought on account of their sin. All those whom God means to give an inheritance in Canaan; He will first take down into Egypt. Even Jesus Christ himself went into Egypt before He appeared publicly as a teacher before the world, that in His instance, as well as in that of every Christian, the prophecy might be fulfilled—"Out of Egypt have I called my Son." Everyone who enjoys the liberty wherewith Christ has made us free must first feel the galling bondage of sin. Our wrists must be made to smart by the fetters of our iniquity, and our backs must be made to bleed by the lash of the Law—the taskmaster which drives us to Jesus Christ.

TRIALS MUST COME BEFORE DELIVERANCE

There is no true liberty which is not preceded by true bondage; there is no true deliverance from sin, unless we have first of all groaned and cried unto God, as did the people of Israel when in bondage in Egypt. We must all serve in the brickkiln; we must all be wearied with toiling among the pots; or otherwise we could never realize that glorious verse—*"Though ye have lien among the pots, yet shall ye be as the wings of a dove covered with silver, and her feathers with yellow gold"* [Psalm 68:13]. We must have bondage before liberty; before resurrection there must come death; before life there must come corruption; before we are brought out of the horrible pit and the miry clay we must be made to exclaim, *"I sink in deep mire, where there is no standing;"* and in the past, like Jonah, we can be fetched out of the whale's belly, and delivered from our sin [Psalm 69:2]. We must have been taken down to the bottoms of the mountains, with the weeds wrapped about our heads, shuddering under a deep sense of our own nothingness and fearing that the Earth with her bars was around us forever. [See Jonah Chapter 2.] Taking this as a key, you will see that the deliverance out of Egypt is a beautiful picture of the deliverance of all God's people from the bondage of the law and the slavery of their sins.

I. FIRST, CONSIDER THE MODE OF THEIR GOING OUT.

When the children of Israel went out of Egypt it is a remarkable thing that they were forced out by the Egyptians. Those Egyptians who had enriched themselves with their slavery, said, *"Get ye hence, for we be all dead men;"*

[Exodus 12:33] they begged and entreated them to go; yes, they hurried them forth, gave them jewels that they might depart, and made them leave the land. It is a striking thing that the very sins which oppressed the child of God in Egypt are the very things that drive him to Jesus. Our sins make slaves of us while we are in Egypt, and when God the Holy Spirit stirs them up against us, they beat us with cruel lashes, until our souls are worn with extreme bondage; but those very sins, by God's grace, are the means made to drive us to the Savior.

The dove flees not to the dove cote unless the eagle pursues it; so sins like eagles pursue the timid soul, making it fly into the clefts of the Rock Christ Jesus to hide itself. Once, beloved, our sins kept us from Christ; but now every sin drives us to Him for pardon. I would not have known Christ if I had not known sin; I would not have known a deliverer, if I had not smarted under the Egyptian lash. The Holy Spirit drives us to Christ, just as the Egyptians drove the people out of Egypt.

Again: the children of Israel went out of Egypt covered with jewels and arrayed in their best garments. The Jews have ever on their feast days been desirous of wearing jewels and all kinds of goodly apparel; and when they were too poor to possess them, they would borrow jewels for the purpose. So it was at this remarkable Passover. They had been so oppressed that they had kept no festival for many a year; but now they all arrayed themselves in their best garments, and at the command of God did borrow of the Egyptians jewels of silver, and jewels of gold, and raiment; "and the things as they required: and they spoiled the Egyptians."

Let none say that this was robbery. It would have been, had it not been commanded of God; but as a king can set aside his own laws, so God is above His laws, and whatsoever He orders is right. Abraham would have been guilty of murder in taking up his knife to slay his son, had not God commanded him to do so; but the fact of God having commanded the action, made it justifiable and right. But, moreover, the word "borrowed" here is by the best translators said to mean nothing more than that the children of Israel asked them for their jewels, and had no intention whatever of returning them, and entered into no agreement to do so; and it was most just, that they should do this, because they had toiled for the Egyptians for years, without having had any remuneration.

SOMETIMES NECESSITY HAS NO LAW

How much more shall that God who is above all necessities be the master of His own laws? The great Potentate, the only wise God, the King of kings, has a right to make what laws He pleases; and let not vain man dare to question His Maker, when his Maker gives him a command. But the fact is very significant. The children of Israel did not go out of Egypt poorly clad; they went out with their best clothing on, and moreover, they had borrowed jewels of gold, and jewels of silver, and raiment; and they went gladly out of the land. Ah! Beloved, that is just how a child of God comes out of Egypt. He does not come out of his bondage with his old garments of self-righteousness on: oh! no; as long as he wears those he will always keep in Egypt; but he marches out with the blood and righteousness of Jesus Christ upon him, and adorned with the goodly graces of the Holy Spirit. Oh! Beloved, if you could see a child of Israel coming out of the bondage of sin, you would say, "Who is this that cometh up from the wilderness?" Is this the poor slave that was making bricks without straw? Is this the wretch who had nothing but rags and tatters on him? Is this the poor creature whose whole person was soiled with the mud of

Egypt's river, and who labored in Goshen's land without a wage or pay? Yes, it is he; and now he is arrayed like a king, and appareled as a prince.

Behold, each of these men of labor comes like a bridegroom decked for his wedding, and their wives seem like royal brides clad in their bridal robes. Every child of God, when he comes out of Egypt, is arrayed in goodly apparel.

> "Strangely, my soul, art thou arrayed,
> By the great sacred Three;
> In sweetest harmony of praise.
> Let all thy powers agree."[22]

Note, moreover, that these people obtained their jewels from the Egyptians. God's people never lose anything by going to the house of bondage. They win their choicest jewels from the Egyptians. "Strangely true it is, sins do me good," said an old writer once, "because they drive me to the Savior; and so I get good by them." Ask the humble Christian where he got his humility, and ten to one he will say that he got it in the furnace of deep sorrow on account of sin. See another who is tender in conscience: where did he get that jewel from? It came from Egypt, I am sure.

We get more by being in bondage, under conviction of sin, than we often do by liberty. That bondage state under which you are now laboring, you poor wayworn child of sorrow, shall be good for you; for when you come out of Egypt you will steal jewels from the Egyptians; you will have won pearls from your very convictions. "Oh!" say some, "I have been for months and years toiling under a sense of sin, and cannot get deliverance." Well, I hope you will get it soon; but if you do not, you will have gained all the more jewels by stopping there, and when you come out, you will

---

22. Hymn, "Awake My Heart, Arise My Tongue" by Isaac Watts.

very likely make the best of Christians.

There was hardly a more noble preacher to sinners than John Bunyan. And who suffered more than he did? For years he was doubting and hesitating, sometimes thinking that Christ would save him, at other times thinking that he was never one of the elect, and continually bemoaning himself; but he got jewels while he was in bondage that he would never have obtained anywhere else. Who could have made a large collection of jewels like *Pilgrim's Progress*[23], if he had not lived in Egypt? It was because he tarried so long in Egypt that he gathered so many jewels. And oh! beloved, let us be content to stop a little while in distress; for the jewels that we shall win there will adorn us all our lives long, and we shall one night come out of Egypt, not with weeping, but with songs and crowns of rejoicing. We shall have *"the garments of praise for the spirit of heaviness;"* [Isaiah 61:3] the sackcloth shall be removed from our loins, and the ashes from our head, and we shall march forth decked with jewels, glittering with gold and silver.

TODAY IS THE DAY OF SALVATION

But there is one more thought concerning the way of their coming out; and that is, they came out in haste. I think a child of God, whenever he has the opportunity of coming out of bondage, will quickly avail himself of it. When a man comes to me, and says, "I am under deep conviction of sin," and so on, and seems to be very well content, talking about tomorrow, and tomorrow, and tomorrow, and saying, "I can repent when I please, and I can believe when I please," and always procrastinating!—Ah! I think to myself that is not the Lord's deliverance, for when His people go forth out of

---

23. A highly popular Pure Gold Classic published by Bridge-Logos.

Egypt, they are always in a hurry to get out. I never met with a poor sinner under a sense of sin, who was not in haste to get his burden off his back.

No man has a broken heart, that doesn't want to have it bound up directly. *"To day if ye will hear his voice, harden not your hearts..."* says the Holy Ghost [Hebrews 3:15]. He never says tomorrow; today is His continual cry, and every true born Israelite will want to get out of Egypt, whenever he has the opportunity. He will not stop to knead his dough, and make his bread to carry with him; but he will be in such a hurry to get away that he will carry the unleavened bread on his shoulders. He, who hates the noxiousness of the dungeon, longs to hear the wards[24] of the lock creak, so that he may find liberty; he who has been long in the pit hastily wants to escape; and he who has suffered the taskmaster's whip flees like a dove to his window, that he may find peace and deliverance in Christ Jesus.

II. THE MAGNITUDE OF THIS DELIVERANCE

But having noticed three points of similarity in the emigration of the Israelites and the deliverance of God's people, we would lead your attention, secondly, to their deliverance. Did it never strike you what a wonderful exodus of the people of Israel this was? Do you know how many people went out? According to the very lowest calculations, there must have been two million and a half, all assembled together in one place, and all coming out of the country at one time. And then, besides these, there went out with them an exceeding great company—a mixed multitude. The number must have been so large that it is impossible to imagine it.

---

24. Part of a lock that has various sized slots that will allow the correctly cut key to turn the lock.

Suppose the people of London should all go out at once to march through a wilderness; it would be a marvelous thing in history, such as we can hardly conceive of; but here were, to say the least, two million people, all at one time coming out from the midst of Egypt, and going forth from the country. *"They journeyed,"* it is said, *"from Rameses to Succoth"* [Exodus 12:37]. Rameses was where they were employed in building a city for the king. They stayed in Succoth, or booths. Because such an immense multitude could not find houses, they therefore made booths; and hence the children of Israel ever afterwards kept "the feast of tabernacles," to commemorate their building of the booths at Succoth, when they first came out of Egypt.

What a mind Moses must have had, to direct so great an army; or rather what a Spirit must that have been that rested on him, so that he could lead them all to one place, and then guide them all through the wilderness; if you bear in mind this mighty number, you will be astonished to think what a quantity of manna it must have required to feed them, and what a stream of water that must have been which followed them! Talk of the armies of Xerxes, or the host of the Persians; speak of the mighty armies that kings and potentates have assembled! Here was an army that outrivaled them all in comparison. But oh! Beloved, how much grandeur is there in the thought of the multitudes Christ redeems with His blood. Christ did not die to save a few; *"he shall see of the travail of his soul, and shall be abundantly satisfied. By his knowledge shall my righteous servant justify many"* [Isaiah 53:11]. *"A multitude which no man can number"* shall stand before the throne of God and of the Lamb. [See Revelation 7:9.]

Oh! Wondrous the stars of Heaven, nor the dust of the Earth, nor the sand of the sea; but let us remember that God has promised to Abraham—*"As the sand upon the sea shore, even so shall thy seed be.*" [See Genesis 15:5 and Genesis 22:17.] "*Who can count the dust of Jacob, and the number of the fourth part of Israel?*" [Numbers 23:10]. They lick up the earth like water, and the land is utterly devoured before them. Oh! Mighty God! How great is that deliverance which brings out a host of your elect, more countless than the stars and as innumerable as the sands upon a thousand shores! All hail to your power that does all this!

You will have another idea of the greatness of this work, when you think of the different stations which the children of Israel must have occupied. I suppose they were not all equally destitute. They were not all toiling in the same brickkilns, but some of them would be in one place, some in another—some working in the king's court, some for the less prominent Egyptians—dispersed everywhere; but whatever their work might be, they all came. If Pharaoh had slaves in his halls, they marched out the selfsame day from his golden gated palace, at Memphis or at Thebes. They all came forth that same day from their different situations, and guided by God they all came to one spot, where they built their booths, and called it Succoth. As when the autumn declines, and the winter approaches, we have seen the chattering swallows gather upon the housetop, prepared for distant flights beyond the purple sea, where they might find another summer in another land, so did these Israelites from all their countries thus assemble, and stand together, about to take their flight across a trackless wilderness to that land of which God had told them saying, "*Behold, I will bring you into a land that floweth with milk and honey*" [Leviticus 20:24].Oh! Great and glorious works of God! "*great are thy works, O Lord, and marvellous are thy doings; and that my soul knoweth right well.*" [Psalm 139:14 and Revelation 15:3].

I WOULD HAVE YOU REMEMBER ONE THING

Beloved, as great as this emigration was, and enormous as were the multitudes that left Egypt, it was only *one* Passover that set them all free. They did not want two celebrations of the supper; they did not need two angels to fly through Egypt; it was not necessary to have two deliverances: but all in one night, all by the Paschal Lamb, all by the Passover supper, they were saved. Look at yonder host above! Do you see the blood-washed throng of souls, chosen of God and precious? Can you tell their number? Can you count the small dust of the beatified[25] ones before the throne? Ah! No; but here is a thought for you. They did not want two Christs to save them; they did not require two Holy Spirits to deliver them; nor did it take two sacrifices to bring them there.

> "Ask them whence their victory came,
> They with united breath
> Ascribe their victory to the Lamb,
> Their triumph in his death."[26]

One agonizing sacrifice, one death on Calvary, one bloody sweat on Gethsemane, one shriek of *"It is finished."* consummated all the work of redemption. Oh! The precious blood of Christ! I love it when I think it saves one sinner; but to think of the multitude of sinners that it saves! Beloved, we do not think and meditate enough on our Lord Jesus Christ; we have not even half an estimation of His precious person as we ought to have. We do not value His blood at the right price. Why, poor sinner, are you saying this morning, "This blood cannot save me." What! Not save

---

25. Blessed
26. Hymn, *Give Me the Wings of Faith by Isaac Watts.*

you, when it is engaged to save thousands upon thousands, and myriads of myriads? Shall the shepherd who gathers the whole flock together, and leads them unto the pastures lose a single lamb? Or perhaps you say, "I am so little." For that very reason then, it will not take much of His power to take care of you.

"But," says one, "I am so great a sinner." Yes, then, so much the better, for He *"came to save sinners, of whom I am chief,"* said Paul; and He came to save you. [See 1 Timothy 1:15.] Ah! do not fear, you sons of God; He who brought the Israelites all out in one night can bring you all out, though you are in the severest bondage. Perhaps there is one of you who not only has to make bricks without straw, but has to make twice as many bricks as anyone else, you think, and your taskmaster has a whip which goes right around you, and cuts the flesh off you every time; you have worse bondage than any one, your slavery is more intense, your oven hotter, your pots harder to make. Very well, I am glad of it: how sweet liberty will be to you!

And I will tell you, you shall not be left in Egypt; for if you were, what would old Pharaoh say? "He said he would bring them all out, but he has not; there is one left;" and he would parade that poor Israelite through the streets, he would take him through Memphis and Thebes, and say, "There is one that God would not deliver; there is one I had so tight in my grasp that He could not get him out!" No, Satan! You shall not say that of one of the Lord's people; they shall all be there, the great and the small; this unworthy hand shall take the hand of the blessed St. Paul; they shall all be in Heaven, shall all be redeemed, shall all be saved; all I say, and mark it down, through *one* sacrifice, *one* covenant, *one* blood, *one* Passover.

III. THE COMPLETENESS OF THEIR DELIVERANCE

This brings us to speak more fully of our third point. Our text says,—*"It came to pass at the end of the four hundred and thirty years, even the selfsame day it came to pass, that all the hosts of the Lord went out from the land of Egypt."* Our dear Arminian friends think that some of the Lord's people will not come out of Egypt, but will be lost at last. Ah! Well, as good Hart says—

> "If one poor saint may fall away,
> It follows so may all;"

Then none of us are safe and secure. Therefore, we do not give way to that. But all the hosts came out of Egypt, every one of them; not a soul was left behind. Look . . . there is a poor man that was lame. Ah, look again! Now you see him throw away his crutches. There is a poor woman sick; yes, but she suddenly rises from her bed. There is another who has palsy, he can by no means lift himself up, but his frame in a moment becomes firm, *"for there was not one feeble person in all their tribes."*—Psalm 105:37. Oh yes, and there is a poor little babe who knows nothing about it; but still it leaves Egypt, carried by its mother.

The old grey-haired sire tottered not on his staff. Though eighty years of age, yet he was a son of Israel, and out he came. There was a youth who had just begun to have his shoulders chafed by the load he was carrying on them; but though he was young the time was come for him, and out he came. They all came out, every one of them; there was not one left behind. I do not suppose they had any hospitals there; but if they had, I am sure they did not leave any of them in the hospital, for all were healed in an instant. There was one Israelite who had rebelled against the government of Moses, and said, "Who made you a judge and a divider over us?" But they did not leave him behind; even he came out. All of them came out; we do not find that there was some poor shriveled creature whose arms and legs were almost useless, and who was sick in the mind left behind.

So beloved, if you are "the smallest lamb in Jesus' fold," you are "one in Jesus now;" though you have very little learning, and very little common sense, you will come out of Egypt. If the Lord has put you there in bondage, and you have been made to groan there, He will make you sing by-and-by, when you are redeemed from it. There is no fear of your being left behind; for if you were, Pharaoh would say, "He delivered the strong ones, but he was not able to bring out the weak;" and then there would be laughter in hell against the mightiness and omnipotence of God. They all came out.

Not a Hoof Is Left Behind

But not only the people; they all had their cattle with them. [See Exodus 10:26.] They were to have all their goods, as well as their persons. What does this teach us? Well, not only that all God's people shall be saved, but that all God's people ever had shall be restored. All that Jacob ever took down to Egypt shall be brought out again. Have I lost a perfect righteousness in Adam? I shall have a perfect righteousness in Christ. Have I lost happiness on Earth in Adam? God will give me much happiness here below in Christ. Have I lost Heaven in Adam? I shall have Heaven in Christ; for Christ came not only to seek and to save the people that were lost, but that which was lost; that is, all the inheritance, as well as the people; all their property. Not the sheep merely, but the good pasture that the sheep had lost: not only the prodigal son, but all the prodigal son's estates.

Everything was brought out of Egypt; not even Joseph's bones were left behind. The Egyptians could not say that they had a scrap of the Israelites' property—not even one of their kneading troughs, or one of their old garments. And when Christ shall have conquered and gathered all things to himself, the Christian shall not have lost one atom by the toils of Egypt, but shall be able to say, *"O death where is thy sting? O grave, where is thy victory?"* [1 Corinthians 15:55]. O hell, where is your triumph? You have not a flag or a pennant to show off your victory; there is not a shield or a helmet left upon the battlefield; there is not a single trophy which you may raise up in hell in scorn of Christ. He has not only delivered His people, but they have gone out with flying colors, taking their shields with them. Stand and admire and love the Lord, who thus delivers all His people.

IV. THE TIME WHEN THE ISRAELITES CAME OUT OF EGYPT

"It came to pass at the end of four hundred and thirty years, even the selfsame day it came to pass, that all the hosts of the Lord went out from the land of Egypt" [Exodus 12:41]. God had promised to Abraham that His people should be in bondage four hundred and thirty years, and they were not in bondage one day more. As soon as God's bond became due, though it had been drawn four hundred and thirty years before, He paid the bill; He required no more time to do it in, but He did it at once. Christopher Ness[27] says they had to tarry for the fulfillment of the promise until the night came; for though He fulfilled it the selfsame day, He made them stay to the end of it, to prove their faith. Ness was wrong there, because Scripture days begin at night. *"The evening and the morning were the second day"* [Genesis 1:8].

27. English preacher and author who lived from 1621-1705.

So that God did not make them wait, but paid them at once. As soon as the day came, beginning with our night, as the Jewish day does now, and the scriptural day always did—as soon as the clock struck—God paid His bond. We have heard of some landlords who come for their rent at twelve o'clock precisely. Well, we admire a man's honesty if he pays him exactly at that minute; but God is never behind in fulfilling His promises, not by the ticking of a clock. Though His promise may seem to tarry, wait for it; you may be mistaken as to the date; if He has promised anything on a certain day, He will not keep you waiting until the next day. The selfsame day that the Lord had promised, the Israelites came out.

And so all the Lord's people shall come out of bondage at the predestined moment: and they cannot possibly come out of bondage before the appointed time. O you poor distressed heir of Heaven, groaning under sin, and seeking rest, but finding none, believe that it is the Lord's will that you should be a little longer where there is a smoking furnace. Wait a little—He is doing you good. Like Jesus of old, He is speaking hardly to you, to try your faith; He is telling you now that thou are a dog, because He wants to hear you say, *"Truth, Lord: yet the dogs eat of the crumbs. . . ."* [Matthew 15:27]. He would not keep you waiting, if your eagerness did not thereby get fresh strength; He would not keep you crying, if He did not mean to make it a sign of better grace to you for the future. Therefore wait; for you shall come out of Egypt, and have a joyous rescue in that day when *". . . they shall come with singing unto Zion, with songs and everlasting joy upon their heads."* [See Isaiah 35:10.]

But now, beloved, we must finish up in a very solemn manner, by reminding you of the companions that came out of Egypt with the children of Israel. When the children of Israel came out of Egypt, there were certain persons in Egypt,

94

dissatisfied with the king—very likely culprits, condemned persons, debtors, bankrupts, and such like persons, who were tired of their country, and who, as is wittily said of those who are transported, "left their country for their country's good." But though these people went with the children of Israel, keep in mind, they were not of them. They escaped, but the door was not opened to let them out; it was only opened to let out the children of Israel.

It is said that the mixed multitude fell into lusting; it was the mixed multitude that taught them to worship the golden calf; it was the mixed multitude that always led them astray. And that mixed multitude have their representatives even now. There are many men that came out of the land of Egypt who never were Israelites. There are many that join with us in church fellowship, and eat that spiritual bread, and drink of that spiritual rock that followed them; and yet with many of them God is not well pleased, just as there were many of old with whom He was not well pleased, and who were overthrown in the wilderness.

"Ah!" says someone, "but I thought if they had been in Egypt, certainly if they came out they must have been Christians; for you have used the metaphors." Yes, but keep in mind how these people were in Egypt. This mixed multitude was never in bondage in Egypt. It was Israel that had to feel the taskmaster's whip, and to make the bricks without straw. But these fellows had nothing to do with that. They were Egyptians themselves—true-born Egyptians—"heirs of sin and children of wrath;" they never had any real bondage, and therefore they could not rejoice as the true Israelite did, when they were set free from the yoke of Pharaoh. These people are represented amongst us today by certain persons, who will tell us, "Ah! I know I have been a sinner." That is as much as to say you have been an Egyptian, and that is all. They have said, "But I cannot say, I have felt my sin, and utterly abhorred it and wept over it." They come and say, "I am a sinner," hear something about Jesus Christ, catch at it with a fancied faith—not with the faith that unites with the Lamb and brings us true salvation, but with a notional, pretended faith, and they get deliverance; and some of these people are marvelously happy. They have no doubts and fears; they are at ease, like Moab; though they have not been emptied from vessel to vessel.

They can tell us about Egypt, of course; they know as much about it as the child of God. If the child of God describes the brickkiln, and how they made bricks without straw, it is because he has seen it, though he has not felt it; and he can talk about it, perhaps better than the poor Israelite. Why? Because the poor Israelite has sometimes been smitten on the mouth by the hard taskmasters so that he stammers, and cannot speak as well as one who never had a blow. He knows all about the bondage; perhaps he has invented some of it, in order to try the poor Israelite; and he can describe very accurately the going out of Egypt and the journey through the wilderness.

But here is the difference between the Israelites and the Egyptians. The Egyptians did not sprinkle the blood on the doorposts; and we do not read of the mixed multitude eating the paschal lamb, for it is written, "No stranger shall eat thereof." Some persons are continually saying, "I believe I am going to Heaven;" but they have never sprinkled the blood, never eaten the paschal Lamb, never had fellowship with Christ, and never had vital union with Him.

FEIGNED CHRISTIANITY

I say this to you members of Christian churches! There are many of you who have an assumed experience and an incomplete religion. There are many of you who have the externals merely of godliness! But you're whitewashed sepulchers, outwardly fair and beautiful, like the garnished gardens of a cemetery; but inwardly you are full of dead men's bones and rottenness! Be persuaded, I beg you, to get deliverance in no other way except by the blood of the Lamb, and by really feasting on Christ. Many a man gets deliverance by stifling his conscience.

"Ah!" says one of these mixed multitude, "here am I in the prison; and this is the night when the children of Israel go out of Egypt; Oh! If only I might go out with them!" What does he do? He calls to the jail keeper who is upset and frightened for he has just lost his eldest son. The prisoner calls to him again and says, "Let me out!" and he bribes the keeper to let him go.

And there is many a man that gets out of Egypt by bribing his conscience and saying to it. "Master conscience, I will never get drunk anymore; I will always go to church; there is my shop, that is always open on Sunday—I will put two shutters up, and that is almost as good as closing it entirely; and I will not do the business myself—I will get a servant to do it for me." And out he comes! But it would be better for him to remain in Egypt than get out like that.

Again, there are some that get out by pure force; the keeper falls down dead, and so they get out of prison. There are also men who not only bribe, but kill their conscience; they go so far that their conscience is almost dead, and one day when the keeper is distracted they rush forth and escape; thereby thinking and saying, "peace, peace, where there is no peace." They wrap themselves up in the folds of their own delusions, and invent for themselves refuges of lies, where they place their trust.

O mixed multitude! You are the ruin of the churches; you set us lusting; the pure Israelite's blood is tainted by union with you; you sit as God's people sit, and yet you are not

His people; you hear as God's people hear, and yet you are *"in the gall of bitterness and in the bonds of iniquity."* [See Acts 8:23.] You take the sacrament as sweetly as others, while you are eating and drinking damnation to yourself; you come to the church meeting, and you sit in the private assembly of the saints; but even when you are there, you are nothing but a wolf in sheep's clothing, entering the flock when you ought not to be there.

My dear hearers, do try yourselves, to see whether you are real Israelites. Could Christ say to you, *"Behold an Israelite indeed, in whom there is no guile?"* [See John 1:47.] Have you the blood on your doorpost? Have you eaten of Jesus? Do you live on Him? Do you have fellowship with Him? Has God the Holy Ghost brought you out of Egypt? Or have you come out yourself? Have you found refuge in Christ's dear Cross and wounded side? If you have, rejoice, for Pharaoh himself cannot bring you back again; but if you have not, I pray my Master to dash your peace into atoms, fair and lovely as it may be; I beseech Him to send the winds of conviction and the floods of His wrath, that your house may fall now, rather than it should stand until your death, and then, in the last solemn hour, the edifice of your own hands would totter.

Mixed multitude! Hear this, you assembled gatherings of professors! *"Examine yourselves, whether ye be in the faith; prove your-own selves. Know ye not your own selves, how that Jesus Christ is in you, except ye be reprobates?"* [2 Corinthians 13:5] But if he is not in you, then you are still reprobates, whom God abhors.

I pray for you now and all those in bondage that through the shed blood of Christ Jesus His Son, the Lord will deliver all His children from the house of bondage, and will bring all His people out of Egypt to His glory and praise.

CHAPTER 4
THE ONLY ATONING PRIEST

A SERMON
(No. 1034)

Delivered on Lord's Day Morning, February 4th, 1872,
by
REVEREND CHARLES H. SPURGEON,
at the Metropolitan Tabernacle,
Newington, London, England

*"And every priest standeth daily ministering and offering
oftentimes the same sacrifices, which can never take away
sins: But this man, after he had offered one sacrifice for
sins for ever, sat down on the right hand of God; From
henceforth expecting till his enemies be made his footstool.
For by one offering he hath perfected for ever them that
are sanctified."—Hebrews 10:11-14.*

WE SHALL HAVE TO REPEAT A TRUTH which has sounded forth from this pulpit many hundreds of times; but we offer no apology for our repetitions, seeing that the truth to be preached is one that cannot be proclaimed too often. What a wonderful variety of celestial scenery there is when you lift up your eyes at night to the stars! The astronomer can turn his telescope first to one quarter of the heavens, and then to another, and find an endless change in the grandeurs that meet his gaze. Such are the doctrines of the Gospel; they are full of variety, beauty, and glory: yet in the heavens one or two conspicuous constellations are more often regarded by the human eye than all the rest put together. The mariner looks for the Great Bear, the Pointers[28], and the Pole Star;[29] or, if he should cross the equator, he gazes on the Southern Cross. Though these stars have often been looked upon, it is never thought to be superfluous that practical men would still observe them. Night by night they have their watchers; for by them ten thousand sails are steered. I would suppose that in those days, now happily past, when slavery reigned in the Southern States of America, the black man, if he desired liberty for his boy would be sure to point out to him the star of liberty and say, "Know well, my child, those friendly stars which point to the lone star of liberty. Follow that light until it leads you to a land where fetters no longer clank on human limbs.

Even so it seems to me that certain doctrines, and especially the doctrines of atonement and justification by faith, are like these guiding stars; and we should frequently point them out and make sure that our children know them. Furthermore, to all who listen to us, whatever else they may be mistaken about, make sure they are clear about these guides of men to the haven of freedom and eternal rest. I believe if I would preach the atonement of our Lord Jesus Christ every Sabbath day, morning and evening, and nothing else, my ministry would not be unprofitable, but perhaps it might be more profitable than it is. Therefore, we will be discussing the same truth we taught last Sabbath evening. Many dishes are

---

28. In the southern hemisphere, Alpha Centauri forms the outer star of *The Pointers* or *The Southern Pointers,* so called because the line through Beta Centauri (Hadar/Agena), some 4.5° west, points directly to the constellation Crux—the Southern Cross. The Pointers easily distinguish the true Southern Cross from the fainter asterism known as the False Cross.

29. A pole star is a visible star, preferably a prominent one, that is approximately aligned with the Earth's axis of rotation; that is, a star whose apparent position is close to one of the celestial poles, and which lies approximately directly overhead when viewed from the Earth's North Pole or South Pole.

put upon the table at intervals, but bread and salt are always placed there; and so we will have the atonement again, and again, and again; for this is the bread and salt of the gospel feast. I purpose, this morning, to handle the text thusly:

Firstly, we will *read, mark, and learn it.*

Secondly, we will ask God's grace that we may *inwardly digest it.*

ONE: THE READING, MARKING, AND LEARNING OF IT.

Come then, and you will observe that in the text there are three things very clearly stated. The atoning sacrifice of Jesus, our great High Priest, is set forth first by way of *contrast;* then its *character* is described; and, then, thirdly, its *consequences* are mentioned. I will comment briefly upon each.

First, it is set forth by way of *contrast*—contrast with that ancient dispensation which was of divine origin that conveyed much blessing to Israel, and had the divine approval resting upon it. In that old dispensation, the first point mentioned in the text is, that there were many priests. *"For every priest standeth"*—implying that there were several. There were many priests at the same time—the sacrifices of the temple were too numerous to have been performed by one man: all the descendants of Aaron were set apart to this work, and even then they required the aid of the Levites in certain inferior duties.

Because there were many priests at one time, there were also many in succession. As a priest died, he was succeeded by his sons. By reason of infirmity, they were not able to continue in their office through the whole of their lifetime; there was a certain period at which they were commanded to surrender their office to younger men. By reason of mortality the priesthood was perpetually changing; one high priest died, and was succeeded by another.

Now the reason for the existence of many priests was because no one priest had accomplished the work of expiation. The good man has gone to his fathers and offered up the last of the morning lambs—but the morning lambs must still be offered. The high priest, being dead, there would be no more opportunity for him to enter into that which is within the veil, but there must be a new high priest appointed, for the work is not finished. There were many priests, and as one generation passed away, another inherited the mitre[30].

Now, herein is the glory of Christ that He is but One, and our attention is called to this by the apostle; that whereas there were many priests, and the sacrifices were hereby proved to be incomplete since others had to take up the work; here is but One priest forever, and He has finished His work, and therefore sits down at the right hand of God.

In further contrast, we observe that as there were many priests, there were also many sacrifices for sins. The sacrifice was offered once, but sin was not put away, and therefore had to be offered again. The great Day of Atonement came every year, wherein sin was brought afresh to remembrance. There was a Day of Atonement last year, but the people are unforgiven, and there must be a Day of Atonement this year. When the Day of Atonement is over and the priest has come forth in his holy and beautiful apparel, with the breastplate gleaming in the light of God, Israel may rejoice for a while, but there is one thought that will sadden her; there must be a Day of Atonement next year, for sin still remains upon Israel, in spite of all that the house of Aaron can do by all their sacrifices.

Yes, and furthermore, remembrance of sin was of necessity made every day. There was the lamb for the morning, the

---

30. A liturgical headdress worn by priests.

innocent victim was slaughtered and burned; but the morning sacrifice did not put away the day's sin, for as the sun began to descend in the west another victim must be brought, and so on each morning and each night, victim, victim, victim, sacrifice, sacrifice, sacrifice, because the expiation was always incomplete. But our blessed Lord, *"the Lamb of God, which taketh away the sin of the world,"* [John 1:29], was sacrificed but *once,* and that *one* sacrifice has completed His expiatory work. In very truth His was a sacrifice of nobler name and richer blood than theirs.

Follow the contrast a little further, and observe the apostle's assertion that the repeated sacrifices of the law could never take away sin. Those who thought they could must have been those strangely blind. How could the blood of bulls and of goats put away sin? What conceivable connection can there be, except in symbol, between the death pangs of a beast and the sin of a man before God? The principle of substitution was by the legal sacrifices clearly set forth, but that was all; those offerings did not and could not provide the actual substitute. The principle of vicarious sacrifice was plainly unfolded, but they provided no real sin-offering. How could they? Where but in the Christ of God could a propitiation be found? Where else is there anyone in our nature who could make recompense to the injured Law of God?

You will observe, dear brethren, that the words used in the text are these, *"Can never take away sin."* The word is, "Can never strip off sin." As if our sins were like filthy garments—the vestures of our disgrace—these could not be taken from us by the daily ministering of priests. There was no power in their sacrifices to remove the polluted coverings. Yet the priests were very diligent, for *"every priest standeth"* in the posture of activity, and they were persevering too, for *"every priest standeth daily."* They were obedient too, for they did not offer sacrifices according to their own devices, but, as the text saith, *"the same sacrifices"*—that is to say, such as were ordained of God. The priests were diligent, constant, and obedient, and the principle of the truth was in their offerings—viz., the doctrine of substitution; yet, sin still remained upon the consciences of the offerers, and none of them were made perfect.

MODERN DAY PRIESTS

Mark well one inference from this. If these offerings were of no service to the taking away of sin, even though they were presented reverently and perpetually according to God's own command by men He had indisputably called into the priesthood, then it is clear enough that the offerings of so-called priests in these modern times cannot have any efficacy. Here is a priesthood, certainly appointed of God, offering victims ordained by divine order, and yet their service does not put away sin. How much less wise can it be to trust in doubtful priests, who present sacrifices unwarranted by the Word of God. Their descent cannot be proved, their title, and their pretensions of one sect are ridiculed by another, and they are all deceivers. Therefore be done with them and rest alone in Christ Jesus, *the Apostle and High Priest of our profession.* [See Hebrews 3:1.] If Jerusalem has no sacrifice in all her flocks, what use can it be to look to Rome? If Aaron's seed cannot put away sin, to what end shall we look to the shavelings[31] of Antichrist?

Second, following along in the apostle's words, we come to the character of our Lord's sacrifice, and we perceive, in reading, that His priesthood was personal, and entirely within himself. There is but one true atoning priest. The twelfth verse says, "this man." The word "man" is not in the original; it is "this priest," if you will; "this man," if you please; but

---

31. Religious person with a shaved head.

its vagueness may make us think that the apostle scarcely knew what to say. You see the stars and the moon in their brightness, but suddenly they are all eclipsed and lost in a superior light. What can this glory be which has paled their fires? It is the sun rising in its strength. So, while we are beholding the priesthood of Aaron with all its excellence, it suddenly ceases to shine because of the glory that excels the radiant presence of One, for whom like Heaven's manna, it is not easy to find one fully descriptive name. Shall we call Him "man?" Blessed be His name; He is so, our near Kinsman, the "Son of Man." Shall we call Him "priest?" He is so. Blessed be His name; He is the true Melchisidec. Shall we call Him "God?" Yes we may do so, for He counts it not robbery to be equal with God. But this one divinely mysterious person—this unique and solitary high priest, accomplishes what the many priests of Aaron's race could not compass. They were weak, but He is all-sufficient. He has wrought out eternal redemption, and made an end of sin.

CHRIST STANDS ALONE

Note well, that no one stands with Him at the altar; no one is appointed to aid Him, neither before Him nor after Him is there one to share His office. He is without father, without mother, without predecessor, and without successor. He stands alone and by himself, this glorious One who looked and there was no man, and therefore His own arm brought salvation; He trod the winepress alone, and of the people there was none with Him. Jesus, the sole sacrificing priest of our profession, has completed what the long line of the Levitical priesthood have left for ever incomplete.

And we are told further, by the apostle that as there was but one priest, so there was only one sacrifice. He *"offered one sacrifice for sins."* [See Hebrews 10:12.] He was the sacrifice; His body the altar, He was the priest, He was also the victim. On Calvary's tree He presented himself a substitute for human guilt, and there He bore the crushing weight of Jehovah's wrath in His own body, on the behalf of all His people. On Him our sins were laid, and He was numbered with the transgressors; [Mark 15:28] and there He, in our stead, suffered what was due to the righteousness of God, and made atonement to divine justice for the sins of His people. This was done, not by many offerings, but by one sacrifice, and one alone. Jesus offered no other sacrifice: He had never made one before, nor since, nor will He ever present another sacrifice. His sin offering is one and done forever.

The text further adds that, as there was but one sacrifice, so it was but once offered forever, or, as Scripture puts it, *"Once for all." "Christ was once offered to bear the sins of many"* [Hebrews 9:28]. There is in the Scriptures no such idea of Christ perpetually offering himself; it is a childish invention of superstition. We are expressly told that He offered himself *"once."* Under the law the lamb was offered many times, the same sacrifices were repeated; but our Lord exclaimed, *"It is finished,"* and concluded all His sacrificial work [John 19:30]. He *"offered one sacrifice for sins for ever."* I do not know how your Bibles happen to be marked as to the comma in the passage; mine, now before me, reads thus:—"After he had offered one sacrifice for sin for ever sat down;" [Hebrews 10:12] but the Bible which I use at home is marked in the other way—*"After he had offered one sacrifice for sins, for ever sat down."*

We do not quite know where the comma should be; some of the best scholars maintain that it should be joined to the preceding words, others that it belongs to the succeeding. It does not involve any point of doctrine; and it may be read whichever way you please, without error. I think, however, the preponderating testimony is in favor of its being read, *"he offered one sacrifice for sins for ever;"* at any rate those words express a great and precious truth.

Look back as far as you can, there was no sacrifice for sins except for Revelation 13:8, the *"lamb slain from the foundation of the world."* Look on as far as you will, until this present dispensation has completed its circle and men shall have passed the judgment seat, and you will find no atonement for sin except this One—it stands alone, shining as a lone star, or a solitary rock in the midst of a raging sea. The propitiation which God has set forth was and ever must be One. The Lord Jesus offered himself once, once only, once only forever: there is no other atoning priest, no other sacrifice, and there is no repetition of that one sacrifice.

Third, we now go on to notice *the results* of Christ's one offering, which is threefold as described in the text—toward *himself,* his *enemies,* and his *people.*

Toward himself: After Christ Jesus, our High Priest, had offered one sacrifice for sins, He sat down for ever at the right hand of God. Every priest, under the old dispensation, stood; but Christ Jesus sat down, and the posture is very instructive. The typical priests stood because there was work to do; they must still present more sacrifices; but our Lord sits down because there is no more sacrificial work to do; atonement is complete, He has finished His task.

There were no seats in the tabernacle. Observe the Levitical descriptions and you will see that there were no resting-places for the priests in the holy place. Not only were none allowed to sit, but there was nothing whatever to sit upon. According to the rabbis, the king might sit in the holy places, and perhaps David sat there; if so, he was a striking type of Christ sitting as king. A priest never sat in the tabernacle, he was under a dispensation which did not afford rest, and was not intended to give it, a covenant of works which gives the soul no repose. Christ Jesus sits in the holy of holies, and herein we see that His work is finished.

There is more teaching in this passage. He "sat down;" this shows that Christ Jesus took possession of the holy place. Under the law, when the priest had done his work, what did he do? He went home. Neither the temple nor the tabernacle was his home. If you had asked a priest, "Where do you dwell" He would have said, "I have my abode yonder among the tribe of Levi." But our High Priest, Christ Jesus, when He had finished His work, sat down in the holy place, because He was at home, not a servant only but a Son, yes, and Lord of the whole house; and, therefore, He took His own seat therein by right. It is a joyful truth that He did this representatively, to show us that while the law gave no permanent possession, and could not establish the seed of Israel in possession of sacred privileges; the Gospel gives us an abiding place amongst the children of God, who dwell in His house for ever.

The apostle tells us where this seat of Christ was. He says, he "sat down at the right hand of God." This indicates the highest glory possible; our poet calls it,

"The highest place that heaven affords."[32]

There was no nobler position, or Jesus would have had it. Note the remark of this same apostle in Hebrews 1:5 of this epistle: "Unto which of the angels said he at any time, sit thou at my right hand?" Angels do not sit at the right hand of God; they are constantly in the place of service, and therefore they stand ready to fly on their Master's commands. But Jesus sits in the highest seat as Lord over His own house, clothed with honor and dignity, enthroned in the place of favor at the right hand of God. Sitting there He is to be viewed as clothed with everlasting power, "able

---

32. Hymn titled "The Head That Once Was Crowned with Thorns", words by Thomas Kelly, 1769-1854, music by Jeremiah Clark.

to save unto the uttermost them that come unto God by him." [See Hebrews 7:25.] *"Exalted to be a Prince and a Savior to give repentance unto Israel, and remission of sins."* [See Acts 5:31.]

No more the "despised and rejected, a man of sorrows, and acquainted with grief," [Isaiah 53:3]. No more in weakness and dishonor taken out to die; He sits as a king upon His throne, distributing royal bounties, coequal with Jehovah himself. As King of kings, Jesus Christ is exalted at the right hand of the Father.

Toward His Enemies: Observe carefully the result of His offering with regard to His enemies. He sits there *"expecting till they be made his footstool"* [Hebrews 10:13]. They are crushed already; sin which is the sting of death has been removed, and the law which was the strength of sin has been satisfied. Sin being put away by Christ's death, He has effectually broken the jaw teeth of all His enemies. When Jesus Christ offered himself unto God He fulfilled that ancient promise, *"The seed of the woman shall bruise the serpent's head."* [See Genesis 3:15.] Christ has set His foot upon the old dragon's head, and crushed out his power. Still, however, a feeble fight is kept up; feeble, I say, for so it is to Christ, though to us it seems vigorous. Sin and Satan within us, and all Christ's enemies without us, including death itself, are vainly raging against the Christ of God, for every day they are being put beneath His feet; every day as the battle rages the victory turns unto the enthroned Christ. In us, I trust sin has been put beneath Christ's feet; in thousands of others it shall yet be so. Jesus upon the throne expects the growth of that victory until all His enemies shall be utterly and ignominiously beaten. "O long expected day, begin!" Father, fulfill your Son's expectations, for your saints expect it in Him. Let the time come when every enemy shall be beneath His feet.

TOWARD HIS OWN PEOPLE

However, we will not tarry on that but will close this exposition of the words of the text by noticing the effect of Christ's death upon *His own people*. We are informed that *"he hath perfected"* them. [See Hebrews 10:14.] What a glorious word! Those for whom Christ has died were perfected by His death. It does not mean that He made them perfect in character so that they are no longer sinners, but that He made those for whom He died perfectly free from the guilt of sin.

When Christ took their sins upon himself, sin remained no longer upon them, for it could not be in two places at the same time. If it was on Christ it was not upon them; they were acquitted at the bar of God when Christ was, on their behalf, *"numbered with the transgressors."* [See Mark 15:28.]

When Christ Jesus suffered the penalty due to His people's sins to the last jot and tittle, then their sins ceased to be, and the covenant was fulfilled: *"Their sins and their iniquities will I remember no more"*. . . . for ever [Hebrews 10:17]. There was a clean sweep made of sin: He has finished transgression, and made an end of sin; and that for all His people. They want no other washing, no further purging, as far as pardon of sin and acceptance with God in the matter of justification are concerned, for they are all perfected by His sacrifice.

His people are described in the text as "them that are sanctified," and you must beware of misunderstanding that word as though it meant those who are made perfectly holy in character. The word implies an inward work of grace, but it means a great deal more. The passage should be read *"He hath perfected for ever them that are being sanctified,"* for it is in the present tense in the Greek. The text is not to be made to say that those who are perfectly sanctified are perfected, that would be a common-place, self-evident truth; but the great High Priest perfected for ever those who are being sanctified.

Now, sanctification means, primarily, the setting apart of a people by God to be holy to himself. Election is virtually sanctification; all God's people were sanctified—set apart and made holy to the Lord—in the eternal purpose and sovereign decree or however long the Earth is. Christ has, by His death, perfected all who are sanctified or set apart in election. This purpose of sanctification is carried out further when those set apart are called out by grace.

When effectual grace separates men from the world by conversion and regeneration they then become, in another sense, the sanctified; they are set apart even as Christ set apart himself, dedicated to God's service, and separated from sinners. As the work which began at regeneration is continued and carried on in them, they are sanctified in another aspect; they are realizing in themselves that sanctification or dedication to God was theirs from before the foundation of the world. The text relates not only to those in Heaven who are perfectly sanctified, but it relates to all who were set apart in the purposes of grace, that as far as their pardon and justification are concerned, Christ perfected them for ever when He offered up himself without spot unto God.

TWO: DIGESTING THESE TRUTHS

We have studied the interpretation of the words, reading, marking, and learning them. Now, I ask your earnest attention while we learn to digest these truths. It is in the digestion that the real nutriment shall come to our hearts. All you who desire eternal life lend me your ears, for this matter concerns you—observe that the whole business of this passage concerns sinners. The verse speaks about the Jewish priests who offered sacrifices for sins, and then it further speaks concerning Christ Jesus who has put away sin. All you who are guilty—the Gospel is meant for you. If there are any of you who are innocent and pure, and without spot, for you I have no words of consolation—but O you sinners—*the Gospel is for you.* The priesthood and the substitution of Jesus *are for you,* His death on Earth *is for you,* His reign and power in Heaven *is for you.*

These facts should encourage every trembling conscience. Are any of you saying, "Ah, I shall never be saved, I am so guilty?" That is a lie of Satan; do not believe it. *"For the Son of man is come to seek and to save that which was lost"* [Luke 19:10].The special aim and intent of the Gospel is the putting away of sin, and therefore it is suitable to your case.

Furthermore, note in the text the position you should labor to escape from. It is the position of those who stand daily ministering and offering sacrifices which can never put away sin. I know what you are doing; you are seeking mercy and trying to establish a righteousness of your own. You thought to yourself, "I will pray very regularly,"—you have done that for months, but prayers can never put away sin. What is there in prayer itself that can have merit in it to make atonement for sin? You have read the Scriptures regularly, for which I am most glad, but this you should always have done, and if you now do it most commendably, in what way will that put away sin?

"Ah" you say, "but I have been a regular attendant at a place of worship." It is well you should, for "faith cometh by hearing;" but I see no connection between the mere fact of your sitting in a place of worship and the putting away of sin. You know it has not eased your conscience yet, but has even increased your sense of sin. Perhaps some of you have been trying to save yourselves for years, and you are no closer than when you began, in fact, you feel further off than you ever were. Why do you spend your money for that which is not bread and your labor for that which does not profit you? Why do you stand daily at the altar offering that which can never put away sin? It would be infinitely wiser to flee to the Sacrifice which can atone.

Now, follow on in the text, and may it come into your very soul, for its practical teaching is that the one sole object of faith for the pardon of sin is the Man, the High Priest, Christ Jesus. *"But this man,"* says the Apostle, *"after he had offered one sacrifice for sins for ever, . . ."* [Hebrews 10:12]. If you want peace of heart, you must get it only from this one glorious Person, the Christ of God. I tell you solemnly, you will damn yourself by your prayers, your tears, your repenting, and your church and chapel going as easily as by blasphemy and fornication, if you trust in them; for if you make a Savior out of your best works they are accursed. Though your idol may be of purest gold, it is as much an abomination unto the living God as if you had made it of filth.

There must be no looking anywhere but to Jesus, not in any measure or degree. He, who looks partly to Jesus, and partly to himself, looks not to Christ at all. If a man puts one foot upon the land and the other on the sea—the foot that is on the land will not avail him, and he will most certainly fall because his other standing place is weak. If a chain is made strong enough to bear heavy weights in every portion except one link, as we all know its strength is not to be measured by the stronger portions, but by the weak link; and if you have one weak link in your hope, if you are resting in anything you are or hope to be, or can do or feel, that one weak link will snap and ruin you forever.

"None but Jesus, none but Jesus, Can do helpless sinners good."[33]

---

33. Hymn: "Come Ye Sinners, Poor and Needy", words by Joseph

From top to bottom, from foundation to pinnacle, our hopes must be in the work of Jesus, and we must trust in Him alone, or else we shall build in vain. *"For other foundation can no man lay than that is laid, which is Jesus Christ"* [1 Corinthians 3:11]. Other hope beneath the skies—there is none. O soul, learn the uselessness of looking to anything but Christ; but, be assured of this, if you will look to Him, and to Him alone, He will put away your sin, for He has done it by the sacrifice of himself.

Furthermore, here is another thought—I wish you would drink it in as Gideon's fleece drank in the dew—it is this: the efficacy of the atonement of Christ for sin is as great today as ever it was. He "offered one sacrifice for sins," for what? For a thousand years? No! But the text says *"for ever!"*—for ever!

"The dying thief rejoiced to see, That fountain in his day, Anal there may I, though vile as he, Wash all my sins away.

Dear dying Lamb, thy precious blood, Shall never lose its power; Till all the ransomed church of God, Be saved to sin no more."[34]

"One sacrifice for sins for ever." The devil tells you it is of no use for you to believe in Christ, there is not efficacy for you, you have sinned away your day of grace; tell him he is a liar, Christ has offered one sacrifice for sins *for ever;* and while a man lives beneath the covenant of mercy, where the Gospel is sounded in his ears, there is efficacy in the atonement for ever. The atoning sacrifice has no limit in its merit; the salvation of some has not drained it of even the smallest degree of its power. As the sunlight, though it is seen by millions of eyes, is as bright as ever it was, so it is with Jesus. Perhaps the Sun's fires may grow dull, and

---

Hart, 1759, music by William Walker, 1835.

34. Hymn: *There Is a Fountain Filled With Blood* by William Cowper in 1772.

become dimmed in the course of ages, but it is certain that the eternal fount of mercy, the Son of Righteousness, will never fail. He will continue to flood His people with the golden sunlight of His forgiving grace. He has made one sacrifice for sins for ever. I will come to Him then, for He is able to save me—He is able to save me even though I may be a sinner of seventy years of age. I will come to Him; I will rest in Him—in Him alone. Oh, believe me, if you do this you have eternal life abiding in you.

A further thought. The text leads me to say to you that it is utterly hopeless to desire salvation if you expect Jesus Christ to do anything more than He has already done. Many are waiting for a *something,* and they do not know what. Now mark my words, when Jesus died and went to Heaven, He perfected His work for ever. Therefore, if you do not believe today in what He has done, there will be no surer grounds for belief tomorrow. If faith is difficult to me today, I must not expect that I shall have any more evidence, or that there will be any more truth for me to rely upon, if I live another twenty years.

God has set forth Christ for you as guilty sinners to rest on; and if that is not enough for you, what more would you have? Christ has offered himself, died and suffered in our stead, was resurrected on the third day, and ascended into glory and sits at the right hand of God, His Father. If you do not believe He is the Son of God and receive Him as your Savior what more would you have Him do? Shall He come and die again? You have rejected Him once; and you would reject Him though He died twice. But that cannot be done; there is enough in His sacrifice to answer all the purposes of mercy, and if you sin willfully by rejecting Him, *"there remaineth no more sacrifice for sin, but a fearful looking for of judgment and of fiery indignation"!* [See Hebrews 10:26-27.] This is the point; all the atonement that could save me in ten years' time is here now; all that I can ever rely upon if I postpone all thoughts of faith is here already. There will be no more sacrifice by Christ. He has perfected His work. Oh, poor troubled soul, rest yourself in Him now. While I put these words, into your eyes and ears and even have you repeat them with your mouths—how I wish I could put them into your hearts!

How foolish you are who are looking for signs and wonders or else you will not believe. May the Spirit of God show you that Christ Jesus is now able and willing to save you, and that all you have to do is to take what He has done, and simply trust Him, and you shall be saved this morning, completely saved, perfected through His one sacrifice. There remains no more to be done by the Redeemer. He sits down, and He will not rise for any further sacrifice. He has finished His atonement and perfected those He means to save; and if you believe not in Him, there remains no more sacrifice for sins.

THE BELIEVER'S POSITION

Yet again, I want you, dearly beloved brethren, to gather from the text before us the true posture of every believer in Christ. *"This man, after he had offered one sacrifice for sins for ever, sat down"* [Hebrews 10:12]. If I am a believer that is my posture, if you are a believer that is yours,—you are to sit down. Under the law there was no sitting down. Even at the Passover the Israelites stood with their loins girt and their staves in their hands. There was no sitting down. It is only at the gospel supper that our proper posture is that of recumbency, reclining, or sitting down, because our warfare is accomplished. They that have believed have entered into rest. Jesus has given us rest, we are not traversing the wilderness, we have come unto Mount Zion, unto the glorious assembly of the Church of the first born whose names are written in Heaven. [See Hebrews 12:23.] Our justifying work is finished, finished by Christ. Sit down Christian, sit down and rest in your Lord. There is much to be done as to fighting your sins, much to be done for Christ in the world, but so far as justification and forgiveness are concerned, rest is your proper place; peace in Christ Jesus is your lawful portion.

SIT EXPECTANTLY

Your position is also to be one of expectancy. When Christ sat down, He sat down with the expectation that His enemies will be made His footstool. Expect, O believer, the time when you shall be rid of all sin. Fight manfully against your inbred corruptions, struggle against sin as you see it in the outside world, and expect every day with holy faith that you shall get the victory. As Christ sits there expecting, He has raised us up together and made us sit together in the heavenly places in himself; and we will sit there and look down upon this erring world, and expect the time when all evil shall be beneath our feet as it is beneath His.

Meanwhile, our posture is, once again, that of those who are perfected in Christ Jesus. How I wish that we could all realize this, and live in the power of it. If I am, indeed, a believer, I have nothing whatever to do in order to put away the guilt of my sins. I have much to do by faith to overcome the power of sin in me, and to seek after holiness; but so far as the guilt of transgression is concerned, Jesus Christ's one offering has perfected all His people, there is not a sin remaining upon them, nor a trace of sin; they are *"without spot, or wrinkle, or any such thing;"* before God's sight they are perfectly lovely; they are not somewhat beautiful, but they are altogether lovely in Christ; they are accepted not in part but altogether, "accepted in the Beloved" [Ephesians

5:27and 1:6].

When I get upon this strain, words are quite inadequate to express the emotions of my soul. This truth might well make David dance before the ark of the Lord—to think that though black in ourselves, we are comely in Christ; though like the smoke-dried tents of Kedar we are foul, yet clothed in our Savior's beauties we are like the curtains of Solomon for glory. The glory of the text is that we are perfected for ever; not for tomorrow, and then suffered to fall from grace; not for the next twenty years, and then turned out of the covenant; *but he hath perfected "for ever" those that are set apart.* It is a work which abides like the worker himself, and while Christ sits on the throne His people cannot die; while His work remains forever perfect, they are also forever perfect in Him.

LABOR AFTER HOLINESS

Now, brethren, another practical point is this, that it becomes us to make the evidence of our interest in this gracious work more and more clear to others. The text says, *"Hath perfected them that are sanctified,"* or set apart as holy unto God. We must be more and more set apart every day, we must labor after holiness; this must be our object, not in order that we may be saved, for we are saved already, but in order that by others it may be clearly seen that we are saved, and they, seeing our good works, may glorify our Father which is in Heaven. If I have in myself no measure of holiness, how shall I be recognized as belonging to Christ? Is it not foolish presumption to say "I am perfect in Christ," if sin still lives in my soul and loves it? May the Lord, by His Spirit, lead us in the ways of holiness, and then, *walking in the light as he is in the light, we shall have fellowship one with another; and the blood of Jesus Christ his Son shall cleanse us from all sin.* [See 1 John 1:7.]

Finally, brethren, it remains for us to remember that Christ will be one of two things to every one of us:

1. Either we shall see Him at the right hand of God and rejoice that He is lifted so high.
2. Or, we shall behold Him there with horror as we writhe beneath His feet.

For His people, perfected forever, it is their Heaven to think that Christ is highly exalted. Oh, would we not exalt Him if we could! Is there anything in this world that we would keep back from Him? Is there any suffering from which we would shrink if we could lift Him high? I hope I can speak for all of God's people and say, the dearest object of our life is to honor Him. Oh for high thrones and bright crowns for Jesus!

"Let him be crowned with majesty Who bowed his head to death! And be his honors sounded high By all things that have breath!"[35]

Let Him have the highest place that Heaven can yield Him.

But, if we will not believe His Godhead, if we will not trust Him as the Mediator, if we have no part in His sacrifice, if we oppose His gospel, if we reject His claims to our obedience, there is another position we shall have to take up, and that is, beneath His feet. Those feet will be heavy indeed! They were pierced once; but if ever those pierced feet come upon you, they will crush you to powder. Nothing is as terrible as love when once it is turned to anger. Oil is soft, but how it burns. Inflame love into jealousy and it is cruel as the grave. Beware, all you that reject the Savior, for in the day when He comes He will smite you with a rod of iron, and even His face, which is full of tenderness today, shall then

---

35. Hymn: "Psalm 8" by Isaac Watts.

be full of terror, and this shall be your cry, "Hide us you mountains, you rocks conceal us, from the face of Him that sits upon the throne, and from the wrath of the Lamb." [See Revelation 6:16.] What a wonderful mixture of words, "The wrath of the Lamb." It is one of the most dreadful expressions in Scripture. The Lord grant we may never feel its terrible meaning. May His blood cleanse us. Amen.

PART TWO
THE BLOOD

CHAPTER 5
THE BLOOD

A SERMON
(No. 228)
Delivered on Sabbath Morning, December 12th, 1858,
by the
REVEREND C. H. SPURGEON,
at the Music Hall, Royal Surrey Gardens, Kennington,
London, England.

*"...When I see the blood, I will pass over
you."—Exodus 12:13*

GOD'S PEOPLE are always safe. *"All the saints are in
his hand;"* [See Deuteronomy 33:3.], and the hand
of God is a place for safety, as well as a place of
honor. Nothing can hurt the man who has made God his
refuge. *"Thou hast given commandment to save me,"* said
David in Psalm 71:3; and every believing child of God may
say the same. Plague, famine, war, tempest,—all these have
received commandment of God to save His people. Though
the Earth may rock beneath the feet of man, yet the Christian
may stand fast, and though the heavens may be rolled up,
and the firmament pass away like a scroll that is burned by
fervent heat, yet a Christian need not fear. God's people *shall*
be saved: if they cannot be saved under the heavens, they shall
be saved in the heavens. If there is no safety for them in the
time of trouble upon this solid Earth, they shall be *"caught
up together with the Lord in the air, and so shall they be ever
with the Lord,"* and ever safe. [See 1 Thessalonians 4:17.]

Now, at the time of which this Scripture in the Book of
Exodus speaks, Egypt was exposed to a terrible peril. Jehovah

himself was about to march through the streets of all the cities of Egypt. It was not merely a destroying angel, but Jehovah himself; for thus it is written, *"I will pass through the land of Egypt this night, and will smite all the first-born in the land of Egypt, both man and beast."* [See Exodus 12:12.] No one less than *I AM,* the great God, had vowed to "cut Rahab" with the sword of vengeance. Tremble, you inhabitants of the Earth, for God has come down among you, provoked, incensed, and at last awakened from His seeming sleep of patience. He has girded on His terrible sword, and He has come to smite you. Quake for fear, all you that have sin within you, for when God walks through the streets, sword in hand, will He not smite you all?

When I See the Blood . . .

But hark! The voice of covenant mercy speaks; God's children are safe, even though an angry God is in the streets. As they are safe from the rod of the wicked, so are they safe from the sword of justice—always and ever safe; for there was not a hair of the head of an Israelite that was so much as touched; Jehovah kept them safe beneath His wings. Though He did rend His enemies like a lion, yet, He protected His children, every one of them. But, beloved, while this is always true, that God's people are safe, there is another fact that is equally true, namely, that God's people are only safe through *the blood.* The reason why God spares His people in the time of calamity is, because He sees the blood mark on their brow.

Scriptural Truth

What is the basis of this great truth? The basis of this great truth is that *"all things work together for good to them that love God"* [Romans 8:28]. What is the cause that all things produce good to them that love God? None but this—that they are bought with the precious blood of Christ! Therefore, that is why nothing can hurt them, because *the blood* is upon them, and every evil thing must pass them by. It was so that night in Egypt. God himself was abroad with His sword; but He spared them, because He saw the blood mark on the lintel and on the two sideposts. And so it is with us. In the day when God in His fierce anger shall come forth from His dwelling place to frighten the Earth with terrors and to condemn the wicked, we shall be secure . . . if we are found in Him, covered with the Savior's righteousness, and sprinkled with His blood.

Do I hear someone say, that I am now coming to an old subject? This thought struck me when I was preparing for preaching, that I should have to tell you an old story over again; and just as I was thinking of that, I happened to turn over a book and read an anecdote of Judson the missionary to Burma[36]. He passed through unprecedented hardships, and performed dangerous exploits for his Master. He returned, after thirty years' absence to America. "Announced that he would address an assembly in a provincial town, and a vast multitude of people gathered from great distances to hear him. He rose at the close of the usual service, and as all eyes were fixed on him and every ear attentive, he spoke for about fifteen minutes with much poignancy of the precious Savior, of what He has done for us, and of what we owe to Him; then he sat down, visibly affected.

"The people are very much disappointed," said a friend to him on their way home; "they wonder why you did not talk of *something else.*"

"Why, what did they want?" Judson asked, "I presented,

---

36. Adoniram Judson, Jr. 1788—1850, a Baptist missionary to Burma. He also translated the Bible into Burmese.

to the best of my ability, the most interesting subject in the world."

"But they wanted something different—a story," said his friend.

"Well" replied Judson, "I am sure I gave them a story—the most thrilling one that can be conceived of."

"But they have heard it before. They wanted to hear something new of a man who had just come from the antipodes."[37]

Judson responded, "Then I am glad they have it to say, that a man coming from the antipodes had nothing better to tell than the wondrous story of the dying love of Jesus. My business is to preach the gospel of Christ; and when I can speak at all, I dare not trifle with my commission. When I looked upon those people today and remembered where I would next meet them, how could I stand up and furnish food to vain curiosity—tickle their fancy with amusing stories, however decently strung together on a thread of religion? That is not what Christ meant by preaching the gospel. And then how could I hereafter meet the fearful charge, 'I gave you one opportunity to tell them of *Me*; you spent it in describing your own adventures!'"

So I thought. Well, if Judson told the old story after he had been away thirty years, and could not find anything better, I will just go back to this old subject that is always new and always fresh to us—*the precious blood of Christ*, by which we are saved.

> **First:** The Blood.
> **Second:** Its Efficacy.
> **Third:** One Condition Appended to it;—
> *"When I see the blood."*
> **Fourth:** The Practical Lesson.

---

37. Any two places or regions on diametrically opposite sides of the Earth. Example: The North Pole and the South Pole are antipodes.

I. THE BLOOD

1. In the case of the Israelites it was the blood of the Paschal Lamb. In our case Beloved, it is the blood of the Lamb of God, Christ Jesus who takes away the sins of the world. The blood of which I solemnly speak this morning is, first of all, the blood of a *divinely appointed victim.* Jesus Christ did not come into this world unappointed. He was sent here by His Father. This indeed is one of the underlying foundations of the Christian's hope. We can rely upon Jesus Christ's acceptance by His Father, because His Father ordained Him to be our Savior from before the foundation of the world.

Sinner, when I preach to you the blood of Christ this morning, I am preaching something that is well pleasing to God; for God himself chose Christ to be the Redeemer; He himself set Him apart from before the foundation of the world, and He himself, even Jehovah the Father, laid upon Him the iniquity of *us* all. The sacrifice of Christ is not brought to you without warrant; it is not a something which Christ did surreptitiously and in secret; it was written in the great decree from all eternity, that He was the Lamb slain from before the foundation of the world.

As He said in Psalm 40:7-9, *"Lo I come; in the volume of the book it is written of me, I delight to do thy will O God."* [See also John 4:34.] It is God's will that the blood of Jesus should be shed. Jesus is God's chosen Savior for men; and here, when addressing the ungodly, here, I say, is one potent argument with them. Sinner, you may trust that Christ is able to save you from the wrath of God, for God himself has appointed Him to save.

DIVINELY APPOINTED AND SPOTLESS

2. Christ Jesus, too, like the lamb, was not only a divinely appointed victim, but He was *spotless.* Had there been one sin in Christ, He would not have been capable of being our Savior; but He was without spot or blemish—without original sin, without any practical transgression. In Him was no sin, though he was *"tempted in all points like as we are."* [See Hebrews 4:15.] Here, again, is the reason why the blood is able to save, because it is the blood of an innocent victim, a victim whose only reason for death lay in us and not Him.

When the poor innocent lamb was put to death in Egypt by the head of the household I imagine that thoughts like these ran through his mind. "Ah" he would say, as he struck the knife into the lamb, "This poor creature dies, not for any guilt that it has ever had, but to show me that I am guilty, and that I deserved to die like this." Turn, then, your eye to the Cross, and see Jesus bleeding there and dying for you. Remember, "He dies to atone for sins not His own;"[38] Sin had no foothold in Him, never troubled Him. The prince of this world came and looked, but he said, "I have nothing in Christ; there is no room for me to plant my foot—no piece of corrupt ground, which I may call my own." O sinner, the blood of Jesus is able to save you because He was perfectly innocent himself, and He died, *". . . the just for the unjust, to bring us to God."* [See 1 Peter 3:18.]

3. But some will say, "From what source has the blood of Christ such power to save?" My reply is, not only because God appointed that blood, and because it was the blood of an innocent and spotless being, but because *Christ himself was God.* If Christ were a mere man, my hearers, you could not be exhorted to trust him; even if he were ever so spotless and holy, there would be no efficacy in His blood to save; but Christ was *"very God of very God;"*[39] the blood that Jesus shed was *Godlike* blood. It was the blood of man,

---

38. Hymn: "Invitation to Sinners (All Ye That Pass By)" by Charles Wesley.

39. From the *Nicene Creed* written in 1549.

for He was man like us; but the divinity was so allied with the manhood, that the blood derived efficacy from it. Can you imagine what must be the value of the blood of God's own dear Son? No, you cannot put an estimate upon it that would so much as reach to a millionth part of its preciousness. I know you esteem that blood as beyond all price if you have been washed in it; but I know also that you do not esteem it enough. It was the wonder of angels that God should condescend to die; it will be the wonder of all wonders, the unceasing wonder of eternity, that God should become man to die.

Oh, when we think that Christ was Creator of the world, and that His all-sustaining shoulders hung the universe, we cannot wonder that His death is mighty to redeem, and that His blood cleanses from sin. Come closer saints and sinners; gather in and crowd around the Cross, and see this man, overcome with weakness, fainting, groaning, bleeding, and dying. This man is also *"God over all, blessed forever,"* [See Romans 9:5.]. Is there not power to save? Is there not efficacy in blood like that? Can you imagine any stretch of sin that can outmeasure the power of divinity—any height of iniquity that shall top the topless steeps of the divine? Can I conceive a depth of sin that shall be deeper than the infinite? Or a breadth of iniquity that shall be broader than the Godhead? Because He is divine, He is *"able to save to the uttermost, them that come unto God by him"* [Hebrews 7:25]. Divinity appointed, spotless, and divine, His blood is the blood whereby you may escape the anger and the wrath of God.

ONCE FOR ALL

4. Once more; *the blood* of which we speak today, is blood *"shed once"* for many for the remission of sin. The paschal lamb was killed every year; but now Christ has appeared and He takes away sin by the offering up of himself and there is now no more mention of sin, for Christ *once for all* has put away sin, by the offering of himself. The Jew had the lamb every morning and every evening, for there was a continual mention of sin; the blood of the lamb could not take it away. The lamb availed for today, but there was the sin of tomorrow, what was to be done with that? Why, a fresh victim must bleed. But oh, my hearer, our greatest joy is, that the blood of Jesus has been *once shed,* and He has said, *"It is finished"* [John 19:30]. There is no more need of the blood of bulls or of goats, or of any other sacrifice; that one sacrifice has *"perfected for ever them that are sanctified"* [Hebrews 10:14].

Trembling sinner, come to the Cross again; your sins are heavy, and many; but the atonement for them is completed by the death of Christ. Look then to Jesus, and remember that Christ needs nothing to supplement His blood. The road between God and man is finished and open; the robe to cover your nakedness is complete, without a rag of yours; the bath in which you are to be washed is full, full to the brim, and needs nothing to be added to it. "It is finished!" Let that ring in your ears. There is nothing now that can hinder your being saved, if God has made you willing now to believe in Jesus Christ. He is a complete Savior, full of grace for an empty sinner.

5. Yet I must add one more thought, and then leave this point. The blood of Jesus Christ is blood that has been accepted. Christ died—He was buried; but neither Heaven nor Earth could tell whether God had accepted the ransom. There was needed God's seal upon the great Magna Charta[40] of man's salvation, and that seal was put, my hearer, in

---

40. Pronounced Magna Carta per dictionary.

that hour when God summoned the angel, and bade him descend from Heaven and roll away the stone. Christ was put in durance vile[41] in the prison house of the grave, as a hostage for His people. Until God had signed the warrant for acquittal of all His people, Christ must abide in the bonds of death. He did not attempt to break His prison; He did not come out illegally by wrenching down the bars of His dungeon; He waited: He wrapped up the napkin, folding it by itself: He laid the grave-clothes in a separate place. Then He waited, waited patiently; and at last down from the skies, like the flash of a meteor, the angel descended, touched the stone and rolled it away; and when Christ came out, rising from the dead in the glory of His Father's power, then the seal was put upon the great Charta of our redemption.

The blood was accepted, and sin was forgiven. And now, soul, it is not possible for God to reject you, if you come this day to Him, pleading the blood of Christ. God cannot—and here we speak with great reverence—the everlasting God cannot reject a sinner who pleads the blood of Christ: for if He did so, it would be to deny himself, and to contradict all His former acts. *He has* accepted the blood, and *he will* accept it; He can never revoke that divine acceptance of the resurrection; and if you go to God, my hearer, pleading simply and only the blood of Him that hung upon the tree, God would have to un-God himself before He could reject you, or reject the blood.

Still, I fear that I have not been able to make you think with depth on the blood of Christ. I beseech you, just for a moment; try to picture Christ on the Cross. Let your imagination see the motley crew assembled around that little hill of Calvary. Now lift your eyes, and see the three crosses put upon that rising knoll. See in the center the thorn-crowned brow of Christ. Do

---

41. A very long prison sentence. Example: life in prison.

you see the hands that have always been full of blessing nailed fast to the accursed wood! See His dear face, more marred than that of any other man? Do you see it now, as His head bows upon His bosom in the extreme agonies of death? Remember, He was a real man. It was a real Cross. Do not think of these things as figments, and fancies, and romances. There was such a being, and He died as I describe it. Let your imagination picture Him, and then sit still a moment and meditate on this thought: "The blood of that man, whom I now behold dying in agony, must be my redemption; and if I would be saved, I must put my only trust in what He suffered for me, when He *'bore our sins in His own body on the tree'*" [1 Peter 2:24]. If God the Holy Spirit helps you, you will then be in a right state to proceed to the second point.

II. THE EFFICACY OF THIS BLOOD

1. *"When I see the blood I will pass over you."* The blood of Christ has such a divine power to save that *nothing but it can ever save the soul*. If some foolish Israelite had despised the command of God and had said, "I will sprinkle something else upon the doorposts," or, "I will adorn the lintel with jewels of gold and silver," he would have perished; nothing could save his household but the sprinkled blood. And now let us all remember the Scriptures in 1 Corinthians 3:11 and Acts 4:12, that *"other foundation can no man lay than that which is laid, Jesus Christ,"* for *"there is none other name given among men whereby we must be saved."* My works, my prayers, my tears, cannot save me; *the blood,* the blood alone, has power to redeem. Sacraments, however well they may be attended to, cannot save me. Nothing but your blood, O Jesus, can redeem me from the guilt of sin. Though I might give rivers of oil, and ten thousand of the fat of fed beasts; and though I should give my firstborn for

my transgression, the fruit of my body for the sin of my soul, all would be useless. Nothing but the blood of Jesus has in it the slightest saving power.

Furthermore, you that are trusting in your infant baptism, your confirmation, and your Lord's Supper, you are trusting in a lie. Nothing but the blood of Jesus can save. I care not how right the ordinance, how true the form, how scriptural the practice, it is all a vanity to you if you rely on it. God forbid I should say a word against ordinances, or against holy things; but keep them in their places. If you make them the basis of your soul's salvation, they are lighter than a shadow, and when you need them most you will find they fail you. There is not, I repeat it again, the slightest atom of saving power anywhere but in the blood of Jesus. That blood has the only power to save, and anything else that you rely upon shall be a refuge of lies. This is the rock, and this is the work that is perfect; but all other things are day dreams; they must be swept away in the day when God shall come to try our work of what sort it is. *The Blood* stands out in solitary majesty, the only rock of our salvation.

2. This blood is not simply the only thing that can save, but *it alone must save.* Put anything with the blood of Christ, and you are lost; trust to anything else with this and you perish. "It is true," says one, "that the sacrament cannot save me, but I will trust in that, and in Christ too." You are a lost man, then. Christ is so jealous of His honor that anything you put with Him, however good it is, becomes, from the fact of it with Him, an accursed thing. And what is it that you would put with Christ? Your good works? What! Will you yoke a reptile with an angel—yoke yourself to the chariot of salvation with Christ? What are your good works? Your righteousnesses are *"as filthy rags;"* and shall filthy rags be joined to the spotless celestial righteousness of Christ? [See Isaiah 64:6.] It must not, and it shall not be. Rely on Jesus only, and you cannot perish; but rely on anything with Him, and you are surely damned as if you would rely upon your sins. Jesus only—Jesus only—Jesus only—this is the rock of our salvation

Let me stop here and do verbal combat with a few forms and shapes which our self-righteousness always takes:

"Oh," says one, "I could trust in Christ *if I felt my sins more.*"

Sir, that is a damning error. Is your repentance, your sense of sin, to be a part-Savior? Sinner, *the blood* is to save you; not your tears, Christ's death; not your repentance. You are bidden this day to trust in Christ; not in your feelings and not in your pangs on account of sin. Many a man has been brought into great soul distress, because he has looked more at his repentance than at the obedience of Christ—

> "Could thy tears for ever flow,
> Could thy zeal no respite know;
> All for sin could not atone,
> Christ must save and *Christ alone.*"[42]

"No," says another, "but I feel that I do not value the blood of Christ as I ought, and therefore I am afraid to believe."

My friend, that is another insidious form of the same error. God does not say, "When I see your estimate of the blood of Christ, I will pass over you; no, but when I see *the blood.*" It is not your estimate of that blood; it is the blood that saves you. As I said before, that magnificent, solitary *blood* must be alone.

"No," says another, "but if I had more faith then I would have hope."

---

42. A hymn by Augustus Toplady written in 1776 called "Rock of Ages"

That, too, is a very deadly shape of the same evil. You are not to be saved by the efficacy of your faith, but by the efficacy of the blood of Christ. It is not your believing, it is Christ's dying.

I bid you believe, but I bid you not to look to your believing as the ground of your salvation. No man will go to Heaven if he trusts to his own faith; you may as well trust to your own good works as trust to your faith. Your faith must deal with Christ not with itself. The world hangs on nothing; but faith cannot hang upon itself, it must hang on Christ. For example, sometimes I find this happening to me when my faith is vigorous and joy is flowing into my heart and after a while I begin to find that my joy suddenly departs. I ask the causes, and I find that the joy came because I was thinking of *Christ;* but when I begin to think about *my joy,* then my joy fled. You must not think of your faith but of Christ. Faith comes from meditation upon Christ. Turn your eye not upon faith but upon Jesus. It is not your hold of Christ that saves you; it is His hold of you. It is not the efficacy of your believing in Him; it is the efficacy of His blood applied to you through the Spirit. I do not know how sufficiently to follow Satan in all his windings into the human heart, but this, I know, he is always trying to keep back this great truth—the blood, and the blood alone has power to save.

"Oh," says another, "if I had such-and-such an experience then I could trust." Friend, it is not your experience, it is the blood. God did not say, "When I see your experience," but "When I see *the blood of Christ."*

"No" another says, "but if I had such-and-such graces, I could hope."

No, He did not say, "When I see your graces," but "When I see *the blood."* Get grace, get as much as you can of faith, and love, and hope, but oh, do not put them where Christ's blood ought to be. The only pillar of your hope must be the Cross, and all else that you put to buttress up the Cross of Christ is obnoxious to God, and ceases to have any virtue in it, because it is an anti-Christ. The blood of Christ, *alone*, saves; but put anything with it, and it does not save.

3. Yet again we may say of the blood of Christ, *it is all-sufficient*. There is no case the blood of Christ cannot meet; there is no sin it cannot wash away. There is no multiplicity of sin it cannot cleanse, and no aggravation of guilt it cannot remove even though:

> You may be double-dyed like scarlet, you may have lain in the stain of your sins seventy years or more, but the blood of Christ can take out the stain.
>
> You may have blasphemed Him almost as many times as you have breathed.
>
> You may have rejected Him as often as you have heard His name.
>
> You may have broken His Sabbath.
>
> You may have denied His existence.
>
> You may have doubted His Godhead.
>
> You may have persecuted His servants.
>
> You may have trampled on His blood; but all this the blood can wash away.
>
> You may have committed whoredom without number.
>
> You may have committed murder itself that has defiled your hands, but this fountain filled with blood can wash all the stains away.

. . . *The blood of Jesus Christ cleanseth us from all sin.* [See 1 John 1:7.] There is no sort of a man; there is no abortion of mankind, no demon in human shape that this blood cannot wash. Hell may have sought to make a paragon of iniquity, it may have striven to put sin, and sin, and sin together, until it had made a monster in the shape of man, a monster abhorred of mankind, *but* the blood of Christ can transform that monster. Magdalene's seven devils it can cast out, the madness of the demoniac it can ease, the deep-seated leprosy it can cure, the wound of the maimed, yes even, the lost limb it can restore. There is no spiritual disease that the great Physician cannot heal. This is the great Catholicon[43], the medicine for all diseases. No case can exceed its virtue, no matter how black or vile; *the blood of Christ Jesus is all-sufficient.*

4. But go further. The blood of Christ saves *surely.* Many people say, "Well, I hope I shall be saved through the blood of Christ;" and perhaps, someone here who is believing in Christ may say, "Well, I hope it will save." My dear friend, that is a slur upon the honor of God. If any man gives you a promise, and you say, "Well, I hope he will fulfill it;" is it not implied that you have at least some small doubt as to whether he will or not? Now, I do not hope that the blood of Christ will wash away my sin. I know it is washed away by His blood; true faith does not hope about Christ's blood, but says, "I know it is so; that blood does cleanse. The moment it was applied to my conscience it cleansed me, and it cleanses me still."

The Israelite, if he was true to his faith, did not go inside, and say, "I hope the destroying angel will pass by me;" but he said, "I know he will; I know God cannot smite me; I know He will not. There is the blood mark on the lentil and doorpost, I am secure beyond a doubt; there is not the shadow of a risk of my perishing. I am, I must be saved." And so I preach a sure gospel this morning: *". . . Whosoever believeth in him should not perish, but have everlasting life"* [John 3:16]. *"And I give unto them eternal life;"* said He, *"and they shall never perish, neither shall any man pluck*

---

43. Cure

them out of my hand" [John 10:28].

O, sinner, I have not the shadow of a doubt as to whether Christ will save you if you trust in His blood. Oh, no, I know He will. I am certain His blood can save; and I beg you, in Christ's name, believe the same; believe that the blood is *sure* to cleanse, not only that it *may* cleanse, but that it *must* cleanse, *"whereby we must be saved,"* says the Scripture in Acts 4:12. If we have that blood upon us we must be saved, or else we are to suppose that God is unfaithful and unkind; and that He is a god who is transformed from everything that is divine and godlike into everything that is base.

5. Moreover, he that has this blood sprinkled upon him is saved *completely.* Not the hair of the head of an Israelite was disturbed by the destroying angel. They were completely saved; so he that believeth in the blood is saved from all things. I like the old translation of the chapter in the Book of Romans. There was a martyr once summoned before Bonner; and after he had expressed his faith in Christ, Bonner[44] said "You are a heretic and will be damned." "Nay" said he, quoting the old version, *"There is therefore now no damnation to them that believe in Christ Jesus."* [See Romans 8:1.] And that brings a sweet thought before us; there is no damnation to the man who has the blood of Christ upon him; he cannot be condemned by God. It is impossible. *There is no such a thing;* there can be no such thing. There is no damnation. He cannot be damned; for there is no damnation to him that is in Christ Jesus. Let the blood be applied to the lintel, and to the doorpost, there is no destruction. There is a destroying angel for Egypt, but there is none for Israel. There is a hell for the wicked, but none for the righteous. And if there is none, they cannot be put there. If there is no damnation they cannot suffer it. Christ saves completely; every sin is

---

44. Catholic clergyman, Joseph Bonner

washed, every blessing ensured, perfection is provided, and glory everlasting *is* the sure result.

I think I have dwelt sufficiently long upon the efficacy of His blood; but no tongue of seraph can ever speak its worth. I must go home to my chamber, and weep because I am powerless to tell this story, and yet I have labored to tell it simply, so that all can understand; and I pray, therefore, that God the Spirit may lead some of you to put your trust simply, wholly, and entirely, on the blood of Jesus Christ.

III. THE ONE CONDITION

This brings us to the third point, upon which I must be very brief, and the third point begins with a question. "What," says someone, "do you preach a conditional salvation?" Yes I do, there is one condition. "When *I see* the blood I will pass over you." What a blessed condition! It does not say when you see the blood, but when *I see* it. Your eye of faith may be so dim, that you cannot see the blood of Christ. Ay, but God's eye is not dim: He can see it, yes, He must see it; for Christ in Heaven is always presenting His blood before His Father's face. The Israelite could not see the blood; he was inside the house; he could not see what was on the lintel and the doorpost; but God could see it; and this is the *only* condition of the sinner's salvation—God's seeing the blood; not your seeing it. O how safe is every one that trusts in the Lord Jesus Christ. It is not His faith that is the condition, not His assurance; it is the simple fact, that Calvary is set perpetually before the eyes of God in a risen and ascended Savior. *"When I see the blood, I will pass over you."* Fall on your knees then in prayer, you doubting souls, and let this be your plea:—"Lord, have mercy upon me for the blood's sake. *I* cannot see it as I could desire, but Lord *you* see it, and you have said, *'When I see it, I will pass over you.'*

Lord, you see it this day, pass over my sin, and forgive me for its dear sake alone."

IV. WHAT IS THE LESSON?

The lesson of the text is this to the Christian. Christian, take care that you always remember, that nothing but the blood of Christ can save you. I preach to myself today what I preach to you. I often find myself like this:—I have been praying that the Holy Spirit might rest in my heart and cleanse out an evil passion, and presently I find myself full of doubts and fears, and when I ask the reason, I find it is this:—I have been looking to the Spirit's work until I put the Spirit's work where Christ's work ought to be. Now, it is a sin to put your own works where Christ's should be; but it is just as much a sin to put the Holy Spirit's work there. You must never make the Spirit of God an anti-Christ, and you virtually do that when you put the Spirit's work as the groundwork of your faith. Do you not often hear Christian men say, "I cannot believe in Christ today as I could yesterday, for yesterday I felt such sweet and blessed enjoyments." Now, what is that but putting your thoughts and feelings where Christ ought to be. Remember, Christ's blood is able to save you in a good frame of mind or in a bad frame of mind. Christ's blood must be your trust, as much when you are full of joy as when you are full of doubt.

It is here that your happiness will be in danger, by beginning to put your good thoughts and good feelings in the room of the blood of Christ. O, brethren, if we could always live with a single eye fixed on the Cross, we would always be happy; but when we get a little peace, and a little joy, we begin to prize the joy and peace so much, that we forget the source from whence they come. As Mr. Brooks[45] says,

---

45. Bishop James Brooks

"A husband that loves his wife will, perhaps, often give her jewels and rings; but suppose she should sit down and begin to think of her jewels and rings so much that she forgets her husband, it would be a kind husband's business to take them away from her so that she might fix her affections entirely on him." And it is so with us. Jesus gives us jewels of faith and love, and we begin trusting to them, and He takes them away in order that we may come again as guilty, helpless sinners, and put our trust in Christ. To quote a verse I often repeat—I believe the spirit of a Christian should be, from his first hour to his last, the spirit of these two lines:—

"Nothing in my hand I bring,
Simply to thy cross I cling."
That is the lesson to the saint.[46]

Just one more minute; there is a lesson here to the sinner. Poor, trembling, guilty self-condemned sinner, I have a word from the Lord for you. *"The blood of Jesus Christ cleanseth us,"* that is you and me, *"cleanseth us from all sin."* [See 1John 1:7.] That "us" includes you, if you are now feeling your need of a Savior. Now that blood is able to save you, and you are told simply to trust that blood, and you shall be saved. But I hear you say, "Sir," you said, "If I feel my need. Now I feel that I do not feel, I only wish I did feel my need enough." Well do not trust in your feelings then; trust only in His shed blood. If you can rely simply on the blood of Christ, whatever your feelings may or may not be then His blood is able to save you.

"But" you are saying, "How am I to be saved? What must I do?" Well there is nothing that *you* can do. You must stop *doing* altogether, in order to be saved. There must be a

---

46. Verse from the hymn called "Rock of Ages" by Augustus M. Toplady.

denial of all your doings. You must put Christ first, and then you may do as much as you like. But you must not trust in your doings. Your business is now to lift up your heart in prayer like this:—"Lord, you have shown me something of myself, show me something of my Savior." See the Savior hanging on the Cross, turn your eyes to Him, and say, "Lord, I trust you. I have nothing else to trust to, but I rely on you; sink or swim, my Savior, I trust you." And sinner, as surely as you put your trust in Christ, you are His and you are as safe as an apostle or prophet. Neither death nor hell can slay that man whose firm reliance is at the foot of the Cross of Christ. *"Believe on the Lord Jesus Christ and thou shalt be saved."* [See Acts 16:31.] *"He that believeth and is baptized shall be saved; but he that believeth not shall be damned"* [Mark 16:16]. He that believes shall be saved, though his sins may be many; he that believes not shall be damned, though his sins may be few, and his virtues many. Trust in Jesus now! Sinner, trust in Jesus only.

"Not all the blood of beasts
On Jewish altars slain
Could give the guilty conscience peace,
Or wash away the stain.
But Christ, the heavenly Lamb,
Takes all our sins away;
A sacrifice of nobler name
And richer blood than they."[47]

---

47. Hymn by Isaac Watts titled: "Not All the Blood of Beasts written in 1709".

CHAPTER 6
THE BLOOD-SHEDDING

A SERMON
(No. 118)
Delivered on Sabbath Morning, February 22, 1857,
by the
REVEREND C. H. SPURGEON,
at Music Hall, Royal Surrey Gardens,
Kennington, London, England

"Without shedding of blood is no remission."
—Hebrews 9:22.

I WILL SHOW YOU THREE FOOLS. One is yonder soldier, who has been wounded on the field of battle, grievously wounded, well nigh unto death; the surgeon is by his side, and the soldier asks him a question. Listen, and judge his folly. What question does he ask? Does he raise his eyes with eager anxiety and inquire if the wound is mortal, if the practitioner's skill can suggest the means of healing, or if the remedies are within reach and the medicine at hand? No, nothing of the sort; strange to tell, he asks, "Can you inform me with what sword I was wounded, and by what Russian I have been thus grievously mauled? I want," he adds, "to learn every minute particular respecting the origin of my wound." The man is delirious or his head is affected. Surely such questions at such a time are proof enough that he is bereft of his senses.

There is another fool. The storm is raging, the ship is flying impetuously before the gale, the dark scud[48] moves swiftly over head, the masts are creaking, the sails are rent

---

48. Heavy, dark, swiftly moving clouds in a windy, stormy sky.

to rags, and still the gathering tempest grows more fierce. Where is the captain? Is he busily engaged on the deck, is he manfully facing the danger, and skillfully suggesting means to avert it? No sir, he has retired to his cabin, and there with studious thoughts and crazy fancies he is speculating on the place where this storm began. "This wind is mysterious, no one has ever yet been able to discover it," he says to himself. And, so regardless of the vessel, the lives of the passengers, and his own life, he is careful only to solve his curious questions. The man is mad, sir; take the rudder from his hand; he has gone clean mad! If he should ever come ashore, shut him up as a hopeless lunatic.

The third fool I shall doubtless find among yourselves. You are sick and wounded with sin, you are in the storm and hurricane of Almighty vengeance, and yet the question which you would ask of me, this morning, would be, "Sir, what is the origin of evil?" You are mad, Sir, spiritually mad; that is not the question you would ask if you were in a healthy and sane state of mind; your question would be: "How can I get rid of the evil?" Not, "How did it come into the world?" but "How am I to escape from it?" Not, "How is it that hail descends from Heaven upon Sodom?" but "How may I, like Lot, escape out of the city to a place like Zoar." [See Genesis 19:22.]

Not, "How is it that I am sick?" but "Are there medicines that will heal me? Is there a physician to be found that can restore my soul to health?" Ah! You trifle with subtleties while you neglect certainties. More questions have been asked concerning the origin of evil than upon anything else. Men have puzzled their heads, and twisted their brains into knots, in order to understand what men can never know—how evil came into this world, and how its entrance is consistent with divine goodness?

The broad fact is this, there is evil; and your question

should be, "How can I escape from the wrath to come, which is engendered of this evil?" In answering that question this verse stands right in the middle of the way (like the angel with the sword, who once stopped Balaam on his road to Barak in Numbers 22:31), *"Without shedding of blood is no remission."* Your real need is to know how you can be saved; if you are aware that your sin must be pardoned or punished, your question will be, "How can it be pardoned?" and then point blank in the very teeth of your enquiry, there stands out this fact: *"Without shedding of blood is no remission."* Remember, this is not merely a Jewish maxim; it is a world-wide and eternal truth.

TO WHOM DOES THE TRUTH APPLY?

It pertains not only to the Hebrews, but to the Gentiles likewise. Never in any time, never in any place, never in any person, can there be remission of sin apart from shedding of blood. This great fact, I say, is stamped on nature; it is an essential law of God's moral government, it is one of the fundamental principles which can neither be shaken nor denied. Never can there be any exception to it; it stands the same in every place throughout all ages—*"Without shedding of blood there is no remission."* It was so with the Jews; they had no remission without the shedding of blood. Some things under the Jewish law might be cleansed by water or by fire, but in no case where absolute sin was concerned was there ever purification without blood—teaching this doctrine, that blood, and blood alone, must be applied for the remission of sin.

Indeed the very heathen seem to have an inkling of this fact. Do I not see their knives gory with the blood of victims? Have I not heard horrid tales of human immolations, of holocausts, of sacrifices; and what these mean, but that there lies deep in the human breast, deep as the very existence of man, this truth,—*"that without shedding of blood there is no remission."* And I assert once more, that even in the hearts and consciences of my hearers there is something which will never let them believe in remission apart from a shedding of blood. This is the grand truth of Christianity, and it is a truth which I will endeavor now to fix upon your memory; and may God by His grace bless it to your souls. *"Without shedding of blood is no remission."*

MOST PRECIOUS BLOOD SHED

First, let me show you the blood-shedding, before I begin to dwell upon the text. Is there not a special blood-shedding meant? Yes, there was a shedding of the most precious blood, to which I must immediately refer you. I shall not tell you now of massacres and murders, nor of rivers of blood of goats and rams. There was a blood-shedding once, which outrivaled all other shedding of blood by far; it was a man—a God—that shed His blood at that memorable season. Come and see it. Here is a garden dark and gloomy; the ground is crisp with the cold frost of midnight; between those gloomy olive trees I see a Man, I hear Him groan out His life in prayer; hearken, angels, hearken men, and wonder; it is the Savior groaning out His soul! Come and see Him.

Behold His brow! O heavens! Drops of blood are streaming down His face, and from His body; every pore is open, and it sweats! But not the sweat of men that toil for bread; it is the sweat of one that toils for Heaven—He *"sweats great drops of blood!"* [See Luke 22:44.] That is the blood-shedding, without which there is no remission. Follow that man further; they have dragged Him with sacrilegious bands from the place of His prayer and His agony, and they have taken Him to the hall of Pilate. They seat Him in a chair and mock Him; a robe of purple is put on His shoulders in mockery; and look at His brow—they have put a crown of thorns around it, and the crimson drops of gore are rushing down His cheeks!

Look, you angels! The drops of blood are running down His cheeks! But turn aside that purple robe for a moment. His back is bleeding. Tell me, demons, who did this? They lift up the whip, still dripping clots of gore; they scourge and tear His flesh, and make a river of blood to run down His shoulders! That is the shedding of blood without which there is no remission. Not yet am I done: they hurry Him through the streets; they fling Him on the ground; they nail His hands and feet to the transverse wood, they hoist it in the air, they dash it into its socket, it is fixed, and there He hangs the Christ of God. Blood from His head, blood from His hands, blood from His feet! In agony unknown He bleeds away His life; in terrible throes He exhausts His soul. *"Eloi, Eloi, lama sabacthani."* [. . . *My God, my God, why hast thou forsaken me?"* (Mark 15:34.).] And then see, they pierce His side, and immediately blood and water run out. This is the shedding of blood, sinners and saints; this is the awful shedding of blood, the terrible pouring out of blood, without which for you, and for the whole human race, there is no remission.

I hope I have brought my text fairly out: without this shedding of blood there is no remission. Now I shall come to dwell upon it more particularly. Why is it that this story does not make men weep? I didn't tell it well, you say. Aye, perhaps I didn't; I will take all the blame. But, sirs, if it were told as badly as men could speak, if our hearts were what they should be, we would bleed away our lives in sorrow. Oh! It was a horrid murder! It was not an act of regicide[49];

---

49. Killing a king.

it was not the deed of a fratricide[50], or of a parricide[51]; it was—what shall I say?—I must make a word—a deicide[52]; the killing of a God; the slaying of Him who became incarnate for our sins. Oh! If our hearts were but soft as iron, we must weep, if they were but tender as the marble of the mountains, we would shed great drops of grief; but they are harder than the nether[53] millstone; we forget the griefs of Him that died this ignominious death, we pity not His sorrows, nor do we account the interest we have in Him as though He suffered and accomplished all for us. Nevertheless, here stands the principle—*"Without shedding of blood is no remission."*

Now, I take it, there are two things here. First, there is a *negative expressed:* "No remission without shedding of blood." And then there is *a positive implied,* however, with shedding of blood there is remission.

I. A NEGATIVE EXPRESSED

There is no remission of sin without blood—without the blood of Jesus Christ. This is of divine authority; when I utter this sentence I have divinity to plead. It is not a thing which you may doubt, or which you may believe; it must be believed and received, otherwise you have denied the Scriptures and turned aside from God. Some truths I utter, perhaps, have little better basis than my own reasoning and inference, which are of little value enough; but this I utter, not with quotations from God's Word to back up my assertion, but from the lips of God himself. Here it stands in great letters, *"There is no remission."* So divine its authority.

---

50. Murder of a sibling.
51. Murder of a parent.
52. The act of killing a being of a divine nature, particularly, the putting to death of Jesus Christ.
53. The infernal nether regions are situated "down below."

REJECTING THE TRUTH

Perhaps you will kick at it: but remember, your rebellion is not against me, but against God, if any of you reject this truth, I will not contradict you; God forbid I should turn aside from proclaiming His gospel, to dispute with men. I have God's irrevocable statute to plead now, here it stands: *"Without shedding of blood there is no remission."* You may believe or disbelieve many things the preacher utters; but this you disbelieve at the peril of your souls. It is God's utterance: will you tell God to His face you do not believe it? That would be impious. The negative is divine in its authority; bow yourselves to it, and accept its solemn warning.

But some men will say that God's way of saving men, by shedding of blood, is a cruel way, an unjust way, an unkind way; and all other kinds of things they may say of it. Sirs, I have nothing to do with your opinion of the matter; it is so. If you have any faults to find with your Maker, fight your battles out with Him. But take heed before you throw the gauntlet down; it will go badly with a worm when he fights with His Maker, and it will go badly with you when you contend with Him. The doctrine of atonement when rightly understood and faithfully received is delightful, for it exhibits boundless love, immeasurable goodness, and infinite truth; but to unbelievers it will always be a hated doctrine. So it must be sirs; you hate your own mercies; you despise your own salvation. I tarry not to dispute with you; I affirm it in God's name: *"Without shedding of blood there is no remission."*

NOTE HOW DECISIVE THIS IS IN CHARACTER

"Without shedding of blood there is no remission." "But, sir, can't I get my sins forgiven by my repentance? If I weep,

and plead, and pray, will God not forgive me for the sake of my tears?" "*No remission,*" says the text, "*without shedding of blood.*" "But, sir, if I never sin again, and if I serve God more zealously than other men, will He not forgive me for the sake of my obedience?" "*No remission,*" says the text, "*without shedding of blood.*" "But, sir, may I not trust that God is merciful, and will forgive me without the shedding of blood?" "*No,*" says the text, "*without shedding of blood there is no remission;*" none whatever. It cuts off every other hope. Bring your hopes here, and if they are not based in blood and stamped with blood, they are as useless as castles in the air, and dreams of the night. "*There is no remission,*" says the text, in positive and plain words; and yet men will be trying to get remission in fifty other ways, until their special pleading becomes as irksome to us as it is useless for them. Sirs, do what you like, say what you please, but you are as far off from remission when you have done your best, as you were when you began, unless you put confidence in the shedding of our Savior's blood, and in the blood-shedding alone, for without it there is no remission.

UNIVERSAL IN CHARACTER

"What! May not I get remission without blood-shedding?" says the king; as he comes with the crown on his head. "May not I in all my robes, with this rich ransom, get pardon without the blood-shedding?" "None," is the reply; "none." Then comes forward the wise man, with a number of letters after his name—"Can I not get remission by these grand titles of my learning?" "None; none." Then comes the benevolent man—"I have dispersed my money to the poor, and given my bounty to feed them; shall not I get remission?" "None;" says the text, "*Without shedding of blood there is no remission.*"

Notice how this puts everyone on an equal level! My

lord, you are no bigger than your coachman; Sir, squire, you are no better off than the groundskeeper, John, that ploughs the ground; minister, your office does not serve you with any exemption—your poorest hearer stands on the very same footing. *"Without shedding of blood there is no remission."* No hope for the best, any more than for the worst, without this shedding of blood. Oh! I love the gospel, for this reason among others, because it is such a leveling gospel.

Some persons do not like a leveling gospel; nor would I, in some senses of the word. Let men have their rank, their titles, and their riches, if they will; but I do like, and I am sure all good men like, to see rich and poor meet together and feel that they are on the same level; for the gospel makes them so. It says "Put up your moneybags, they will not procure you remission; roll up your diploma, that will not get you remission; forget your farm and your park, they will not get you remission; just cover up that shield, that coat of arms will not get you remission. Come, you ragged beggars, filthy off-scourings of the world, penniless; come hither; here is remission as much for you, ill-bred and ill-mannered though you may be, it is the same for you as for the noble, the honorable, the titled, and the wealthy. All stand on an equal level here; the text is universal: *"Without shedding of blood there is no remission."*

Note How Perpetual the Text Is

Paul said, *"there is no remission;"* I must repeat this testimony too. When thousands of years have rolled away, some minister may stand on this spot and say the same. This will never alter at all; it will always be so, in the next world as well as this: *no remission without shedding of blood.*

"Oh yes there is" says one, "the priest takes the shilling, and he gets the soul out of purgatory." That is a mere pretence;

it never was in. But without shedding of blood there is no real remission. There may be tales and fancies, but there is no true remission without the blood of propitiation. Never, though you strained yourselves in prayer; never, though you wept yourselves away in tears; never, though you groaned and cried until your heartstrings break; never in this world, nor in that which is to come, can the forgiveness of sins be procured on any other ground than *redemption by the blood of Christ, and never can the conscience be cleansed but by faith in that sacrifice.* The fact is, Beloved; there is no use for you to satisfy your hearts with anything less than what satisfied God the Father. Without the shedding of blood nothing would appease His justice; and without the application of that same blood nothing can purge your consciences.

II. It is Implied That Without the Blood There Is No Remission

Mark this down, this remission is a *present* fact. The blood having been already shed, the remission is already obtained. I took you to the Garden of Gethsemane and the Mount of Calvary to see the blood-shedding. I will now conduct you to another garden and another mount to show you the grand proof of the remission. Another garden, did I say? Yes, it is a garden, fraught with many pleasing and even triumphant reminiscences. Aside from the haunts of this busy world, in it was a new sepulchre, hewn out of a rock where Joseph of Arimathea thought his own poor body would presently be laid. But there they laid Christ Jesus after His crucifixion.

He had stood surety for His people, and the law had demanded His blood; death had held Him with strong grasp; and that tomb was, as it were, the dungeon of His captivity, when, as the Good Shepherd, He laid down His life for the sheep. Why, then, do I see in that garden, an open, unoccupied grave? I will tell you. The debts are paid, the sins are canceled—the remission is obtained. "How" you ask? That great Shepherd of the sheep had been brought again from the dead by the blood of the everlasting covenant, and in Him also we have obtained redemption through His blood. There, beloved, is the first proof.

Do you ask for further evidence? I will take you to Mount Olivet. You shall behold Christ Jesus there with His hands raised like the High Priest of old to bless His people, and while He is blessing them, He ascends, the clouds receiving Him out of their sight. But why, you ask, why has He ascended, and where has He gone? Behold, He enters not into the holy place made with hands, but He enters into Heaven itself with His own blood, there to appear in the presence of God for us. Therefore, we now have boldness to draw near to God by the blood of Christ. The remission is obtained, here is the second proof. Oh believer, what springs of comfort are here for you.

And now let me commend this remission by the shedding of blood to those who have not yet believed. Mr. Innis[54], a great Scotch minister, once visited an infidel who was dying. When he came to him the first time, the infidel said, "Mr. Innis, I am relying on the mercy of God; God is merciful, and He will never damn a man for ever." When he got worse and was nearer death, Mr. Innis went to him again, and the man said, "Oh! Mr. Innis, my hope is gone; for I have been thinking if God is merciful, God is just too; and what if, instead of being merciful to me, He should be just to me? What would then become of me? I must give up my hope in the mere mercy of God; tell me how to be saved!" Mr. Innis

---

54. Anglican clergyman, George Innis, 1717-1781.

told him that Christ had died in the stead of all believers—that God could be just and yet the justifier through the death of Christ." Ah!" said the man, "Mr. Innis, there is something solid in that; I can rest on that; I cannot rest on anything else;" and it is a remarkable fact that none of us ever met with a man who thought he had his sins forgiven unless it was through the blood of Christ.

Meet a Mussulman[55]; he never had his sins forgiven; he does not say so. Meet an Infidel[56]; he never knows that his sins are forgiven. Meet a Legalist[57]; he says, "I hope they will be forgiven;" but he does not pretend they are. No one ever gets even a fancied hope apart from this that Christ, and Christ alone, must save by the shedding of His blood.

George Whitfield's Brother

Let me tell a story to show how Christ saves souls. George Whitfield had a brother who had been like him, an earnest Christian, but he had backslidden; he went far from the ways of godliness; and one afternoon, after he had been recovered from his backsliding, he was sitting in a room in a chapel house. He had heard his brother preaching the day before, and his poor conscience had been cut to the very quick. George Whitfield's brother said when he was at tea,

"I am a lost man," and he groaned and cried, and could neither eat nor drink.

Lady Huntingdon, who sat opposite him said, "What did you say, Mr. Whitfield?"

"Madam," he said, "I said, I am a lost man."

"I'm glad of it," she replied; "I'm glad of it."

"Your ladyship, how can you say so? It is cruel to

---

55. Muslim
56. Heathen
57. Strict conformist to the Law.

say you are glad that I am a lost man," he retorted.

"I repeat it, sir," she said; "I am heartily glad of it."

He looked at her, more and more astonished at her barbarity.

"I am glad of it," she said, "because it is written, 'The Son of Man came to seek and to save that which was lost." [Luke 19:10]

With the tears rolling down his cheeks, he said, "What a precious Scripture; and how is it that it comes with such force to me? O Madam," he said, "madam, I bless God for that; then He will save me; I trust my soul in His hands He has forgiven me." Mr. Whitfield then got to his feet and went outside the house, felt ill, fell upon the ground, and expired.

I may have a *lost man* here this morning. As I cannot say much more, I will leave you good people, for you do not seem to be in want of anything. Ah no, but I cannot leave! Have I got a lost man here? A lost man! Or a lost woman! Where are you? Do you feel yourself to be lost? If so, I am so glad of it; for there is remission by the blood-shedding. O sinner, are there tears in your eyes? Look through them. Do you see that Man in the Garden of Gethsemane? That Man sweats drops of blood for you. Do you see that Man on the Cross? That Man was nailed there for you.

Oh! If I could be nailed on a cross this morning for you all, I know what you would do: you would fall down and kiss my feet, and weep that I should have to die for you. But sinner, lost sinner, Jesus died for you—for you; and if He died for you; you cannot be lost. Christ died in vain for *no one*. Are you a sinner? Are you convinced of sin because you believe not in Christ?

I have authority to preach to you. Believe in His name

and you cannot be lost. Do you say you are not a sinner? Then I do not know that Christ died for you. Do you say that you have no sins to repent of? Then I have no Christ to preach to you. He did not come to save the righteous; He came to save the wicked. Are you wicked? Do you feel it? Are you lost? Do you know it? Are you sinful? Will you confess it?

Sinner! If Jesus were here this morning, He would put out His bleeding hands, and say, "Sinner, I died for you, will you believe me?" He is not here in person; He has sent His servant to tell you. Won't you believe Him?

"Oh!" but you say, "I am such a sinner;"
"Ah!" Christ says, "That is just why I died for you, because you are a sinner."
"But," you say, "I do not deserve it."
"Yes!" He says, "That is just why I did it."
You say, "I have hated you Lord."
"But," He says, "I have always loved you."
"But, Lord, I have spat on your minister, and scorned your Word."
The Lord replies, "It is all forgiven, all washed away by the blood which ran from my side. Only believe me; that is all I ask. And even that I will give you; I will help you to believe."

"Ah!" another one says, "but I do not want a Savior." Sir, I have nothing to say to you except this—"The wrath to come! The wrath to come!"

But there is another who says, "Sir, you do not mean what you say! Do you mean to preach to the most wicked men or women in the place?" Yes, I mean what I say. There she is! She is a harlot; she has led many into sin, and many into hell. There she is; her own friends have turned her out-of-doors; her father called her a good-for-nothing hussy, and said she should never come to the house again." I say to you, "Woman, do you repent? Do you feel yourself to be guilty? Christ died to save you, and you shall be saved."

There he is! I can see him. He was drunk; he has been drunk very often. Not many nights ago I heard his voice in the street, as he went home at a late hour on Saturday night, disturbing everybody; and he beat his wife, too. He has broken the Sabbath; and as to swearing, if oaths be like soot, his throat must want sweeping badly, for he has cursed God often. Do you feel yourself to be guilty, my hearer? Do you hate your sins, and are you willing to forsake them? Then I bless God for you. Christ died for you. Believe!

I had a letter a few days ago, from a young man who heard that during this week I was going to a certain town. He said, "Sir, when you come, do preach a sermon that will fit me; for you know, sir, I have heard it said that we must all think ourselves to be the wickedest people in the world, or else we cannot be saved. I try to think so, but I cannot, because I have not been the wickedest. I want to think so, but I cannot. I want to be saved, but I do not know how to repent enough."

Now, if I have the pleasure of seeing him, I shall tell him, God does not require a man to think himself the wickedest in the world, because that would sometimes be to think a falsehood; there are some men who are not so wicked as others are. What God requires is that a man should say, "I know more of myself than I do of other people; I know little about them, and from what I see of myself, not of my actions, but of my heart, I do think there can be few worse than I am. They may be more guilty openly, but then I have had more light, more privileges, more opportunities, more warnings, and therefore I am still guiltier." I do not want you to bring your brother with you, and say, "I am more wicked than he is;" I want you to come yourself, and say,

"Father, I have sinned;" you have nothing to do with your brother William, whether he has sinned more or less; your cry should be, "Father, I have sinned;" you have nothing to do with your cousin Jane, whether or not she has rebelled more than you. Your business is to cry, "Lord, have mercy upon me, a sinner!" That is all. Do you feel yourselves lost? Again, I say,—"Come, and welcome, sinner, come!"

To conclude. There is not a sinner in this place who knows himself to be lost and ruined, who may not have all his sins forgiven, and *"rejoice in the hope of the glory of God."* [See Romans 5:2.] Though your sins are as black as hell you may be white as Heaven this very instant. I know it is only by a desperate struggle that faith takes hold of the promise, but the very moment a sinner believes that conflict is past. It is his first victory, and a blessed one. Let this verse be the language of your heart; adopt it, and make it your own:

> "A guilty, weak, and helpless worm,
> Into Thy hands I fall;
> Be Thou my strength and righteousness,
> My Savior, and my all."[58]

---

58. Hymn: "How Sad Our State By Nature Is!" by Isaac Watts.

CHAPTER 7
THE VOICE OF THE BLOOD OF CHRIST

A SERMON

No. 211

Delivered on Sabbath Morning, August 29, 1858,

by the

REVEREND C. H. SPURGEON,

at the Music Hall, Royal Surrey Gardens,

Kennington, England

"The blood of sprinkling, that speaketh better things than that of Abel."—Hebrews 12:24.

OF ALL SUBSTANCES blood is the most mysterious, and in some senses the most sacred. Scripture teaches us,—and there is very much philosophy in Scripture,—that *"the blood is the life thereof,"*—that the life lies in the blood.

For the life of the flesh is in the blood; and I have given it to you for making atonement for your lives on the altar; for, as life, it is the blood that makes atonement [Leviticus 17:11].

Blood, therefore, is the mysterious link between matter and spirit. How it is that the soul would in any degree have an alliance with matter through blood, we cannot understand; but it is certain that this is the mysterious link that unites these apparently dissimilar things together, so that the soul can inhabit the body, and the life can rest in the blood. God has attached extreme sacredness to the shedding of blood.

Under the Jewish dispensation, even the blood of animals was considered as sacred. Blood was never to be eaten by the Jews; it was too sacred a thing to become the food of man. The Jew was under sacred laws regarding the killing of his own food: most importantly he must not kill it until he poured out the blood as a sacred offering to Almighty God. Blood was accepted by God as the symbol of the atonement. *"Without the shedding of blood there is no remission of sin"* [Hebrews 9:22, NRSV]. Because the blood has a strong affinity with life, inasmuch as God would accept nothing but blood, He signified that there must be a life offered to Him, and that His great and glorious Son must surrender His life as a sacrifice for His sheep.

Now, in our text we have "blood" mentioned—two-fold blood. We have the blood of murdered Abel, and the blood of murdered Jesus. We have also two things in the text:—a *comparison* between the blood of sprinkling, and the blood of Abel; and then a certain *condition* mentioned. As we read the whole verse in order to get its meaning, we find that the righteous are spoken of as coming to the blood of sprinkling, *"that speaketh better things than the blood of Abel"*; so that the condition which will constitute the second part of our discourse, is coming to that blood of sprinkling for our salvation and glory. Without further introduction I shall now introduce to you:

I. THE CONTRAST AND COMPARISON IMPLIED IN THE TEXT

"The blood of sprinkling, that speaketh better things than that of Abel." I confess I was very much astonished when looking at Dr. Gill[59] and Albert Barnes[60], and several of the more eminent commentators, while studying this passage, to find that they attach a meaning to this verse which had never occurred to me before. They say that the meaning of

---

59. Dr. John Gill, 11/23/1697—10/14/1771, English theologian.
60. 12/1/1798—12/24/1870. American theologian.

the verse is not that the blood of Christ is superior to the blood of murdered Abel, although that is certainly a truth, but that the sacrifice of the blood of Christ is better, and speaks better things than the sacrifice which Abel offered. Now, although I do not think this is the meaning of the text and I have my reasons for believing that the blood here contrasted with that of the Savior, is the blood of the murdered man Abel, yet on looking to the original there is so much to be said on both sides of the question. Therefore, I think it fair in explaining the passage to give you both the meanings. They are not conflicting interpretations; there is indeed a shade of difference but still they amount to the same idea.

First of all, so that we may understand here a comparison between the offerings Abel presented, and the offerings Jesus Christ presented, when He gave His blood to be a ransom for the flock. Let me describe Abel's offering. I have no doubt Adam had offered a sacrifice to God after his expulsion from the Garden of Eden. And we have some dim hint that this sacrifice was of a beast, for we find that the Lord God made Adam and Eve skins of beasts to be their clothing, and it is probable that those skins were procured by the slaughter of victims offered in sacrifice. However, that is but a dim hint: the first absolute record that we have of an obligatory[61] sacrifice is the record of the sacrifice offered by Abel.

Now, it appears that very early there was a distinction among men. Cain was the representative of the seed of the serpent, and Abel was the representative of the seed of the woman. Abel was God's elect, and Cain was one of those who rejected the Most High. However, both Cain and Abel united together in the outward service of God. They both brought a sacrifice on a certain high day. Cain took a different view of the matter of sacrifice from that which presented itself

---

61. Required, mandatory.

to the mind of Abel. Cain was proud and haughty: he said "I am ready to confess that the mercies which we receive from the soil are the gift of God, but I am not ready to acknowledge that I am a guilty sinner, deserving God's wrath, therefore," he said, "I will bring nothing but the fruit of the ground." "Ah, but" said Abel, "I feel that while I ought to be grateful for temporal mercies, at the same time I have sins to confess, I have iniquities to be pardoned, and I know that without shedding of blood there is no remission of sin. Therefore," he said, "O Cain, I will not be content to bring an offering of the ground, of the ears of corn, or of first ripe fruits, but I will bring of the firstlings of my flock, and I will shed blood upon the altar, because my faith is, that there is to come a great victim who is actually to make atonement for the sins of men, and by the slaughter of this lamb, I express my solemn faith in him."

Not so Cain; he cared nothing for Christ; he was not willing to confess his sin; he had no objection to presenting a thank-offering, but a sin-offering he would not bring. He did not mind bringing to God that which he thought might be acceptable as a return for favors received, but he would not bring to God an acknowledgment of his guilt, or a confession of his inability to make atonement for it, except by the blood of a substitute.

Cain, moreover, when he came to the altar, came entirely without faith. He piled the unhewn stones, as Abel did, he laid his sheaves of corn upon the altar, and there he waited, but it was to him a matter of comparative indifference whether God accepted him or not. He believed there was a God, no doubt, but he had no faith in the promises of that God. God had said that the seed of the woman would bruise the serpent's head—that was the gospel as revealed to our first parents in Genesis 3:15; but Cain had no belief in that gospel—whether it were true or not, he cared not—it was sufficient for him that he acquired enough for his own sustenance from the soil; he had no faith.

But holy Abel stood by the side of the altar, and while Cain the infidel perhaps laughed and jeered at his sacrifice, Abel boldly presented there the bleeding lamb as a testimony to all men, both of that time and all future times that he believed in the seed of the woman—that he looked for Him to come who would destroy the serpent, and restore the ruins of the fall. Do you see holy Abel, standing there, ministering as a priest at God's altar? Do you see the flush of joy which comes over his face, when he sees the heavens opened, and the living fire of God descend upon the victim? Do you note with what a grateful expression of confident faith he lifts his eyes to Heaven which had been before filled with tears, and cries, "I thank thee O Father, Lord of Heaven and Earth, that you have accepted my sacrifice, inasmuch as I presented it through faith in the blood of your Son, my Savior, who is to come."

Abel's sacrifice, being the first on record, and being offered in the teeth of opposition, has very much in it which puts it ahead of many of the other sacrifices of the Jews. Abel is to be greatly honored for his confidence and faith in the coming Messiah. But compare for a moment the sacrifice of Christ with the sacrifice of Abel and the sacrifice of Abel shrinks into insignificance. What did Abel bring? He brought a sacrifice which showed the necessity of blood-shedding but Christ brought the blood-shedding itself.

Abel taught the world by his sacrifice that he looked for a victim, but Christ brought the actual victim. Abel brought but the type and the figure, the Lamb which was but a picture of the Lamb of God which takes away the sins of the world; but Christ was that Lamb. [See John 1:29.] He was the substance of the shadow, the reality of the type. Abel's sacrifice had no merit in it apart from the faith in the

Messiah with which he presented it; but Christ's sacrifice had merit of itself; it was in itself meritorious.

What was the blood of Abel's lamb? It was nothing but the blood of a common lamb that might have been shed anywhere, except for the fact that Abel had faith in Christ, the blood of the lamb was but as water, a contemptible thing. But the blood of Christ was a sacrifice indeed, richer far than all the blood of beasts that ever were offered upon the altar of Abel, or the altar of all the Jewish high priests. We may say of all the sacrifices that were ever offered, however costly they might be, and however acceptable to God, though they might be rivers of oil and tens of thousands of fat beasts, yet they were less than nothing. They were contemptible in comparison with the one sacrifice which our high priest has offered once for all, whereby He has eternally perfected them that are sanctified.

We have therefore found it very easy to set forth the difference between the blood of Christ's sprinkling and the blood which Abel sprinkled. But now I believe there is a deeper meaning than this, despite what some commentators have said. I believe that the allusion here is to the blood of murdered Abel. Cain smote Abel, and doubtless his hands and the altar were stained with the blood of Abel who had acted as a priest. "Now," says our apostle, "that blood of Abel spoke." We have evidence that it did, for God said to Cain, *"The voice of thy brother's blood crieth unto me from the ground,"* [See Genesis 4:10.] and the apostle's comment upon that in another place is—*"By faith Abel offered unto God a more excellent sacrifice than Cain, by which he obtained witness that he was righteous, God testifying of his gifts, and by it he being dead yet speaketh,"* speaketh through his blood, his blood crying unto God from the ground. [See Hebrews 11:4.]

Now, Christ's blood speaks too. What is the difference

between the two voices?—for we are told in the text that it *"speaketh better things than that of Abel."* Abel's blood spoke in a threefold manner. It spoke in Heaven; it spoke to the sons of men; it spoke to the conscience of Cain. The blood of Christ speaks in a like threefold manner, and it speaks better things.

First: the Blood of Abel Spoke in Heaven

Abel was a holy man, and all that Cain could bring against him was, "His own works were evil, and his brother's were righteous." You see the brothers going to the sacrifice together. Note the black scowl upon the brow of Cain, when Abel's sacrifice is accepted while his remains untouched by the sacred fire. You note how they begin to talk together— how quietly Abel argues the question, and how ferociously Cain denounces him. You note again how God speaks to Cain, and warns him of the evil which He knew was in his heart; and you see Cain, as he goes from the presence chamber of the Most High, warned and forewarned; but yet with the dreadful thought in his heart that he will drench his hands in his brother's blood. He meets his brother; he talks friendly with Abel: he gives him, as it were, the kiss of Judas; he entices him into the field where he is alone; Cain comes upon him unawares; he smites him, and smites him yet again until there lays the murdered bleeding corpse of his brother. O earth! earth! earth! Cover not his blood! This is the first murder you have ever seen; the first blood of man that ever stained your soil.

Hark! There is a cry heard in Heaven, the angels are astonished; they rise up from their golden seats, and they inquire, "What is that cry?" God looks upon them, and He says, "It is the cry of blood, a man has been slain by his fellow; a brother by him who came from the bowels of the self-same mother has been murdered in cold blood, through malice. One of my saints has been murdered, and here he comes. Abel entered into Heaven blood-red, the first of God's elect who had entered Paradise, and the first of God's children who had worn the blood-red crown of martyrdom. And then the cry was heard, loud and clear and strong; and thus it spoke—"Revenge! revenge! revenge!" And God himself, rose from His throne, summoned the culprit to His presence, questioned him, condemned him out of His own mouth, and made him henceforth a fugitive and a vagabond, to wander over the surface of the Earth, which was to be sterile from then on to his plow.

And now, beloved, just contrast this with the blood of Christ. That is Jesus Christ, the Incarnate Son of God; He hangs upon a tree; He is murdered—murdered by His own brethren. *"He came unto his own, and his own received him not,"* but His own led Him out to death. [See John 1:11.] He bleeds; He dies; and then is heard a cry in Heaven. The astonished angels rise again startled by the cry and say, "What is this cry that we hear?" And the Mighty Maker answers yet again, "It is the cry of blood; it is the cry of the blood of my only-begotten and well-beloved Son!" And God, rising from His throne, looks down from Heaven and listens to the cry. And what is the cry? It is not revenge; but the voice cries, "Mercy! Mercy! Mercy!" Did you not hear it? It cried, *"Father, forgive them; for they know not what they do"* [Luke 23:34.]. Herein, the blood of Christ *"speaketh better things than that of Abel,"* for Abel's blood said, "Revenge!" and made the sword of God start from its scabbard; but Christ's blood cried "Mercy!" and sent the sword back again, and bade it sleep for ever.

"Blood hath a voice to pierce the skies,
'Revenge!' the blood of Abel cries;
But the rich blood of Jesus slain,
Speaks peace as loud from every vein."[62]

You will note also that Abel's blood cried for revenge upon one man only—upon Cain; it required the death of but one man to satisfy for it, namely the death of the murderer. "Blood for blood!" The murderer must die the death. But what says Christ's blood in Heaven? Does it speak for only one? Ah! No, beloved; *the free gift hath abounded unto many.* [See Romans 5:15.] Christ's blood cries mercy! mercy! mercy! Not on one, but upon a multitude whom no man can number—ten thousand times ten thousand.

Again: Abel's blood cried to Heaven for revenge for one transgression that Cain had done, worthless and vile before, the blood of Abel did not demand any revenge: it was for the one sin that blood clamored at the throne of God, and not for many sins. Not so the voice of the blood of Christ. It is "for many offences unto justification." [See Romans 5:16.]. Oh, could you hear that cry, that all-prevailing cry, as now it comes up from Calvary's summit—*"Father, forgive them!"* not one, but many. *"Father, forgive them."* And not only forgive them this offense, but forgive them all their sins, and blot out all their iniquities. Ah beloved, we might have thought that the blood of Christ would have demanded vengeance at the hands of God. Surely, if Abel is revenged seven fold, then Christ must be revenged seventy times seven. If the earth would not swallow up the blood of Abel until it had its fill, surely we might have thought that the earth never would have covered the corpse of Christ, until God had struck the world with fire and sword, and banished all

---

62. Hymn written by Isaac Watts titled: "Blood Has a Voice to Pierce the Skies".

men to destruction. But, O precious blood! You say not one word of vengeance! All that this blood cries is peace, pardon, forgiveness, mercy, and acceptance! Truly it *"speaketh better things than that of Abel."*

SECOND: ABEL'S BLOOD HAD A SECOND VOICE

Abel's blood had a second voice. It spoke to the whole world. *"He being dead yet speaketh"*—not only in Heaven, but on Earth. [See Hebrews 11:4.] God's prophets are a speaking people. They speak by their acts and by their words as long as they live, and when they are buried they speak by their example which they have left behind. Abel speaks by his blood to us. And what does it say? When Abel offered up his victim upon the altar he said to us, "I believe in a sacrifice that is to be offered for the sins of men," but when Abel's own blood was sprinkled on the altar he seemed to say, "Here is the ratification of my faith; I seal my testimony with my own blood; you have now the evidence of my sincerity, for I was prepared to die for the defense of this truth which I now witness unto you."

It was a great thing for Abel to thus ratify his testimony with his blood. We would not have believed the martyrs half so easily if they had not been ready to die for their profession. The gospel in ancient times would never have spread at such a marvelous rate, if it had not been that all the preachers of the gospel were ready at any time to bear witness to their message with their own blood. But Christ's blood *"speaketh better things than that of Abel."* Abel's blood ratified his testimony, and Christ's blood has ratified His testimony too; but Christ's testimony is better than that of Abel. What is the testimony of Christ? The covenant of grace—that everlasting covenant. He came into this world to tell us that God had from the beginning chosen His people.

He ordained them to eternal life, and He had made a covenant with His son Jesus Christ that if He would pay the price they would go free. That price being His willingness to suffer in their stead and they would be delivered. And Christ cried out before *"he bowed his head and gave up the ghost"*— *"It is finished."* [See John 19:30.] The covenant purpose is finished. That purpose was "to finish the transgression, and to make an end of sins, and to make reconciliation for iniquity, and to bring in everlasting righteousness." Such was the testimony of our Lord Jesus Christ, as His own blood gushed from His heart, to be the die-stamp[63], and seal, that the covenant was ratified. When I see Abel die I know that his testimony was true; but when I see Christ die I know that the covenant is true.

> "This covenant, O believer, stands
> Thy rising fears to quell;
> 'Tis signed and sealed and ratified,
> In all things ordered well."[64]

When He bowed His head and gave up the ghost, He as much as said, "All things are made sure unto the seed by my giving myself as the victim." Come, saint, and see the covenant all bloodstained, and know that it is sure. He is *"the faithful and true witness, the prince of the kings of the earth."* [See Revelation 1:5 and 3:14.] First of the martyrs, my Lord Jesus, you have a better testimony to witness than they all, for you have witnessed to the everlasting covenant; you have witnessed that you are the shepherd and bishop

---

63. To produce a word or image that stands out in relief such as in embossing.
64. Hymn titled: "Come Saints and Sing in Sweet Accord by John Kent".

of souls; you have witnessed to the putting away of sin by the sacrifice of yourself.

Again: I say, come, you people of God, and read over the golden roll. It begins in election—it ends in everlasting life, and all this the blood of Christ cries in your ears. All this is true; for Christ's blood proves it to be true, and to be sure to all the seed. It *"speaketh better things than that of Abel."*

THE THIRD VOICE OF THE BLOOD OF ABEL

The blood of Abel had a three-fold sound. It spoke in the conscience of Cain. Hardened though he was, and like a very devil in his sin, yet he was not so deaf in his conscience that he could not hear the voice of blood. The first thing that Abel's blood said to Cain was this: Ah, guilty wretch, to spill your brother's blood! As he saw it trickling from the wound and flowing down in streams, the sun shone on it, and as the red glare came into his eye it seemed to say, "Ah, you cursed wretch, for the son of your own mother you have slain! Your wrath was vile enough your countenance fell when you saw Abel's sacrifice but to rise up against your brother and take away his life, Oh, how vile!" The voice seemed to say to him, "What had he done that you would take his life? How had he offended you? Was not his conduct blameless, and his conversation pure? If you had smitten a villain or a thief, men might not have blamed you; but this blood is pure, clean, perfect blood; how could you kill such a man as this?"

Cain put his hand across his brow, and felt there was a sense of guilt there that he had never felt before. And then the blood said to him again, "Why, where will you go? You shall be a vagabond as long as you live." A cold chill ran through him, and he said, "Whosoever finds me will kill me." And though God promised him he would live, no doubt he was always afraid. If he saw a company of men together, he would hide himself in a thicket, or if in his solitary wanderings he saw a man at a distance, he turned back, and sought to bury his head, so that none should observe him.

In the stillness of the night he awoke startled by his dreams but it was only his wife that slept by his side; but he thought he felt someone's hands gripping his throat, and about to take away his life. Then he would sit up in his bed and look around at the grim shadows, thinking some fiend was haunting him and seeking after him. Then, as he rose to go about his business, he trembled. He trembled to be alone, and trembled to be in company. When he was alone he felt like he wasn't alone; the ghost of his brother seemed to be staring him in his face; and when he was in company he dreaded the voice of men, for he seemed to think everyone cursed him.

He thought everyone knew the crime he had committed, and no doubt they did, and every man shunned him. No man would shake his hand, for it was red with blood, and his own child upon his knee was afraid to look up into his father's face, for there was the mark which God had set upon him. His very wife could scarcely speak to him,—for she was afraid that from the lips of him who had been cursed of God some curse might fall on her. The very earth cursed him. He no sooner put his foot upon the ground, then suddenly it turned to desert where it had been a garden before, and the fair rich soil became hardened into an arid rock. Guilt, like a grim chamberlain[65], with bloody-red fingers would draw the curtain of his bed each night. His crime refused him sleep. It spoke in his heart, and the walls of his memory reverberated

---

65. A person such as a butler or a nobleman or gentleman's valet.

the dying cry of his murdered brother. No doubt that blood spoke one more thing to Cain. It said:

> "Cain, although you may be spared now there is no hope for you; you are a man accursed on Earth, and accursed forever, God has condemned you here, and He will damn you hereafter."

And so wherever Cain went, he never found hope. Though he searched for it in the mountain top, yet he found it not. Hope that was left to all men was denied to him: a hopeless, homeless, helpless vagabond, he wandered up and down the surface of the Earth. Oh, Abel's blood had a terrible voice indeed.

But now see the sweet change as you listen to the blood of Christ. It *"speaketh better things than that of Abel."* Friend, have you ever heard the blood of Christ in your conscience? I have, and I thank God I heard that sweet soft voice.

> "Once a sinner near despair;
> Sought the mercy seat by prayer."[66]

He prayed: he thought he was praying in vain. The tears gushed from his eyes; his heart was heavy within him; he sought, but he found no mercy. Again, again, and yet again, he besieged the throne of the heavenly grace and knocked at mercy's door.

Oh who can tell the millstone[67] that lay upon his beating heart, and the iron that ate into his soul. He was a prisoner in sore bondage; deep in the bondage of despair and chained to perish forever.

One day that prisoner heard a voice, which said to him,

---

66. Verse 4 of a hymn called "Lord I Cannot Let Thee Go by John Newton".
67. A heavy load.

"Away, away Calvary!" But he trembled at the voice and said, "Why should I go there, for there my blackest sin was committed; there I murdered the Savior by my transgressions? Why should I go to see the murdered corpse of Him who became my brother born for adversity?"

But mercy beckoned, and she said, "Come, come away, sinner!"

And from the feet, and from the side, and mercy touched his ears and said:

> "Listen!" and he heard that blood speak; and
> as it spoke the first thing it said was, "Love!"
> And the second thing it said was, "Mercy!"
> The third thing it said was, "Pardon."
> The next thing it said was, "Acceptance."
> The next thing it said was, "Adoption."
> The next thing it said was, "Security."
> And the last thing it whispered was, "Heaven."

As the sinner heard that voice, he said within himself, "And does that blood speak to me?" And the Spirit said, "To you—to you it speaks."

As he listened, the words of the voice were like beautiful music to his poor troubled heart, for in a moment all his doubts were gone. He had no sense of guilt. He knew that he was vile, but he saw that his vileness was all washed away. He knew that he was guilty, but he saw his guilt all atoned for, through the precious blood that was flowing there. He had been full of dread before; he dreaded life, he dreaded death; but now he had no dread at all; a joyous confidence took possession of his heart. He looked to Christ, and he said, "I know that my Redeemer liveth."[68] He clasped the Savior

---

68. Hymn titled: "I Know That My Redeemer Liveth". Music by James H. Filllmore, Sr. and Words by Jessie B. Pounds.

in his arms, and he began to sing:—"Oh! Confident am I; for this blest blood was shed for me." Then Despair fled and Destruction was driven clean away and in its place came the bright white-winged angel of Assurance, and she dwelt in his bosom, saying evermore to him, "You are accepted in the Beloved: you are chosen of God and precious: you are His child now, and you shall be His favored throughout eternity." *"The blood of Christ speaketh better things than that of Abel."*

COMPARISON OF THE BLOOD OF CHRIST AND OF ABEL

Now I must have you notice that the blood of Christ bears a *comparison* with the blood of Abel in one or two respects, but the blood of Christ excels. The blood of Abel cried "Justice!" It was but right that the blood should be revenged. Abel had no personal anger against Cain; no doubt Abel could not have done so for he would have forgiven his brother, but the blood spoke justly, and only asked its due when it shouted "Vengeance! vengeance! vengeance!"

Furthermore, Christ's blood also speaks justly, when it says, "Mercy!" Christ has as much right to demand mercy upon sinners, as Abel's blood had to cry vengeance against Cain. When Christ saves a sinner, He does not save Him on the sly, or against law or justice, but He saves him justly. Christ has a right to save whom He will save, to have mercy on whom He will have mercy, for He can do it justly. He can be just, and yet be the justifier of the ungodly.

Again, Abel's blood cried effectively. It did not cry in vain. It said, "Revenge!" and revenge it had. And Christ's blood, blessed be His name, never cries in vain. It says, "Pardon;" and pardon every believer shall have; it says, "Acceptance," and every penitent is accepted in the Beloved. If that blood cries for me, I know it cannot cry in vain. That all-prevailing blood of Christ shall never miss its due; it must, and it shall be heard. Shall Abel's blood startle Heaven, and shall not the blood of Christ reach the ears of the Lord God of Sabaoth?

And again, Abel's blood cries continually, there is the mercy seat, and there is the Cross, and the blood is dropping on the mercy seat. I have sinned a sin. Christ says, "Father, forgive him." There is one drop. I sin again: Christ intercedes again. There is another drop. In fact, it is the drop that intercedes, Christ need not speak with His mouth; the drops of blood as they fall upon the mercy seat, each seems to say, "Forgive him! Forgive him! Forgive him!"

Dear friend, when you hear the voice of conscience, stop and try to hear the voice of the blood too. Oh! What a precious thing it is to hear the voice of the blood of Christ. You who do not know what that means, do not know the very essence and joy of life; but you who understand that, can say, "The dropping of the blood is like the music of Heaven upon Earth."

Poor sinner! I would ask you to come and listen to that voice that speaks in your ears and your heart today. You are full of sin; the Savior bids you to lift your eyes to Him. See, there, His blood is flowing from His head, His hands, His feet, and every drop that falls, still cries, "Father, O forgive them! Father, O forgive them!" And each drop seems to cry also as it falls, "It is finished: I have made an end of sin, I have brought in everlasting righteousness." Oh! Sweet, sweet language of the dropping of the blood of Christ." It *"speaketh better things than that of Abel."*

II. THE CONDITION EVERY CHRISTIAN IS BROUGHT INTO

Having thus, I trust, sufficiently enlarged upon this subject I shall now close by addressing you with a few earnest words concerning the above point. He is said to have "*come to the blood of sprinkling*" [Hebrews 12:24]. I shall make this a very brief matter, but a very solemn and pointed one. My friends, have you come to the blood of Christ? I do not ask you whether you have come to a knowledge of doctrine, or of an observance of ceremonies, or of a certain form of experience; but I ask you if you have come to the blood of Christ. If you have, I know how you come. You must come to the blood of Christ with no merits of your own. Guilty, lost, and helpless, you must come to that blood and to that blood alone. For your hopes; you come to the Cross of Christ and to that blood too, I know, with a trembling and an aching heart.

Some of you remember how you first came, cast down and full of despair; but that blood recovered you. And this one thing I know: if you have come to that blood once, you will come to it every day. Your life will be just this—"*Looking unto Jesus.*" [See Hebrews 12:2.] And your whole conduct will be epitomized in this—"*To whom coming as unto a living stone.*" [See 1 Peter 2:4.] Not to whom I have come, but to whom I am always coming. If you have ever come to the blood of Christ you will feel the need of coming to it every day. He that does not desire to wash in that fountain every day has never washed in it at all. I feel it every day to be my joy and my privilege that there is still a fountain opened for me to go to. I trust I came to Christ years ago but oh I could not trust to that, unless I could come again today. Past experiences are doubtful things to a Christian; it is present coming daily to Christ that gives us joy and comfort. Did some of you at twenty years of age sing that hymn:

> "My faith doth lay her hand
> On that dear head of thine

> While like a penitent I stand,
> And there confess my sin."[69]

Why, beloved you can sing it as well today as you did then. I was reading a book the other day, in which the author states, that we are not to come to Christ as sinners as long as we live; he says we are to grow into saints. Ah! He did not know much, I am sure; for saints are sinners still, and they have always to come to Christ as sinners. If ever I go to the throne of God as a saint, I get repulsed; but when I go just as a poor humble seeking sinner, relying upon nothing but your blood, O Jesus, I never can get a repulse, I am sure. To whom coming as unto *blood that speaketh better things than that of Abel.*" Let this be our experience every day.

But there are some here who confess that they never did come. I cannot exhort you, then, to come every day, but I exhort you to come now for the first time. But you say, "May I come?" Yes, if you are wishing to come you may come; if you feel that you have need to come you may come.

> "All the fitness he requireth,
> Is to feel your need of him;
> And even
> This he gives you,
> 'Tis his Spirit's rising beam."
> But you say, "I must bring some merits."[70]

Listen to the blood that speaks! It says, "Sinner, I am full of merit: why bring your merits here?"

"Ah, but," you say "I have too much sin."

Listen to the blood: as it falls, it cries, "Of many offenses unto justification of life." "Ah, but," you say, "I know I am

---

69. Hymn: "O God Our Help in Ages Past", by Isaac Watts.
70. Hymn: "Come Ye Sinners Poor and Wretched" by William Walker.

too guilty."

Listen to the blood! *"Though your sins be as scarlet I will make them as wool; though they be red like crimson they shall be whiter than snow."*

"No" says another, "but I have such a poor desire, I have such a little faith."

Listen to the blood! "The bruised reed I will not break, and smoking flax I will not quench."

"No, but," you say, "I know he will cast me out, if I do come."

Listen to the blood! *"All that the Father giveth me shall come to me, and him that cometh to me I will in no wise cast out"* [John 6:37].

"Oh no, but," you say, "I know I have so many sins that I cannot be forgiven."

Now, hear the blood once more, and I will be done. *"The blood of Jesus Christ, his Son, cleanseth us from all sin"* [1 John 1:7]. That is the blood's testimony, and its testimony to you. *"There are three that bear witness on earth, the Spirit, and the water, and the blood;"* [See 1 John 5:8.] and behold the blood's witness is—*"The blood of Jesus Christ, his Son, cleanseth us from all sin."* Come, poor sinner, cast yourself simply on that truth. Away with your good works and all your trusting! Simply cast yourself on that sweet Word of Christ. Trust His blood; and if you can put your trust in Jesus alone, in His sprinkled blood, it shall speak in your conscience better things than that of Abel.

I am afraid there are many that do not know what we mean by believing. Good Mr. Chalmers[71] once visited a poor old woman and told her to believe in Christ, and she said, "But that is just the thing I do not know what you mean by." So Dr. Chalmers said, *"Trust Christ."* Now, that is just

---

71. Thomas Chalmers, Scottish minister.

the meaning of believing. Trust Him with your soul; trust Him with your sins; trust Him with the future; trust Him with the past; trust Him with everything. Say,

> "A guilty, weak, and worthless worm,
> On Christ's kind arms I fall
> Be thou my strength and righteousness,
> My Jesus and my all."[72]

May the Lord now give you his blessing; for Jesus Christ's sake. Amen.

---

72. Poem by Isaac Watts.

CHAPTER 8

THE PRECIOUS BLOOD OF CHRIST

Delivered on Sunday Morning, March 26, 1865,
by REVEREND CHARLES H. SPURGEON,
At the Metropolitan Tabernacle in
Newington, London, England.

"The precious blood of Christ."—1 Peter 1:19.

IT IS FREQUENTLY MY FEAR that I might fall into the habit of preaching about the Gospel rather than directly preaching the Gospel. And then I labor to return to the first principle of our faith and often take a text upon which it would not be possible to say anything new, but which will compel me to recapitulate in your hearing those things that are vital, essential and fundamental to the life of our souls. With such a text as this before me, if I do not preach the Gospel I shall do violence both to the sacred Word and to my own conscience. Surely I may hope that while endeavoring to unfold my text and to proclaim the saving Word, the Holy Spirit will be present to take of the things of Christ and to show them unto us and make them saving to our souls.

INGESTING THE BLOOD OF MAN OR ANIMAL IS FORBIDDEN

God has regarded blood as a most precious thing from the very beginning. He has hedged around this fountain of vitality the most solemn sanctions. The Lord thus commanded Noah and his descendants, *"Flesh with the life thereof, which is the blood thereof, shall you not eat."* [See Genesis 9:4.]

Man had every moving thing that lives given him for meat, but they were by no means to eat the blood with the flesh. Things strangled were to be considered unfit for food; because God would not have man became too familiar with blood by eating or drinking it in any shape or form. Therefore, even the blood of bulls and goats had a sacredness put upon it by God's decrees. As for the blood of man, you remember how God's threats ran,

> "And surely your blood of your lives will I require; at the hand of every beast will I require it and at the hand of man; at the hand of every man's brother will I require the life of man." Whoso sheddeth man's blood, by man shall his blood be shed: for in the image of God made He man." [Genesis 9:5-6]

It is true that the one who committed the first murder did not have his blood shed by man, but then the crime was new and the penalty had not then been settled and proclaimed. Therefore the case was clearly exceptional and one by itself. And, moreover, Cain's doom was probably far more terrible than if he had been slain upon the spot—he was permitted to fill up his measure of wickedness, to be a wanderer and a vagabond upon the face of the Earth—and then to enter into the dreadful heritage of wrath, which his life of sin had doubtless greatly increased.

Under the theocratic dispensation, in which God was the King and governed Israel, murder was always punished in the most exemplary manner and there was never any toleration or excuse for it. Eye for eye, tooth for tooth, and life for life was the stern inexorable law. It is expressly written, *"You shall take no satisfaction for the life of a murderer which is guilty of death: but he shall surely be put to death"* [Numbers

35:31]. Even in cases where life was taken in chance medley[73] or misadventure[74], the matter was not overlooked. The slayer fled at once to a City of Refuge, where, after having his case properly tried, he was allowed to reside. But there was no safety for him elsewhere until the death of the high priest. The general law in all cases was,

> "So you shall not pollute the land wherein you are: for blood defiles the land: and the land cannot be cleansed of the blood that is shed there, but by the blood of him that shed it. Defile not, therefore, the land which you shall inhabit, wherein I dwell: for I, the Lord, dwell among the children of Israel" [Numbers 35:33-34]

It is strange that that very thing which defiles should turn out to be that which alone can cleanse! It is clear, then, that blood was ever precious in God's sight and He would have it so in ours.

INGESTING BLOOD OF MAN OR ANIMAL FORBIDDEN

He first forbids the blood of beasts as food of man, and then avenges the blood of man shed in anger. Furthermore, He takes care that even accidents shall not pour it out unheeded. That is not all. We hear within us the echo of that Law. We feel that God has truly made blood a sacred thing. Though some can, through use and habit, read the story of war with patience, if not with pleasure—though the sound of the trumpet and the drum and the tramp of soldiery will stir our heart and make us, for the moment, sympathize with the martial spirit—yet, if we could see war as it really is, if we

---

73. Unpremeditated killing.
74. Misfortune, mishap, or accidentally.

could only walk but halfway across a battlefield or see but one wounded man, a cold shiver would shoot through the very marrow of our bones and we would have experimental proof that blood is, indeed, a sacred thing.

The other night, when I listened to one who professed to have come from battlefields of the American war, I felt a faintness and clammy sweat steal over me as he shocked and horrified us with the details of mutilated bodies and spoke of standing up to the tops of his boots in pools of human gore. The shudder that ran through all of us was a sure confirmation of the sanctity with which God has forever guarded the symbol and nutriment of life. We cannot even contemplate the probability of the shedding of blood without fear and trembling.

Comforts that entail high risks in their production or procuring will lose all sweetness to men of humane dispositions. Who does not sympathize with David in his action with regard to the water procured by his three mighties![75] The three heroes broke through the hosts of the Philistines to bring David water from the well of Bethlehem. But as soon as he received that water, though very thirsty and longing much for it, he felt he could not touch it because these men had risked their lives three times by breaking through the Philistine hosts to bring it to him! Therefore, he took the water and poured it out before the Lord, as he felt it was not right that man should run the risk of his life for any except God who gave life!

His words were very touching, *"And he said, Be it far from me, O Lord, that I should do this: is not this the blood of the men that went in jeopardy of their lives? therefore he would not drink it. These things did these three mighty*

---

75. Adino the Eznite, Eleazar, son of Dodo the Ahohite, and Shammah, son of Agee the Hararite.

men" [2 Samuel 23:17]. I wonder at the cruelty of the great crowds who delight to see men and women running such fearful risks of life in rope-dancing.[76] How is it that they can feed their morbid curiosity on such dreadful food and greet the man who is foolish enough to run such hazards with acclamations because of his foolhardiness? How much more Christlike the regret of David that he should have led any man to risk his life for his comfort! How much more laudable was his belief that nothing short of the highest benevolence to man, or the highest devotion to God can justify such jeopardy of life!

Furthermore, permit me to observe that the seal of the sanctity of blood is usually set upon the conscience even of the most depraved of men—not merely upon gentle souls and sanctified spirits—but even upon the most hardened. You will notice that men, bad as they are, shrink from the disgrace of taking blood money. Even those high priests who could sit down and gloat their eyes with the sufferings of the Savior would not receive the price of blood into the treasury.

And even Judas, that son of perdition, who could contemplate without horror the treachery by which he betrayed his Master—yet when he had the thirty pieces of silver in his palm, found the money too hot to hold! He threw it down in the temple, for he could not bear or abide the sight of *"the price of blood."* [See Matthew 27:3-6.] This is another proof that even when virtue has become extinct and vice reigns, yet God has put the broad arrow of His own Sovereignty so manifestly upon the very thought of blood that even these worst of spirits are compelled to shrink from tampering with it.

Now, if in ordinary cases the shedding of life is so

---

76. A person who walks across or performs acrobatics or dancing upon a rope stretched at some height above the floor or ground.

precious, can you guess how fully God utters His heart's meaning when He says, *"Precious in the sight of the Lord is the death of his saints?"* [Psalm 116:15]. If the death of a rebel is precious, what must be the death of a child? If He will not contemplate the shedding of the blood of His own enemies and of them that curse Him without proclaiming vengeance, what do you think He feels concerning His own elect, of whom He says, *"Precious shall their blood be in His sight."* [See Psalm 72:12-14.] Will He not avenge them, though He bears long with them?

Shall the cup which the Harlot of Rome filled with the blood of the saints long remain unavenged? Shall not the martyrs from Piedmont[77] and the Alps and from our Smithfield[78] and from the hills of covenanting Scotland yet obtain from God the vengeance due for all that they suffered and all the blood which they poured forth in the defense of His cause? I have taken you up, you see, from the beast to man—from man to God's chosen men—the martyrs. I have another step to indicate to you—it is a far larger one.

THE BLOOD OF JESUS CHRIST

Here powers of speech would fail to convey to you an idea of the preciousness! Behold here, a Person, innocent—without taint within, or flaw without! A Person meritorious who magnified the Law and made it honorable—a Person who served both God and man even unto death. Here you have a Divine Person—so Divine that in the Acts of the Apostles Paul calls His blood the *"blood of God."* [See Acts 20:28.] Place innocence and merit and dignity and position and Godhead itself in the scale and then conceive what must

---

77. Valley of Piedmont massacres of Protestants in the 1700's.
78. Smithfield massacres in England.

be the inestimable value of the blood which Jesus Christ poured forth!

Angels must have seen that matchless blood-shedding with wonder and amazement, and even God himself saw what never before was seen in creation or in Providence—He saw himself more gloriously displayed than the whole universe. Let us come nearer to the text and try to show forth the preciousness of the blood of Christ. We shall confine ourselves to an enumeration of some of the many properties possessed by this precious blood.

I felt as I was studying that I would have so many divisions this morning that some of you would compare my sermon to the bones in Ezekiel's vision. They were very many and they were very dry; but I am in hopes that God's Holy Spirit may so descend upon the bones in my sermon—that would of themselves be dry—but they being quickened and full of life you may admire the exceeding great army of God's thoughts of loving-kindness towards His people in the sacrifice of His own dear Son.

The precious blood of Christ is useful to God's people in a thousand ways—we intend to speak of twelve of them. After all, the real preciousness of a thing in the time of pinch and trial must depend upon its usefulness. A bag of pearls would be to us, this morning, far more precious than a bag of bread. But you have all heard the story of the man in the desert who stumbled upon a bag when near to death. He opened it, hoping that it might be the wallet of some passerby, and he found in it nothing but pearls! If they had been crusts of bread, how much more precious would they have been! I say, in the hour of necessity and peril, the use of a thing really constitutes the preciousness of it. This may not be according to political economy, but it is according to common sense.

REDEEMING POWER

1. The precious blood of Christ has redeeming power. It redeems from the Law. We were all under the Law which says, "Do this and live." We were slaves to it, but Christ has paid the ransom price and the Law is no longer our tyrant master. We are entirely free from it. The Law had a dreadful curse—it threatened that whoever would violate one of its precepts would die—*"Christ hath redeemed us from the curse of the law, being made a curse for us"* [Galatians 3:13].

By the fear of this curse the Law inflicted a continual dread on those who were under it. They knew they had disobeyed it and all their lifetime they were subject to bondage, fearful lest death and destruction should come upon them at any moment. But we are not under the Law, but under Grace, and consequently, "We [ye] *have not received the spirit of bondage again to fear; but* we [ye] *have received the spirit of adoption, whereby we cry, 'Abba, Father'"* [Romans 8:15]. We are not afraid of the Law now—its worst thunders cannot affect us for they are not hurled at us!

The most powerful lightning cannot touch us for we are sheltered beneath the Cross of Christ, where the thunder loses its terror and the lightning its fury. We read the Law of God with pleasure now! We look upon it as in the Ark of the Covenant covered with the Mercy Seat and not thundering in tempests from Sinai's fiery brow. Happy is that man who knows his full redemption from the Law, its curse, its penalty, and its present dread!

My brethren, the life of a Jew, happy as it was compared with that of a heathen, was perfect drudgery compared to yours and mine! He was hedged in with a thousand commands and prohibitions. His forms and ceremonies were abundant and their details minutely arranged. He was always in danger of making himself unclean. If he sat upon a bed or upon a stool he might be defiled. If he drank out of an earthen pitcher, or even touched the wall of a house—a leprous man might have put his hand there before him and he would thus become defiled. A thousand sins of ignorance were like many hidden pits in his way. He was perpetually in fear lest he should be cut off from the people of God.

When he had done his best any one day, he knew he had not finished—no Jew could ever talk of a finished work. The bullock was offered, but he must bring another. The lamb was offered this morning, but another must be offered this evening, another tomorrow and another the next day. The Passover is celebrated with holy rites—it must be kept in the same manner next year. The high priest has gone within the veil once, but he must go there again. The thing is never finished—it is always beginning. He never comes any nearer to the end. The Law could not make those under it "perfect."

But see our position—we are redeemed from this! Our Law is fulfilled, for Christ is the end of the Law for righteousness! Our Passover is slain, for Jesus died! Our righteousness is finished, for we are complete in Him! Our victim is slain, our High Priest has gone within the veil, and the blood is sprinkled! We are clean and clean beyond any fear of defilement, *"For He has perfected for ever those that were set apart."* [See Hebrews 10:14.] Value this precious blood, my beloved, because it has redeemed you from the thralldom[79] and bondage which the Law imposed upon its votaries.[80]

ATONING EFFICACY

2. The value of the blood lies much in its atoning efficacy. We are told in Leviticus, that, *"it is the blood that maketh an atonement for the soul"* [Leviticus 17:11]. God never

---

79. Slavery
80. Adherents

forgave sin apart from blood under the Law. This stood as a constant text—*"Without shedding of blood there is no remission"* [Hebrews 9:22]. Meal and honey, sweet spices and incense would not avail without shedding of blood. There was no remission promised to future diligence or deep repentance—without shedding of blood, pardon never came. The blood, and the blood alone, put away sin and permitted a man to come to God's courts to worship—because it made him one with God. The blood is the great at-one-ment. There is no hope of pardon for the sin of any man except through its punishment being fully endured. God must punish sin. It is not an arbitrary arrangement that sin shall be punished, but it is a part of the very constitution of moral government that sin must be punished. Never did God swerve from that and never will He. "He will by no means clear the guilty." *["The Lord is longsuffering, and of great mercy, forgiving iniquity and transgression, and by no means clearing the guilty, visiting the iniquity of the fathers upon the children unto the third and fourth generation"* [Numbers 14:18].

ONE WITH GOD

Therefore, Christ came and was punished in the place of all His people. Ten thousand times ten thousand are the souls for whom Jesus shed His blood. He, for the sins of all the elect, has made a complete Atonement. For every man born of Adam who has believed or shall believe on Him, or who is taken to Heaven before being capable of believing, Christ has made a complete Atonement. And there is no other plan by which sinners can be made *one* with God, except by Jesus' precious blood.

I may make sacrifices. I may mortify my body. I may be baptized. I may receive sacraments. I may pray until my knees grow hard with kneeling. I may read devout words until I know them by heart. I may celebrate masses. I may worship in one language or in fifty languages—but I can never be *one* with God except by blood—and that blood, "the precious blood of Christ."

My dear Friends, many of you have felt the power of Christ's redeeming blood! You are not under the Law now, but under Grace—you have also felt the power of the atoning blood—you know that you are reconciled unto God by the death of His Son. You know He is not angry with you, that He loves you with an unchangeable love. However, this is not the case with all of you. Oh that it were! I do pray that you may know this very day the atoning power of the blood of Jesus! Creature, do you want to be one with your Creator? Puny man, would you not want to have Almighty God your Friend? You cannot be *one* with God except through the at-one-ment. God has set forth Christ to be a propitiation for our sins. Oh, take the propitiation by faith in His blood and be *one* with God!

CLEANSING POWER

3. Thirdly, the precious blood of Jesus Christ has cleansing power. John tells us in 1 John 1:7, *"The blood of Jesus Christ His Son, cleanses us from all sin."* Sin has a directly defiling effect upon the sinner, from which comes the need of cleansing. Suppose that God, the Holy One, were perfectly willing to be *one* with an unholy sinner which is supposing a case that cannot be. Yet, should even the pure eyes of The Most High God wink at sin? As long as we are unclean we never will feel in our hearts anything like joy and rest and peace.

Sin is a plague to the man who has it, as well as a hateful thing to the God who abhors it. I must be made clean. I must have my iniquities washed away or I can never be happy. The first mercy that is sung in Psalm 103 is, *"Who forgives all your iniquities."* Now we know it is by the precious blood that sin is cleansed. Murder, adultery, theft—whatever the sin may be—there is power in the veins of Christ to take it away at once and forever! No matter how many, nor how deeply-seated our offenses may be, the blood cries, *"Though your sins are as scarlet, they shall be as white as snow; though they be red like crimson, they shall be as wool"* [Isaiah 1:18].

It is the song of Heaven—*"We have washed our robes and made them white in the blood of the Lamb."* [See Revelation 7:14.] This is the experience of Earth, for none was ever cleansed except in this fountain opened for the house of David for sin and for uncleanness. You have heard this so often that perhaps if an angel told it to you, you would not take much interest in it—unless you have known experientially the horror of uncleanness and the blessedness of being made clean. Beloved, it is a thought that ought to make our hearts leap within us, that through Jesus' blood there is not a spot left upon any believer, not a wrinkle nor any such thing—

"Though in myself defiled I am, And black as Kedar's tent, appear, Yet when I put Your garment on, Fair as the courts of Solomon."[81]

You have no spiritual beauty, beloved, apart from Christ. But, having Christ, He himself says, "You are all fair, My Love, there is no spot in you." [See Song of Solomon 1:8.] Oh, precious blood which makes the sin-blackened white as snow and takes out the leopard's spots! Oh, precious blood removing the hell stains of abundant iniquity and permitting me to stand accepted in the Beloved, in spite of all the many ways in which I have rebelled against my God!

---

81. Song of Solomon 1:5

THE BLOOD'S PRESERVING POWER

4. A fourth property of the blood of Christ is its preserving power. You will rightly comprehend this when you remember that dreadful night in Egypt, when the destroying angel was sent to slay God's enemies. A bitter cry went up from house to house as the first-born of all Egypt—from Pharaoh on the throne to the first-born of the woman behind the mill and the slave in the dungeon—all fell dead in a moment! The angel sped with noiseless wings through every street of Egypt's many cities.

However, there were some houses which he could not enter—he sheathed his sword and breathed no threat of injury there. What was it that preserved the houses? The inhabitants were not better than others. Their habitations were not more elegantly built—there was nothing except the bloodstain on the lintel and on the two side posts—and it is written, *"When I see the blood I will pass over you"* [Exodus 12:13]. There was nothing whatever that gained the Passover for Israel but the sprinkling of blood! The father of the house had taken a lamb and killed it—had caught the blood in a basin. And while the lamb was roasted that it might be eaten by every inhabitant of the house, he took a bunch of hyssop, stirred the basin of blood and went outside with his children and began to strike the lintel and doorposts with the blood. As soon as this was done they were all safe, all safe—no angel could touch them—the fiends of hell themselves could not venture there.

Beloved, see now with your eye of faith how we are preserved in Christ Jesus! Did not God see the blood before you and I saw it and was not that the reason why He spared our forfeited lives when, like barren fig trees, we brought forth no fruit for Him? When we saw the blood, let us remember it was not our seeing it which really saved us—one sight of it gave us peace, but it was God's seeing it that saved us. *"When I see the blood I will pass over you."*

And today, if my eye of faith is dim and I see the precious blood so as to rejoice that I am washed though I can scarcely see it, yet God can see the blood and as long as the undimmed eyes of Jehovah look upon the atoning Sacrifice of the Lord Jesus, He cannot smite one soul that is covered with its scarlet mantle. Oh, how precious is this blood-red shield! My soul, cower yourself down under it when the darts of hell are flying! This is the chariot, the covering of purple—let the storm come and the deluge rise, let even the fiery hail descend beneath that crimson pavilion—my soul must rest secure, for what can touch me when I am covered with His precious blood?

The preserving power of that blood should make us feel how precious it is. Beloved, let me beg you to try and realize these points. You know I told you before I cannot say anything new upon the subject; neither can I put these old thoughts in new words. I would only spoil them and be making a fool of myself by trying to make a display of myself and my own powers, instead of the precious blood. Let me ask you to come here, right under the shelter of the Cross. Sit down, now, beneath the shadow of the Cross and feel, "I am safe, I am safe, O you devils of hell, or you angels of God—I could challenge you all and say, *'Who shall separate me from the love of God in Christ Jesus, or who shall lay anything to my charge, seeing that Christ has died for me'"*? [See Romans 8:35, Romans 8:33.]

When Heaven is ablaze. When Earth begins to shake. When the mountains rock. When God divides the righteous from the wicked, happy will be they who can find a shelter beneath the blood! But where will you be who have never trusted in its cleansing power? You will call to the rocks to hide you and to the mountains to cover you, but all in vain. God help you now, for even the blood will not help you then!

THE BLOOD'S PLEADING PREVALENCE

5. Fifthly, the blood of Christ is precious because of its pleading prevalence. Paul says in Hebrews 12:24, "... *speaks better things than that of Abel."* Abel's blood pleaded and prevailed. Its cry was, "Vengeance!" and Cain was punished. Jesus' blood pleads and prevails. Its cry is "Father, forgive them!" and sinners are forgiven through it. When I cannot pray as I want to, how sweet it is to remember that the blood prays! There is no voice in my tongue, but there is always a voice in the blood. When I bow before my God and can get no farther to say than, *"God be merciful to me, a sinner,"* [Luke 18:13], my Advocate before the throne of God is not unable to speak as I am and His plea has not lost its power because my faith in it may happen to be diminished. The blood is always prevalent with God. The wounds of Jesus are as many mouths to plead with God for sinners, and what if I say His wounds are as many chains with which love is lead captive and sovereign mercy is bound to bless every favored child? What if I say that the wounds of Jesus have become doors of divine grace through which divine love comes forth to the vilest of the vile and doors through which our wants go up to God and plead with Him that He would be pleased to supply them? The next time you cannot pray and you are crying and striving and groaning in that upper room, praise the value of the precious blood which makes intercession before the eternal throne of God!

THE BLOOD'S MELTING INFLUENCE

6. Sixthly, the blood is precious where perhaps we little expect it to operate. It is precious, because of its melting

influence on the human heart. "*. . . they shall look upon me whom they have pierced, as one mourneth for his only son, and shall be in bitterness for Him, as one that is in bitterness for his first-born*" [Zechariah 12:10].

There is a great complaint among sinners that when they are a little spiritually awakened they feel their hearts are hard. The blood of Jesus mightily melts the hard hearts. Alchemists of old sought after a universal solvent—the blood of Jesus is that. There is no nature so stubborn that a sight of the love of God in Christ Jesus cannot melt it, if grace shall open the blind eye to see Christ. The stone in the human heart shall melt away when it is plunged into a bath of divine blood. Can you not say, dear friends, that Toplady was right in his hymn—?

> "Law and terrors do but harden All the while they work alone. But a sense of blood-bought pardon, Soon dissolves a heart of stone"?[82]

Sinner, if God shall lead you to believe this morning in Christ to save you—if, then, you will trust your soul in His hands to have it saved—that hard heart of yours will melt at once! You would think differently of sin, my friends, if you knew that Christ suffered for it. Oh, if you knew that out of those dear listless eyes there looked the loving heart of Jesus upon you, I know you would say, "I hate the sin that made Him mourn and fastened Him to the accursed tree." I do not think that preaching the Law generally softens men's hearts.

PREACHING LOVE

Hitting men with a hard hammer may often drive the particles of a hard heart more closely together and make

---

82. Hymn by Augustus M Toplady titled, "A Debtor to Mercy Alone".

the iron even harder. But oh, to preach Christ's love—His great love with which He loved us even when we were dead in sins and to tell sinners that there is life in a look at the crucified One—surely this will prove that Christ was exalted on high to give repentance and remission of sins! Come for repentance, if you cannot come repenting! Come for a broken heart, if you cannot come with a broken heart! Come to be melted, if you are not melted. Come to be wounded, if you are not wounded.

POWER OF THE BLOOD TO PACIFY

7. But then comes in a seventh property of the precious blood. The same blood that melts has a gracious power to pacify. John Bunyan speaks of the Law as coming to sweep a chamber like a maid with a broom. As she began to sweep there was a great dust that almost choked people and got into their eyes. However, then came the Gospel with its drops of water that settled the dust so the broom might be used efficiently and as intended. Now it sometimes happens that the Law of God makes such a dust in the sinner's soul that nothing but the precious blood of Jesus Christ can make that dust settle down. The sinner is so disquieted that nothing can ever give him any relief except to know that Jesus died for him.

When I felt the burden of my sin, I confess that all the preaching I ever heard never gave me one single atom of comfort. I was told to do this and to do that and when I had done it all; I had not advanced one inch farther. I thought I must feel something, or pray a certain amount. And when I had done that, the burden was still quite heavy. But the moment I saw that there was nothing whatever for me to do, that Jesus did it long, long ago—that all my sins were put on His back and that He suffered all I ought to have suffered—I then had peace in my heart and peace with God. Real peace by believing peace through the precious blood!

ROCK OF GIBRALTAR

Two soldiers were on duty in the citadel of Gibraltar. One of them had obtained peace through the precious blood of Christ; the other was in very great distress of mind. It happened to be their turn to stand sentinel that night. There are many long passages in the rock, and these passages are adapted to convey sounds a very great distance. The soldier in distress of mind was ready to beat his breast because of grief he felt at rebelling against God and could not find how he could be reconciled. Suddenly there came through the air what seemed to him to be a mysterious voice from Heaven saying these words, "The precious blood of Christ." In a moment he saw it all and understood it was that which reconciled us to God, and he rejoiced with joy unspeakable and full of glory!

Now did those words come directly from God? No. They did as far as the effect was concerned for they came from the Holy Spirit of God but who had actually spoken those words aloud? Curiously enough, the other sentinel at the far end of the passage was standing still and meditating when an officer came by and it was the sentinel's duty to give the password for the night and with soldierlike promptness he gave it, not accurately however, for instead of giving the proper word, he was so taken up by his meditations that he said to the officer, "The precious blood of Christ." He quickly corrected himself, but he had said it and it had passed along the passage and reached the ear for which God meant it. The soldier who had been in distress of mind found peace and spent the rest of his life loving and working for God. After serving his soldiering time, he spent many years and means completing one of our excellent translations of the Word of God into the Hindu language.

Who can tell, dear friends, how much peace you may give by only telling the story of our Savior! If I only had about a dozen words to speak and knew I must die, I would say, *"This is a faithful saying, and worthy of all acceptation, that Christ Jesus came into the world to save sinners; . . ."* [1 Timothy 1:15]. The doctrine of Substitution is the heart and marrow of the Gospel, and if you can hold that forth, you will prove the value of the precious blood by its peace giving power.

THE SANCTIFYING INFLUENCE OF THE BLOOD

8. We can only spare a minute now upon its sanctifying influence. The apostle tells us in Hebrews 9:14 that Christ sanctified the people by His own blood. It is certain that the same blood that justifies by taking away sin does, in its after action, act upon the new nature and lead it onward to subdue sin and to follow out the commands of God. There is no motive for holiness as great as that which streams from the veins of Jesus. If you want to know why you should be obedient to God's will my brethren, go and look upon Him who sweat, as it were, great drops of blood and the love of Christ will constrain you, because you will thus judge, *"That if one died for all, then were all dead: and that He died for all, that we which live might not henceforth live unto ourselves, but unto Him that died for us and rose again"* [2 Corinthians 5:14-15].

POWER OF THE BLOOD
TO GIVE ENTRANCE

9. In the ninth place, another blessed property of the blood of Jesus is its power to give entrance. We are told that the high priest never went within the veil without blood. Therefore, we can never get into God's heart, or into the secret of the Lord which is with them that fear Him, or into any familiar communion with our great Father and Friend, except by the sprinkling of the precious blood of Jesus.

"We have access with boldness into this grace wherein we stand," but we never dare go a step towards God unless we are sprinkled with this precious blood. [See Ephesians 3:12.] I am persuaded some of us do not come near to God because we forget the blood. If you try to have fellowship with God in your graces, your experiences, and your believing; you will fail. But if you try to come near to God as you stand in Christ Jesus; you will have courage to come. On the other hand, God will run to meet you when He sees you in the face of His Anointed. Oh, for power to get near to God! However, there is no getting near to God until we get near to the Cross. Therefore, praise the blood for its power of giving you nearness to God.

THE CONFIRMING POWER
OF THE BLOOD

10. Tenthly, the blood is very precious for its confirming power. No covenant, we are told, was ever valid unless victims were slain and blood sprinkled. It is the blood of Jesus which has ratified the New Covenant and made its promises sure to all the seed. Therefore it is called *"the blood of the Everlasting Covenant."* [See Hebrews 13:20.] The Apostle Paul says that a testament is not in force until the testator is

dead. The blood is a proof that the Testator died and now the Law holds good to every inheritor because Jesus Christ has signed it with His own blood.

Beloved, let us rejoice that the promises are yes, and amen, for no other reason than this—Christ Jesus died and rose again. Had there been no bowing of the head upon the tree, no slumbering in the sepulcher, no rising from the tomb, then the promises would have been uncertain, fickle things—not *"immutable things wherein it is impossible for God to lie,"* [See Hebrews 6:18.] and consequently they could never have afforded strong consolation to those who have fled for refuge to Christ Jesus. Now you can clearly see and understand the confirming nature of the blood of Jesus and count it very precious.

THE INVIGORATING POWER OF THE BLOOD

11. I am almost done. But there remains another. It is the eleventh one, the invigorating power of the precious blood. If you want to know that, you must see it set forth, as we often do, at the communion table holding the bread and wine. What do we mean by this ordinance? We mean by it that Christ suffered for us and that we, being already washed in His precious blood and made clean, come to the table to drink wine as an emblem of the way in which we live and feed upon His body and upon His blood.

He tells us, *"Except a man shall eat My flesh and drink My blood, there is no life in him."* [See John 6:53, 55.] We do therefore, in a spiritual manner, drink His blood and He says, *"My blood is drink, indeed."* Superior drink! Transcendent drink! Strengthening drink—such drink as angels never taste though they drink before the eternal Throne. Oh beloved, whenever your spirit faints, this wine shall comfort you!

When your griefs are many, drink and forget your misery and remember your sufferings no more!

When you are very weak and faint, take not a little of this for your soul's sake, but drink a full draught of the wine, well refined, which was set free by the soldier's spike and flowed from Christ's own heart! *"Drink to the full. Yes, drink abundantly O Beloved,"* says Christ to the spouse. [See Song of Solomon 5:1.] Do not linger when He invites. You see the blood has power without to cleanse and then it has power within to strengthen. O precious Blood, how many are your uses! May I prove them all!

THE OVERCOMING POWER OF THE BLOOD

12. Lastly and twelfth—twelve is the number of perfection. We have brought out a perfect number of its uses—the blood has an overcoming power. It is written in the Book of Revelation, *"They overcame through the blood of the Lamb."* [See Revelation 12:11.] How could they do otherwise? He that fights with the precious blood of Jesus fights with a weapon that will cut through soul and spirit, joints and marrow—a weapon that makes hell tremble and makes Heaven subservient and Earth obedient to the will of the men who can wield it!

The blood of Jesus! Sin dies at its presence, death ceases to be death, and hell itself would be dried up if that blood could operate there. The blood of Jesus! Heaven's gates are opened! Bars of iron are pushed back. The blood of Jesus! My doubts and fears flee, my troubles and disasters disappear! The blood of Jesus! Shall I not go on conquering and to conquer as long as I can plead it? In Heaven this shall be the choice jewel which shall glitter upon the head of Jesus—that He gives to His people "Victory, victory, through the blood of the Lamb."

Is this blood to be had? Can we receive it? Yes, it is FREE, as well as full of virtue—free to every soul that believes. Whoever cares to come and trust in Jesus shall find the virtue of this blood in his life this very morning. Turn away from your own works! Turn those eyes of yours to the full Atonement made, to the utmost ransom paid! Poor soul, if God enables you this morning to say, "I take that precious blood to be my only hope," you are saved and you may sing with the rest of us—

"Now, freed from sin, I walk at large; The Savior's blood's my full discharge. At His dear feet my soul I'll lay, A sinner saved and homage pay." [83]

God grant it may be so, for His name's sake. Amen.

---

83. A hymn in the hymnbook titled "A Collection of Original Gospel Hymns by John Kent".

CHAPTER 9
THE BLOOD OF SPRINKLING
PART ONE OF TWO
A SERMON
(No. 1888)

Delivered on Lord's-day Morning, February 28th, 1886,

by

REVEREND C. H. SPURGEON,
At the Metropolitan Tabernacle,
Newington, London, England

"And to Jesus the mediator of the new covenant, and to the blood of sprinkling, that speaketh better things than that of Abel. See that ye refuse not him that speaketh. For if they escaped not who refused him that spake on earth, much more shall not we escape, if we turn away from him that speaketh from heaven."
—Hebrews 12:24, 25

WHAT WE HAVE NOT COME TO

We are joyfully reminded by the Apostle Paul that we have *not* come to Mount Sinai and its overwhelming manifestations. After Israel had kept the feast of the Passover, God was pleased to give His people a sort of Pentecost, and more fully to manifest himself and His law to them at Sinai. They were in the wilderness, with the solemn peaks of a desolate mountain as their center; and from the top in the midst of fire, blackness, darkness, and tempest, and with the sound of a trumpet, God spoke with them. *"The earth shook, the heavens also dropped at the presence of God: even Sinai itself was moved at the presence of God, the God of Israel"* [Psalm 68:8]. We are not come to the dread and terror of the old covenant, of which our apostle says in another place, *"The covenant from the Mount Sinai gendereth unto bondage."* [See Galatians 4:24.]

Upon the believer's spirit there now rests no slavish fear nor the abject terror and fainting alarm, which swayed the tribes of Israel; for the manifestation of God that he beholds, though not less majestic, is far more full of hope and joy. Over us there rests not the impenetrable cloud of apprehension; we are not buried in a present darkness of despair; nor are we are tossed about with a tempest of horror—therefore, we do not exceedingly fear and quake. How thankful we should be for this! Israel was privileged even in receiving a fiery law from the right hand of Jehovah; but we are far more favored, since we receive "the glorious gospel of the blessed God."

WHAT WE HAVE COME TO

I suppose the Apostle Paul is speaking of all the saints after the death and resurrection of our Lord and the descent of the Holy Ghost. He refers to the whole Church, in which the Holy Spirit now dwells in the midst. We are come to a more joyous sight than Sinai, and the mountain burning with fire. The Hebrew worshipper, apart from his sacrifices, lived continually beneath the shadow of the darkness of a broken law; he was often startled by the tremendous note of the trumpet, which threatened judgment for that broken law; and thus he ever lived in a condition of bondage. To what else could the law bring him? To convince of sin and to condemn the sinner is its utmost power.

The believer in the Lord Jesus Christ lives in quite another

206

atmosphere. He has not come to a barren crag[84], but to an inhabited city, Jerusalem above, the metropolis of God. He has left the wilderness for the land which flows with milk and honey, and the material mountain which can be touched for the spiritual and heavenly Jerusalem. He has entered into fellowship with an innumerable company of angels, who are to him, not cherubim with flaming swords to keep men back from the Tree of Life, but *"ministering spirits, sent forth to minister for them who shall be heirs of salvation"* [Hebrews 1:14].

He is come to the joyous assembly of all pure intelligences who have met, not in trembling, but in joyous liberty, to keep the feast with their great Lord and King. He thinks of all who love God throughout all worlds, and he feels that he is one of them; for he has come to *"the general assembly and church of the first-born, which are written in heaven."* Moreover, he has come *"to God the Judge of all,"* the umpire and rewarder of all the chosen citizens who are enrolled by His command, the ruler and judge of all their enemies [Hebrews 12:23]. God is not to them a dreadful person who speaks from a distance; but he is their Father and their Friend, in whom they delight themselves, in whose presence there is fullness of joy. Brethren, our fellowship is with the Father, our God. To Him we have come through our Lord Jesus Christ. Moreover, in the power of the Spirit of God we realize the oneness of the Church both in Heaven and Earth, *"and to the spirits of just men made perfect,"* who are in union with us.

No gulf divides the militant from the triumphant; we are one army of the living God. We sometimes speak of the holy *dead;* but they are not dead for they live unto God; they are perfected in their spirits even now, and they are waiting for

---

84. A steep rugged rock or cliff.

the moment when their bodies also shall be raised from the tomb to be again inhabited by their immortal souls. We no longer shudder at the sepulcher, but sing of resurrection. Our condition of heart, from day to day, is that of men who are in fellowship with God, fellowship with angels, fellowship with perfect spirits.

TO JESUS CHRIST OUR SAVIOR

We have also come to Jesus, our Savior, who is all and in all. *"In Him we live";* we are joined unto Him in one spirit; He is the Bridegroom of our souls, the delight of our hearts. [See Acts 17:28.] We have come to Him as the Mediator of the new covenant. [See 1 Timothy 2:5.] What a blessed thing it is to know that covenant of which He is the Mediator! There are some people in these days that despise the covenant; but saints delight in it. To them the everlasting covenant, *"ordered in all things, and sure,"* is all their salvation and all their desire [2 Samuel 23:5]. We are covenanted ones through our Lord Jesus. God has pledged himself to bless us. There are two immutable things wherein it is impossible for Him to lie, He has given us strong consolation, and good hope through grace, even to all of us who have fled for refuge to the Lord Jesus. We are happy to live under the covenant of grace, the covenant of promise, the covenant symbolized by Jerusalem above, which is free, and the mother of us all.

TO THE BLOOD OF SPRINKLING

Then comes the last thing of all, mentioned last for a purpose. We have come *"to the blood of sprinkling."* On that first day at Sinai no blood of sprinkling was presented, but afterwards it was used by divine order to ratify the national covenant which the tribes made with Jehovah at the foot of the hill. Of that covenant the Lord says, *"which my covenant they brake, although I was an husband unto them"* [Jeremiah 31:32], He never broke His covenant, but they broke it; for they failed to keep that condition of obedience without which a covenant founded upon works falls to the ground. We have come to the blood of sprinkling which has fallen upon a covenant which never shall be broken; for the Lord has made it to endure though rocks and hills remove. This is called by the Holy Ghost *"a better covenant, which was established upon better promises"* [Hebrews 8:6]. We are come to the covenant of grace, to Jesus the Mediator of it, and to His blood, which is the seal of it. Of this last we are going to speak at this time—*"The blood of sprinkling which speaketh better things than that of Abel"* [Hebrews 12:24].

This morning I need to occupy all the time with what I regard as only the first head of my discourse.

1. **What is it?** "The blood of sprinkling."
2. **Where we are?**—it will be our duty afterwards to consider where we are—"we are come unto this blood."
3. **What then?** "See that ye refuse not him that speaketh."

1. WHAT IS IT?

What is this "blood of sprinkling?" In a few words, "the blood of sprinkling" represents the pains, the sufferings, the humiliation, and the death of the Lord Jesus Christ, which He endured on the behalf of guilty man. When we speak of the blood, we wish not to be understood as referring solely or mainly to the literal material blood that flowed from the wounds of Jesus. We believe in the literal fact of His shedding His blood; but when we speak of His Cross and blood we mean those sufferings and that death of our Lord Jesus Christ by which He magnified the law of God. We mean what Isaiah intended when he said, *"He shall make his soul an offering for sin;"* [See Isaiah 53:10.] We mean all the griefs which Jesus vicariously endured on our behalf at Gethsemane, and Gabbatha, and Golgotha, and especially His yielding up His life upon the tree of scorn and doom. *"The chastisement of our peace was upon him, and with his stripes we are healed"* [Isaiah 53:5]. *"Without shedding of blood there is no remission"* [Hebrews 9:22] and the shedding of blood intended is the death of Jesus, the Son of God.

Remember that His sufferings and death were not only apparent, but true and real; and that they involved an incalculable degree of pain and anguish. To redeem our souls cost our Lord an exceeding sorrowfulness *"even unto death"* [See Matthew 26:38.]; it cost Him the bloody sweat, the heart broken with reproach, and especially the spiritual agony He had never known before of being spiritually separated from and forsaken by His Father, until He cried, *"My God, my God, why hast thou forsaken me?"* [Matthew 27:46] Our Mediator endured death under the worst possible aspects, bereft of those supports which are in all other cases of godly men afforded by the goodness and faithfulness of God. His was not merely a natural death, but a death aggravated by supernatural circumstance, which infinitely intensified its woe. This is what we mean by the blood of Christ, His sufferings, and His death.

These were voluntarily undertaken by Christ out of pure love for us, and in order that we might thereby be justly saved from deserved punishment. There was no natural reason on His own account why He should suffer, bleed, and die. Far from it,—*"He only hath immortality."* [See 1Timothy 6:16.] But out of supreme love for us, that man might be forgiven without the violation of divine rectitude, the Son of God assumed human flesh, and became in very deed a Man, in order that He might be able to offer in man's place a full vindication to the righteous and unchangeable Law of God. Being God, He thus showed forth the wondrous love of God to man by being willing to suffer personally rather than the redeemed having to die as the just result of their sin. The matchless majesty of His divine person lent supreme efficacy to His sufferings.

FULLY MAN AND FULLY GOD

It was a man that died, but He was also God, and the death of incarnate God reflects more glory upon the Law than the deaths of myriads of condemned creatures could have done. See the yearning of the great God for perfect righteousness: He would sooner die than stain His justice even to indulge His mercy. Jesus the Lord, out of love to the Father and to mankind, undertook willingly and cheerfully for our sakes to magnify the Law of God, and bring in perfect righteousness. This work was carried out to the utmost, that not a jot of the suffering was mitigated, nor a particle of the obedience foregone: *"he became obedient unto death, even the death of the cross."* [Philippians 2:8]. Now He has finished transgression, made an end of sin, and brought in everlasting righteousness: for He has offered such an expiation that God is just, and the justifier of him that believeth. God is at once the righteous Judge, and the infinitely loving Father, through what Jesus has suffered.

Brethren, though I have said that there was no reason why the Son of God should bleed and die on His own account, yet towards us there was a reason. Our Lord from of old in the eternal covenant was constituted the head and representative of all who were in Him; and so, when the time came, He took the place, bore the sin, and suffered the penalty of those whom the Father gave Him from before the foundations of the world. He is as much the representative man as the first Adam was the representative man; and as in Adam the sin was committed which ruined us, so in the second Adam the atonement was made which saves us. *"For as in Adam all die, even so in Christ shall all be made alive"* [1 Corinthians 15:22]. There was no other person fit to undertake the enterprise of our redemption as this second man, who is the Lord from Heaven. He properly, but yet most generously and spontaneously, came and shed His precious blood, in the room, place, and stead of sinners, to reconcile the guilty to God.

But the text does not merely speak of the *shed* blood, which I have explained to you, but of *"the blood of sprinkling."* This is the atonement applied for divine purposes, and specially applied to our own hearts and consciences by faith. For the explanation of this sprinkling we must look to the types of the Old Testament. In the Old Testament the blood of sprinkling meant a great many things; in fact, I cannot tell you just now all that it signified. We meet with it in the Book of Exodus, at the time when the Lord smote all the first-born of Egypt. Then the blood of sprinkling meant *preservation*. The basin filled with blood was taken, and a bunch of hyssop was dipped into it, and the lintel and the two side-posts of every house tenanted by Israelites were smeared with the blood; and when God saw the blood upon the house of the Israelite, He bade the destroyer to pass that family by, and leave their first-born unharmed. The sprinkled blood meant preservation: it was Israel's Passover and safeguard.

CONFIRMATION

The sprinkled blood very frequently signified the *confirmation* of a covenant. So it is used in Exodus 24, which I read to you just now. The blood was sprinkled upon the Book of the Covenant, and also upon the people, to show that the covenant was, as far as it could be, confirmed by the people who promised, *"All that the Lord hath spoken will we do"* [Exodus 19:8].The blood of bulls and of goats in that case was but a type of the sacrificial blood of the Lord Jesus Christ. The lesson we learn from Exodus 24 is: that the blood of sprinkling means the blood of ratification or confirmation of the covenant, which God has been pleased to make with men in the person of our Lord Jesus Christ. Jesus died, therefore, the promises are Yea and Amen to all believers, and most assuredly must be fulfilled. The covenant of grace had but one condition, and that condition Jesus has fulfilled by His death, so that it has now become a covenant of pure and unconditional promise to all the seed.

PURIFICATION

In many cases the sprinkling of the blood meant *purification*. If a person had been defiled, he could not come into the sanctuary of God without being sprinkled with blood. The ashes of a red heifer were collected and laid by, then as needed, they were mixed with blood and water. By their being sprinkled on the unclean, his ceremonial defilement was removed. There were matters incident to domestic life, and accidents of outdoor life, which engendered impurity, and this impurity was put away by the sprinkling of blood. This sprinkling was used in the case of recovery from infectious disease, such as leprosy; before such persons could mingle in the solemn assemblies, they were sprinkled with the blood, and thus were made ceremonially pure. In a higher sense this is the work of the blood of Christ. It preserves us, it ratifies the covenant, and wherever it is applied it makes us pure; for *"the blood of Jesus Christ his Son cleanseth us from all sin."* [1 John 1:7] We have our hearts sprinkled from an evil conscience; for we have come unto the obedience and sprinkling of the blood of Jesus Christ.

SANCTIFICATION

The sprinkling of the blood also meant *sanctification*. Before a man entered upon the priesthood the blood was put upon his right ear, and on the great toe of his right foot, and on the thumb of his right hand, signifying that all his powers were thus consecrated to God. The ordination ceremony included the sprinkling of blood upon the altar round about. Even thus has the Lord Jesus redeemed us unto God by His death, and the sprinkling of His blood has made us kings and priests unto God forever. He is made of God unto us sanctification, and all else that is needed for the divine service.

ACCEPTANCE AND ACCESS

One other signification of the blood of the sacrifice was *acceptation and access*. When the high priest went into the most holy place once a year, it was not without blood, which he sprinkled upon the Ark of the Covenant, and upon the Mercy Seat, which was on the top thereof. All approaches to God were made by blood. There was no hope of a man drawing near to God, even in symbol, apart from the sprinkling of the blood. And now today our only way to God is by the precious sacrifice of Christ; the only hope for the success of our prayers, the acceptance of our praises, and the reception of our holy works, is through the ever-abiding merit of the atoning sacrifice of our Lord Jesus Christ. The Holy Ghost bids us enter into the holiest by the blood of Jesus; there is no other way.

There were other uses besides these, but it may suffice to put down the sprinkling of the blood as having these effects, namely, that of preservation, satisfaction, purification, sanctification, and access to God. This was all typified in the blood of bulls and of goats, but actually fulfilled in the great sacrifice of Christ.

With this as an explanation, I desire to come still closer to the text, and view it with great care; for to my mind it is singularly full of teaching. May the Holy Spirit lead us into the truth which lies herein like treasure hid in a field!

First. *The blood of sprinkling is the center of the divine manifestation under the Gospel.* Observe its innermost place in the passage before us. You are privileged by almighty grace to come first to Mount Zion, to climb its steeps, to stand upon its holy summit, and to enter the city of the living God, the heavenly Jerusalem. In those golden streets, surrounding the hallowed shrine, you behold an innumerable company of angels. What a vision of glory! But you must not rest here; for the great general assembly, the festal gathering, the solemn convocation of the enrolled in Heaven, is being held, and all are there in glad attire, surrounding their God and Lord. Press onward to the throne itself, where sits the Judge of all, surrounded by those holy spirits who have washed their robes, and, therefore, stand before the throne of God in perfection. [See Hebrews 12:22-24.]

Have you not come a long way? Are you not admitted into the very center of the whole revelation? Not yet. A step further lands you where stands your Savior, the Mediator, with the New Covenant. Now your joy is complete; but you have a further object to behold. What is in that innermost shrine? What is that which is hidden away in the holy of holies? What is that which is the most precious and costly thing of all, the last, the ultimatum, God's grandest revelation? The precious blood of Christ, as of a lamb without blemish and without spot—*the blood of sprinkling.* This comes last; it is the innermost truth of the dispensation of grace under which we live. Brethren, when we climb to Heaven itself, pass the Gate of Pearl, wend our way through the innumerable hosts of angels, and come even to the throne of God, see the spirits of the just made perfect and hear their holy hymn,

215

we shall not have gone beyond the influence of the blood of sprinkling; no, we shall see it more truly present there than in any other place.

"What!" you say, "the blood of Jesus in Heaven?" Yes. We are told that the earthly sanctuary was purified with the blood of bulls and of goats, "but the heavenly things themselves with better sacrifices than these" (Hebrews 9:23). When Jesus entered once for all into the holy place, He entered by His own blood, having obtained eternal redemption for us: so says the apostle in the ninth chapter of this epistle. Let those who talk lightly of the precious blood correct their view before they are guilty of blasphemy; for the revelation of God knows no lower depth, this is the heart and center of all.

The manifestation of Jesus under the Gospel is not only the revelation of the Mediator, but especially of His sacrifice. The appearance of God the Judge of all, the vision of hosts of angels and perfect spirits leads to that sacrifice which is the source and focus of all true fellowship between God and His creatures. This is the character which Jesus wears in the innermost shrine where He reveals himself most clearly to those who are nearest to Him. He looks like a lamb that has been slain. There is no sight of Him which is more full, more glorious, and more complete, than the vision of Him as the great sacrifice for sin. The atonement of Jesus is the concentration of the divine glory; all other revelations of God are completed and intensified here. You have not come to the central sun of the great spiritual system of grace until you have come to the blood of sprinkling—to those sufferings of Messiah which are not for himself, but are intended to bear upon others, even as drops when they are sprinkled exert their influence where they fall. Unless you have learned to rejoice in that blood which takes away sin, you have not yet caught the keynote of the Gospel dispensation. The blood of

Christ is the life of the Gospel. Apart from atonement you may know the skin, the rind, and the husk of the Gospel; but its inner kernel you have not discovered.

Second. I next ask you to look at the text and observe that *this sprinkling of the blood,* as mentioned by the Holy Ghost in this passage, *is absolutely identical with Jesus himself.* Read it. *"To Jesus the mediator of the new covenant, and to the blood of sprinkling, that speaketh better things than that of Abel. See that ye refuse not him that speaketh."* He says it is the blood that speaks; and then He proceeds to say, *"See that ye refuse not him that speaketh"* [Hebrews 12:24-25],

This is a very unexpected turn, which can only be explained upon the supposition that Jesus and the blood are identical in the writer's view. By what we may call a singularity in grammar, in putting *him* for *it,* the Spirit of God intentionally sets forth the striking truth, that the sacrifice is identical with the Savior. *"We are come to the Savior, the mediator of the new covenant, and to the blood of sprinkling that speaketh; see that ye refuse not him."*

Beloved friends, there is no Jesus if there is no blood of sprinkling; there is no Savior if there is no sacrifice. I put this strongly, because the attempt is being made nowadays to set Jesus apart from His Cross and atonement. He is held up as a great ethical teacher, a self-sacrificing spirit, who is to lead the way in a grand moral reformation, and by His influence to set up a kingdom of moral influence in the world. It is even hinted that this kingdom has never had prominence enough given to it because it has been overshadowed by His Cross. But where is Jesus apart from His sacrifice? He is not there if you have left out the blood of sprinkling, which is the blood of sacrifice. Without the atonement, no man is a Christian, and Christ is not Jesus. If you have torn away the sacrificial blood, you have drawn the heart out of the Gospel of Jesus Christ, and robbed it of its life. If you have trampled on the blood of sprinkling, and counted it a common thing, instead of putting it above you upon the lintel of the door, and all around you upon the two side-posts, you have fearfully transgressed.

As for me, God forbid that I should glory save in the Cross of our Lord Jesus Christ, since to me that Cross is identical with Jesus himself. I know no other Jesus but He who died as the just for the unjust. You can separate Jesus and the blood materially; for by the spear-thrust and all His other wounds the blood was drawn away from the body of our Lord; but spiritually this *"blood of sprinkling"* and the Jesus by whom we live, are inseparable. In fact, they are one and indivisible, the self-same thing, and you cannot truly know Jesus, or preach Jesus, unless you preach Him as slain for sin; you cannot trust Jesus unless you trust Him as making peace by the blood of His Cross.

If you do not accept the blood of sprinkling, you have not accepted Jesus completely; for He will never part with His mediatorial glory as our sacrifice, neither can we come to Him if we ignore that character. Is it not clear in the text that Jesus and the blood of sprinkling are one? *"What God hath joined together, let no man put asunder"* [Mark 10:9]. Note this very carefully.

Thirdly, observe that this *"blood of sprinkling"* is put in close contact with *"the New Covenant."* I do not wonder that those who are lax in their views of the atonement have nothing honorable to say concerning the covenants, old or new. The doctrine of the covenants is the marrow of divinity; but these vainglorious spirits willfully disregard it. This is natural, since they speak slightingly of the atonement. What covenant is there without blood? If it is not ratified, if there is no sacrifice to make it sure, then it is not a covenant in the sight of God or of enlightened men.

But, O beloved, you who know your Lord, and follow

on to know Him more, to you the covenant of promise is a heritage of joy, and His atonement is most precious as the confirmation of it. To us the sacrificial death of our Lord is not *a* doctrine, but *the* doctrine, not an outgrowth of Christian teaching, but the essence and marrow of it. To us Jesus in His atonement is Alpha and Omega; in Him the covenant begins and ends. You see how it was confirmed by blood. If it is a man's covenant, if it is confirmed, it stands but this is God's covenant, confirmed with promises, oaths and blood, and it stands fast for ever and ever. Every believer is as much interested in that covenant as was Abraham the father of believers; for the covenant was made with Abraham and his spiritual seed; and in Christ it is confirmed to all that seed forever by His most precious blood. That is also evident enough in the text: *fail not to consider it well.*

But, fourthly, I want you to notice that according to the text *the blood is the voice of the new dispensation.* Observe that on Sinai there was "the sound of a trumpet and the voice of words; which voice they that heard pleaded that the word would not be spoken to them anymore." [See Deuteronomy 5:22-27 and Hebrews 12:19.] You look, therefore, under the new dispensation, for a voice, and you do not come to any until you reach the last object in the list, and there see *"the blood of sprinkling that speaketh."* Here, then, is the voice of the Gospel; it is not the sound of a trumpet, nor the voice of words spoken in terrible majesty; but the blood speaks, and assuredly there is no sound more piercing, more potent, more prevailing. God heard the voice of Abel's blood and visited Cain with fitting punishment for killing his brother; and the precious blood of Jesus Christ, the Son of God, cries in the ears of God with a voice which is ever heard. How can it be imagined that the Lord God should be deaf to the cry of His Son's sacrifice? Lo, these many ages the blood has cried—"Forgive them! Forgive them! Accept

219

them! Deliver them from going down into the pit, for I have found a ransom!"

The blood of sprinkling has a voice of instruction to us even as it has a voice of intercession with God. It cries to us, "See the evil of sin! See how God loves righteousness! See how He loves men! See how impossible it is for you to escape from the punishment of sin except by this great sacrifice in which the love and the justice of God equally appear! See how Jehovah 'spared not his own Son, but freely delivered him up for us all'" [Romans 8:32].

What a voice there is in the atonement!—a voice which pleads for holiness and love, for justice and grace, for truth and mercy. *"See that ye refuse not him that speaketh."* Do you not hear it? If you take away the blood of sprinkling from the Gospel, you have silenced it. It has no voice if this is gone. "Oh," they say, "the Gospel has lost its power!" Why should they wonder when they have made it a dumb Gospel! How can it have power when they take away that which is its life and speech? Unless the preacher is evermore preaching this blood, and sprinkling it by the doctrine of faith, his teaching has no voice either to rouse the careless or to cheer the anxious.

If ever there should come a wretched day when all our pulpits will be full of modern thought, and the old doctrine of a substitutionary sacrifice is exploded, then there will remain no word of comfort for the guilty or hope for the despairing. Hushed will be for ever those silver notes that now console the living and cheer the dying; a dumb spirit will possess this sullen world, and no voice of joy will break the blank silence of despair. The Gospel speaks through the propitiation for sin, and if that is denied, it speaks no more. Those who preach not the atonement exhibit a dumb and dummy Gospel; a mouth it has, but it speaks not; they that make it are like unto their idol.

Let me draw you nearer still to the text. Observe, that *this voice is identical with the voice of the Lord Jesus;* for it is put so. *"The blood of sprinkling that speaketh. See that ye refuse not him that speaketh."* Whatever the doctrine of the sacrifice of Jesus may be, it is the main teaching of Jesus himself. It is good to notice that the voice which spoke from Sinai was also the voice of Christ. It was Jesus who delivered that law, the penalty of which He was to endure. He that read it out amidst the tempest was Jesus. Notice the declaration—*"Whose voice then shook the earth."* Whenever you hear the Gospel, the voice of the precious blood is the voice of Jesus himself, the voice of Him that shook the Earth at Sinai.

This same voice shall by-and-by shake not only the Earth, but also Heaven. What a precious and powerful voice there is in the blood of sprinkling, since indeed it is the voice of the eternal Son of God, who both makes and destroys! Would you have me silence the doctrine of the blood of sprinkling? Would any one of you attempt so horrible a deed? Shall we be censured if we continually proclaim the heaven-sent message of the blood of Jesus? Shall we speak with bated breath because some delicately affected person shudders at the sound of the word *"blood?"* or some "cultured" individual rebels at the old-fashioned thought of sacrifice? No, truly, we will sooner have our tongue cut out than cease to speak of the precious blood of Jesus Christ. For me there is nothing worth thinking of or preaching about than this grand truth, which is the beginning and the end of the whole Christian system, namely, that God gave His Son to die that sinners might live. This is not only the voice of the blood, but the voice of our Lord Jesus Christ himself. So says the text, and who can contradict it?

Furthermore, my brethren, from the text I learn another truth, namely, that *this blood is always speaking.* The text does not say "the blood of sprinkling that spoke," but *"that speaketh."* It is always speaking; it always remains a plea with God and a testimony to men. It will never be silenced, either one way or the other. In the intercession of our risen and ascended Lord His sacrifice ever speaks to the Most High. By the teaching of the Holy Ghost the atonement will always speak in edification to believers upon the Earth. It is the blood that speaks, according to our text, this is the only speech that this dispensation yields us. Shall that speech ever be still? Shall we decline to hear it? Shall we refuse to echo it? God forbid. By day, by night, the great sacrifice continues to cry to the sons of men, "Turn from your sins, for they cost your Savior dearly."

The times of your ignorance God winked at, but now commands all men everywhere to repent, since He is able to forgive and yet be just. Your offended God has himself provided a sacrifice; come and be sprinkled with its blood, and be reconciled once for all. The voice of this blood speaks wherever there is a guilty conscience, wherever there is an anxious heart, wherever there is a seeking sinner, and wherever there is a believing mind. It speaks with a sweet, familiar, tender, and inviting voice. There is no music like it to the sinner's ear: it soothes away his fears. It shall never cease its speaking so long as there is a sinner still out of Christ; and furthermore so long as there is one on Earth who still needs its cleansing power because of fresh backslidings. Oh, hear its voice! Incline your ear and receive its blessed accents: it says, *"Come now, and let us reason together, saith the Lord; though your sins be as scarlet, they shall be as white as snow; though they be red like crimson, they shall be as wool"* [Isaiah 1:18].

This part of my discourse will not be complete unless I bid you notice that we are expressly told that *this precious blood speaks "better things than that of Abel."* I do not think that the whole meaning of the passage is exhausted if we say that Abel's blood cries for vengeance, and that Christ's blood speaks for pardon. Dr. Watts puts it:—

> "Blood has a voice to pierce the skies:
> 'Revenge!' the blood of Abel cries;
> But the dear stream when Christ was slain
> Speaks peace as loud from ev'ry vein."[85]

That is quite true; but I believe that it is not all the sense, and perhaps not even *the* sense intended here. Revenge is scarcely a good thing; yet Abel's blood spoke good things, or we would hardly read that Christ's blood speaks *"better things."* What does the blood of Abel speak? The blood of Abel speaks to a complete and believing obedience to God. It shows us a man who believes God, and in spite of the enmity of his brother, brings to God the appointed sacrifice of faith, strictly following up to the bitter end his holy obedience to the Most High. That is what the blood of Abel says to me; and the blood of Jesus says the same thing most emphatically.

THE BLOOD OF JESUS SAYS FAR MORE THAN THE BLOOD OF ABEL

The death of Jesus Christ was the crown and close of a perfect life; it was a fit completion of a course of holiness. In obedience to His Father, Jesus laid down His life. But if this is all the blood of Jesus speaks, as some say that it is, then it does not speak better things than the blood of Abel; for it only says the same things in a louder voice. The martyrdom of any saint has a voice for obedience to God as truly as the martyrdom of Jesus; but the death of our Lord says far more, infinitely more, than this: it not only witnesses to complete

---

85. Hymn titled: "Blood Has a Voice to Pierce the Skies", words by Isaac Watts, 1709, music by Johann Crüger, 1598-1662.

obedience, but it provides the way by which the disobedient may be forgiven and helped to obedience and holiness. The Cross has a greater, deeper, grateful, thankful, and cheerful Gospel for fallen men than that of a perfect example which they are unable to follow.

The blood of Abel said this, too—that he was not ashamed of his faith, but witnessed a good confession concerning his God, even to the death. He put his life in His hand, and was not ashamed to stand at the altar of God, and avow his faith by obediently offering the ordained sacrifice. Now, I grant you that the blood of Jesus also declares that he was a faithful and true witness, who willingly sealed his witness with his blood. He proved by shedding His blood that He could not be turned aside from truth and righteousness, even though death stood in His way; *but* if that is all that the blood of sprinkling speaks it says no better things than the blood of Abel. "Be faithful unto death," is the voice of Abel as well as of Jesus. Jesus must have said more than this by His blood-shedding.

The blood of Abel said good things; that is implied in the fact that the blood of Jesus Christ says better things; and no doubt the blood of Abel rises to the dignity of teaching self-sacrifice. Here was a man, a keeper of sheep, who by his mode of life laid out his life for the good of those committed to his charge; and at the last, in obedience to God, he yielded himself up to die by a brother's hand. It was the first blueprint of a picture of self-sacrifice. Our Lord Jesus Christ also made a complete self-sacrifice. All His life He gave himself to men. He lived never for himself. The glory of God and the good of men were united in one passion which filled His whole soul. He could say, *"The zeal of thine house hath eaten me up"* [John 2:17]. His death was the completion of His perfect self-sacrifice. But if that were all, the blood of Jesus says no better thing than Abel's death said, though it may say it more emphatically.

Our Lord's blood says *"better things than that of Abel;"* and what does it say? It says, *"There is redemption through his blood, the forgiveness of sins, according to the riches of his grace"* [Ephesians 1:7]. *"He his own self bare who bare our sins in his own body on the tree, that we, being dead to sin, should live unto righteousness: by whose stripes ye were healed"* [1 Peter 2:24]. *"He hath made him to be sin for us, who knew no sin; that we might be made the righteousness of God in him"* [2 Corinthians 5:21], The voice of the blood is this, *"For I will be merciful to their unrighteousness, and their sins and their iniquities will I remember no more"* [Hebrews 8:12]. *"The blood of Jesus Christ his Son cleanseth us from all sin"* [1John 1:7b]. Now, my brethren, these are better things than Abel's blood could say, and they are what the blood of Jesus speaks to everyone upon whom it is sprinkled by faith. It must be applied to each one of us by faith, or it says nothing to us. But when it falls on each believing individual, it says to him words of blessing that pacify his conscience and delight his soul.

The apostle says that *"Ye are come to the blood of sprinkling"* [Hebrews 12:24]. Is it so with you? Has that blood of sprinkling ever been applied to you? Do you feel it? Are you preserved? Are you cleansed? Are you brought near to God? Are you sanctified unto God's service by the atoning sacrifice? If so, then go out, and in firm confidence that never can be shaken, make your glory in the blood of sprinkling. Tell every sinner whom you meet that if the Lord Jesus washes him he shall be whiter than snow. Preach the atoning sacrifice of the Lamb of God and then sing of it. Recollect that wondrous threefold song in the fifth chapter of the Revelation, where, first of all, the elders and living creatures round about the throne, sing a new song, saying, *"Thou wast slain, and hast redeemed us to God by thy blood*

out of every kindred, and tongue, and people, and nation"
[Revelation 5:9].

Then ten thousand times ten thousand and thousands of
thousands of angels take up the strain and cry, *"Worthy is the
Lamb that was slain."* [See Revelation 5:12.] Nor is this all;
for the apostle tells us, *"Every creature which is in heaven,
and on the earth, and under the earth, and such as are in
the sea, and all that are in them, heard I saying, Blessing,
and honor, and glory, and power, be unto him that sitteth
upon the throne, and unto the Lamb for ever and ever."*
[Revelation 5:13] Do you not see that they all extol the Lord
Jesus in His sacrificial character as the Lamb slain? I have
scant patience with those who dare to put this great truth
into the background, and even sneer at it or misrepresent
it on purpose.

Brothers and Sisters, if you would be saved you must have
the blood of Jesus sprinkled upon you. He that believeth not
in Christ Jesus, in Jesus the atoning sacrifice, must perish.
The eternal God must repulse with infinite disgust the man
who refuses the loving sacrifice of Jesus. Inasmuch as He
counted himself unworthy of this wondrous sacrifice, this
marvelous expiation, there remains no other sacrifice for sin,
and nothing for him but that eternal blackness and darkness
and thunder which were foreshadowed at Sinai. Those who
refuse the atonement which wisdom devised, which love
provided, and which justice has accepted, have signed their
own death warrant, and no one can wonder that they perish.
The Lord lead us to glory in Christ crucified. Amen.

CHAPTER 10
THE BLOOD OF SPRINKLING
PART TWO OF TWO

A SERMON
(No. 1889)

Delivered on Lord's-day Evening, February 28th, 1886,

by

REVEREND CHARLES H. SPURGEON,

At the Metropolitan Tabernacle, Newington,
London, England

"Ye are come . . . to Jesus the mediator of the new covenant, and to the blood of sprinkling, that speaketh better things than that of Abel. See that ye refuse not him that speaketh."—Hebrews 12:24, 25

IN PART ONE of this sermon the text inspired me so greatly that it was quite impossible to express all its meaning. In as condensed a manner as possible I explained what was meant by *"the blood of sprinkling,"* and I also enlarged upon the high position this precious blood occupies in the Gospel dispensation; but I was obliged to leave for this second occasion two practical questions which the text is sure to raise if it is carefully thought upon.

The doctrinal portion of our meditation was greatly blest to our hearts, for God the Holy Ghost refreshed us by it. May He now fulfill His sacred office with equal power, by revealing the things of Christ to us in a way that will cause self-examination, and arouse us to give more earnest heed than ever to the voice of Him that speaks from Heaven. No theme can excel in value and excellence than the precious blood of Jesus. Unless the Holy Spirit shall prepare our hearts, even with such a topic as this before us, we shall be profited nothing; but if He will show these choice truths unto us, we will be comforted, quickened, edified, and sanctified by them.

It is a considerable disadvantage to some of you that did not hear Part One of the sermon; but I hope you will read it at your leisure, and then, if you read this in connection with it, the whole subject will be before you. Not that I can set it all out in words: I only mean that it will be before you as the ocean is before us when we sit on the beach, or as the heavens are before us when we gaze upon Arcturus[86] with his sons. Finite language fails to convey the infinite; and if ever there was a text which deserved to be called infinite, it is that which is now before us.

2. WHERE ARE WE?

Having touched, as with a swallow's wing, the surface of our great theme under the first division of the sermon, I have now to speak with you upon the second: Where are we in reference to this blood of sprinkling? The text says, "*Ye are come.*" We are not come to Mount Sinai, but we are come to Mount Zion; to angels and their God; to saints and their Mediator, and to the blood of sprinkling. This having had its share of our thoughts, we will then conclude with the question, *what then?* If we have come to this blood of sprinkling, what then? The answer is, "*See that ye refuse not him that speaketh.*" Let us give to the wondrous truths revealed to us by the sacrifice of Jesus the most earnest

---

86. Arcturus of the constellation Boötes is orange and the brightest star in the northern celestial hemisphere. The sons of Arcturus are the three constellations Pleiades, Orion, and Mazzaroth.

heed, that our souls may hear and live. May the Holy Spirit enable us to hear the heavenly voice at this hour! *"Faith cometh by hearing;"* may it come at this time by our reverently hearing the voice of the blood of sprinkling! [See Romans 10:17.]

My business under the second head of my discourse is to answer the question, Where Are We? I have to explain what is meant by the expression which is found in the twenty-second verse of the chapter *"Ye are come."* Link the twenty-second with this twenty-fourth, and read, *"Ye are come to the blood of sprinkling."*

Well, first of all, you are come to the hearing of the Gospel of the atoning sacrifice. The Israelites left Egypt, and after passing the Red Sea they entered the desert, and at length came to that terrible mountain called Mount Sinai, the mountain of God. In the valley around that mountain of God they were gathered together in the thousands. What a sight that vast multitude must have been! Probably two millions or more were encamped before the mount. Then, *"The Lord came from Sinai, and rose up from Seir unto them; he shined forth from Mount Paran; and he came with ten thousands of his saints; from his right hand went a fiery law for them"* [Deuteronomy 33:2]. Israel crouched in the valley below, subdued by the terrible majesty of the scene, and overawed by the trumpet voice which pealed forth from the midst of the thick darkness. The Lord spoke with them, but their uncircumcised ears could not bear His glorious voice, and they pleaded that Moses might act as mediator, and speak in God's stead.

You and I have not come to such a terrible sight at this hour. No quivering mountain smokes before you, no terrible lightning appalls you, and no thunders distress you.

"Not to the terrors of the Lord.
The tempest, fire, and smoke;
Not to the thunder of that word
Which God on Sinai spoke:
"But we are come to Sion's hill
The city of our God,
Where milder words declare his will,
And spread his love abroad."[87]

Among the great things that you are called upon to consider under the Gospel is *the blood of sprinkling.* Count yourselves happy that you are privileged to hear of the divinely appointed way of reconciliation with God. You have come to hear, not of your sin and its doom, not of the last judgment and the swift destruction of the enemies of God; but of love to the guilty, pity for the miserable, mercy for the wicked, and compassion for those who are out of the way.

You have come to hear of God's great means of wisdom, by which He, by the same act and deed, condemns sin, and lets the sinner live; honors His law, and yet passes by transgression, iniquity, and sin. You have come to hear, not of the shedding of your own blood, but of the shedding of His blood who, in His infinite compassion, deigned to take the place of guilty men—to suffer, that they might not suffer, and that they might not die. Blessed are your ears that they hear of the perfect sacrifice! Happy are your spirits, since they are found where free grace and boundless love have set forth a great propitiation for sin! Divinely favored are you to live where you are told of pardon freely given to all who will believe on the name of the Lord Jesus, as the Lamb of God which takes away the sin of the world.

You hear at this hour not Law, but Gospel; not the

---

87. Hymn titled: "Not to the Terrors of the Lord", written by Isaac Watts in 1707, and music by Israel Holdroyd in 1722.

sentence of judgment, but the proclamation of grace. *"See that ye refuse not him that speaketh."* It is no small thing for the Kingdom of God to have come so near unto you. Awake to a sense of your privilege: you do not sit in heathen midnight, or in popish gloom, or in Jewish mist; but day has dawned on you: do not refuse the light.

In a better sense, going a little further, we have not only come to the blood of sprinkling by hearing about it, but we have come to it because *our great God now deals with us upon methods which are founded and grounded upon the atoning sacrifice of Christ.* If God were to deal with us upon the terms laid down at Sinai, He would not be long in finding the *"two or three witnesses"* to prove that we have broken His law [Deuteronomy 17:6]. We should be compelled to plead guilty; no witnesses would be required. Truly, He has not dealt with us after our sins. We are so faulty that we can draw no comfort from the prospect of judgment by law; we appeal to mercy alone; for on any other ground our case is hopeless. "This do, and thou shalt live" is a covenant which brings us no ray of comfort; for its only word to us is that thunderbolt—*"The soul that sinneth, it shall die"* [Ezekiel 18:20].

JUSTIFICATION DOES NOT COME BY THE LAW

By the works of the Law none can be justified, for by that Law we are all condemned. Read the Ten Commandments, and pause at each one, and confess that you have broken it either in thought, or word, or deed. Remember that by a glance we may commit adultery, by a thought we may be guilty of murder, by a desire we may steal. Sin is any act, word, or thought that does not conform to perfect holiness, and that want of conformity is justly chargeable upon every one of us. Yet the Lord does not, under the Gospel dispensation, deal with us according to Law. He does not now sit on the Throne of Judgment, but He looks down upon us from the Throne of Grace. Not the iron rod, but the silver scepter, is held over us. The long-suffering of God rules the age, and Jesus the Mediator is the gracious Lord-lieutenant[88] of the dispensation. Instead of destroying offending man from off the face of the Earth, the Lord comes near to us in loving condescension, and pleads with us by His Spirit, saying, "You have sinned, but my Son has died. In Him I am prepared to deal with you in a way of pure mercy and unmingled grace."

PATIENT FORBEARANCE

O sinner, the fact that you are alive proves that God is not dealing with you according to strict justice, but in patient forbearance; every moment you live is another instance of omnipotent long-suffering. It is the sacrifice of Christ that stays the axe of justice that otherwise must execute you. The barren tree is spared because the great Dresser of the vineyard, who bled on Calvary, intercedes and cries, *"Let it alone this year also."* [See Luke 13:8.] O my hearer, it is through the shedding of the blood and the mediatorial reign of the Lord Jesus that you are at this moment on praying ground and pleading terms with God! Apart from the blood of atonement you would now be past hope, shut up forever in the place of doom. But see how the great Father bears with you! He stands prepared to hear your prayer, to accept your confession of sin, to honor your faith, and to save you from your sin through the sacrifice of His dear Son.

---

88. Lord Lieutenant is a British title bestowed upon a representative of the reigning King or Queen.

GUILTY TO BELOVED

Through our Lord Jesus sovereign grace and infinite love find a free way to the most undeserving of the race. Through the divine sacrifice the Lord saith, *"Come now and let us reason together: though your sins be as scarlet, they shall be as white as snow;"* [Isaiah 1:18] *"Believe on the Lord Jesus Christ, and thou shalt be saved"* [Acts 16:31]. Thus the rebel is treated as a child, and the criminal as a beloved one. Because of Christ's death on Calvary's cruel tree, God can invite guilty men to come to Him, and He can receive them to the bosom of His love. O my dear hearers do remember this! I am not sent to scold you, but to woo you, not sent to thunder at you, but to let the soft cleansing drops from the heart of Jesus fall upon you. I beg you not to turn away, as men may well do when the tidings are heavy; but listen diligently, for the message is full of joy. You are now in the house of prayer, addressed by one of the Lord's ambassadors, and the tidings are of peace through a propitiation which God himself has provided and accepted. We cry not to you, "Prepare for vengeance;" but we proclaim, "A God ready to pardon." We do not threaten that He will no more have mercy upon you; but we tell you that He waits to be gracious. If I had to say, "You have provoked Him past bearing, and He now means to destroy you," what a miserable man would I be! How could I bring such evil tidings to my fellow-creatures? Then it would have been woe to me that my mother bore me for so hard a fate. Thank God, it is not so. By virtue of the blood of sprinkling the language of boundless love is heard among our apostate race, and we are earnestly pleaded with to acquaint ourselves with God, and be at peace.

No, my hearer, the day of grace is not over: you have not come to Sinai. No, you are not yet condemned past all hope; for you are still within reach of Jesus the Mediator. There is forgiveness. The fountain which was opened of old for sin and for uncleanness is open still. If you have sinned like David, if you will but accept the sprinkling of the blood of Jesus, I am able to speak to you as Nathan did to the guilty king, and say, *"The Lord hath put away thy sin; thou shalt not die"* [2 Samuel 12:13]. At any rate, God is dealing with you now on Gospel terms; He sits on Zion, not on Sinai; He pronounces invitations of grace, and does not utter the stern sentence of justice.

Further, there is a far more effectual way of coming to the blood of sprinkling than this—*when by faith that blood is sprinkled upon our souls.* This is absolutely needed: the *shed* blood must become to each one of us the blood *sprinkled.* "How can I know," says one, "that the blood of Christ is upon me?" Do you trust yourself with Christ? Do you believe that He made atonement on the Cross; and will you venture your eternal destiny upon that fact, *trusting* in what Jesus did, and in that alone? If you do thus trust, you shall not trust in vain. Do you apply your heart to the precious blood of Jesus? Then that precious blood is applied to your heart. If your heart bleeds for sin, bring it to the bleeding heart of Jesus and it shall be healed. I showed, in the early part of this discourse, that the blood sprinkled on the lintel and the two side-posts of the door preserved the Israelites on the night of the Passover: it shall also preserve you. The blood sprinkled upon the defiled made them ceremonially clean: it shall cleanse you. Have I not often quoted those blessed words: *"The blood of Jesus Christ his Son cleanseth us from all sin?"*

That blood put upon the sons of Aaron dedicated them to God; and if it is applied to you, it shall consecrate you to God, and you shall become the accepted servant of the Most High. Oh, what a blessed thing to know assuredly that we have come to the blood of sprinkling by a true and humble faith! Can you say that you do rely on Jesus alone for salvation? Can you call Heaven and Earth to witness that you have no other confidence? Then remember the Word of the Lord: *"He that believeth in him hath everlasting life"* [John 3:16]. *"He that believeth in him is not condemned"* [John 3:18]. *"Therefore being justified by faith, we have peace with God"* [Romans 5:1].

Are not these words full of strong assurance? Indeed, we have not come to Mount Sinai, the place of trembling; but to Zion, the place which is *beautiful for situation, the joy of the earth;* [See Psalm 48:2.], the vision of peace, the home of infinite blessedness. Conscience no longer thunders at you for your sins, for your sins are gone. The expiation has covered them: the sprinkling of the blood has put them all away. Your iniquities are cast into the depths of the sea; God has cast them behind His back. The handwriting of ordinances that was against you Christ has taken away, nailing it to His Cross, as a record in which there is no more condemning force. The debt is paid, the bill is receipted. *Who can lay anything to the charge of God's elect?* [Romans 8:33]. O beloved! It is a most blessed thing to come to the blood of sprinkling.

> "The terrors of law and of God
> With me can have nothing to do;
> My Savior's obedience and blood
> Hide all my transgressions from view."[89]

The act of faith, whereby we accept and trust in the Lord Jesus as our Mediator and Sacrifice is the true and effectual coming to the blood of sprinkling. May none of us forget to come! The Apostle John said in John 1:29, *"He is the Lamb of God, which taketh away the sin of the world"* and those

---

89. Hymn titled: "A Debtor to Mercy Alone" written by Augustus Toplady in 1771, music by Joseph Parry 1841-1903.

who come to him shall be led into full salvation. Have you come? If you have not, why do you delay? He saith, *"Him that cometh to me I will in no wise cast out"* [John 6:37b]. Come to Him, for He is calling you; come to Him, even as you now are, and He will receive you without fail.

Furthermore, to come to this blood of sprinkling means *thankfully to enjoy all that comes to us through the blood of sprinkling.* I have spoken upon this somewhat already. Brothers and sisters, if you have come to the blood of sprinkling, believe in the full pardon which God has given you, and in your consequent peace with God. It is a blessed word in the Creed,[90] "I believe in the forgiveness of sins." Do you believe in the forgiveness of sins? I have seen some of the children of God who have believed in Jesus, but it has been with a faith that did not realize the full blessing promised to it; for they were as troubled about their sins as if they had never been forgiven. Now, a man who receives a free pardon from the Queen, and goes his way out of prison, rejoices in that pardon as a reality, and therefore walks abroad without fear. You must believe in the pardon of God as a reality, and act accordingly. If He has absolved you for Jesus' sake, then you are absolved. Why tremble like a guilty wretch waiting for the verdict? Why talk about fearing divine wrath? If you are pardoned, the deed of grace is done, and can never be undone; for the gifts and calling of God are without repentance on His part. His remission of sin is a clear delivery from Sheol, a sure plea, a full acquittal.

> "Oh! how sweet to view the flowing
> Of our Lord's atoning blood,
> With divine assurance knowing
> He has made my peace with God!"[91]

---

90. The Apostles' Creed
91. Author unknown.

I want every child of God in his inmost soul to come to the blood of sprinkling by full assurance of his justification, and then to go on to enjoy constant access to the mercy seat, and communion with the Lord God. We may now speak with holy boldness with God in prayer, for the mercy seat is sprinkled with the blood. O pardoned one, be not backward to enjoy your liberty of fellowship! You are clean through the blood, and therefore you may enter into the closest communion with the divine Father; you are consecrated by the blood, and therefore you may abound in the service of your God.

Treat your God as a child should treat a father, and be not so awed by His majesty as to be cast down and distressed because of past sin, seeing it is pardoned. Take the good that God provides you; enjoy the peace the blood has bought you; enter into the liberty that your ransom price has ensured you. Do not stand in feelings, and fears, and dreams; but come unto this blood of sprinkling, and rest there, and be filled with joy and peace through believing. With such a ransom found for you, dream not of going down into the pit, but ascend with gladness into the hill of the Lord, and stand in His holy place.

I think, once more, that this coming to the blood of sprinkling means also that *we feel the full effect of it in our lives*. The man who knows that Jesus shed His blood for him, and has had that blood applied to his conscience, becomes a sin-hating man, consecrated to Him who has cleansed him. *"The love of Christ constraineth us; because we thus judge, that if one died for all, then were all dead: and that he died for all, that they which live should not henceforth live unto themselves, but unto him which died for them, and rose again"* [2 Corinthians 5:14-15]. I believe that there is no fruitful source of virtue like faith in the precious blood of Jesus. I hope your conduct will always support me in this assertion. Those who are debtors for salvation to their dying Lord should be the most holy of men.

You people who think that you will get to Heaven by some other way than by "the blood of sprinkling" have no sure bonds to hold you to holiness. You trust partly to your own works, and partly to what Jesus has done. Well, you do not owe Him much, and therefore you will not love Him much, and therefore you will not feel bound to live strict, holy, gracious lives. But the man who knows that his many sins are all washed away through the blood of Jesus, and that he is saved, he is the man who will serve the Lord with all his heart. He who has received a finished righteousness and complete salvation is under boundless obligations of gratitude, and the force of these obligations will urge him to a consecrated life.

Over him the supreme power of gratitude will exert its sacred influence, and he will be not only carefully obedient, but ardently zealous in the service of his Redeemer. We know it is so, and we mean to prove it by our daily conduct. Brethren, I would have you exhibit more and more the influence of the precious blood in sanctifying your lives. Are there not Christians who hold the doctrine of the atoning blood, and yet are no better than others? Alas! It is so. But it is one thing to hold a doctrine, and another thing for that doctrine to take hold upon your heart and influence your life. Oh, if we believed practically what we believe professionally, what manner of persons we would be in all holy conversation and godliness! Hear me, my brethren, and answer the appeals I make to you as in the presence of the Lord. Blood-bought; can you live your life for yourself? Blood-washed; can you defile your garments? Marked with the King's own name, in the King's own blood; how can you yield yourself to other rulers? God grant that we may come unto the blood of sprinkling until it purifies our nature and fills us with an all-consuming enthusiasm for Him whose heart was pierced for us!

I ask you, then, to put the question close to home, "Have I come unto this blood of sprinkling? If not, why should I not come at once?" I read the other day an imaginary story, which describes the need of looking well into this great business. Receive it as a parable:—a little daughter of the house of Israel had heard the commandment concerning the Passover night, and as she lay ill in her bed she cried, "Father, have you sprinkled the blood upon the lintel and the two side-posts?" Her father answered, "Not yet, my child. It shall be done." The daughter was distressed, and filled with fear. After waiting a little while she again cried, "Father, father, have you sprinkled the blood upon the door?" He answered carelessly, "Child, I have told Simeon to sprinkle it, and I have no doubt it is done." "But, father," cried she, "it is near midnight, and the destroying angel will soon be abroad; are you *sure* that the blood is over the door? Jehovah our God has said that we must sprinkle the blood upon the lintel and the two side-posts, or else the destroyer will not pass over us. Father, are you sure it is done?" The father passed over her enquiry: he had been eating of the lamb with his friends, and thought that this was sufficient; he did not care to give too much prominence to the ghastly idea of blood. He was of a liberal mind, and would not believe that a merciful God would smite his household for so small an omission.

Then his daughter arose from her bed, made strong by the God of Israel. Nothing would content her until she had been outside into the street, and seen for herself whether the saving mark was over the door of her father's house. It was almost midnight, but by the light of the moon she looked, and no blood-mark was there! How great was her distress! "Father," she cried, "make haste and bring the basin." There it stood, filled with blood; for the Paschal Lamb had been slain. The father, at her entreaty, dashed the hyssop into it, struck the lintel and the two side-posts and shut the door, and as he did so, the midnight hour arrived. They were saved as by fire. The daughter's obedient care and reverence of the Lord had warded off the sword of the destroyer. Oh that the holy anxiety of someone now present would work the like blessing for other households! Ask, dear child, ask the question, "Father, have you come to the blood of sprinkling? Is the blood of the Lamb above your head, between you and God? Is it on both sides of you, when you come in and go out?" O soul, be anxious about yourself, and rest not until by faith you have been purged with hyssop, and cleansed by the blood of the one sacrifice for sin.

3. WHAT THEN?

The last part of our subject is this: What Then? According to our text, the blood of Jesus is the voice of the new dispensation. It is the blood that speaks, and it speaks better things than the blood of Abel. What then is our duty? How does the apostle express our obligation? *"See that ye refuse not him that speaketh."*

I would like to have a quarter of an hour's very quiet talk with you, without excitement or quibbling debate. Listen to me in all earnestness, for I speak in love for your souls. Dear friends, I want this great truth of atonement which I so often preach to have a fair hearing and not be left to lie among the number of forgotten things.

Do not refuse the voice of Jesus by cold indifference. God was made flesh, and dwelt among men, and in due time He took upon himself our sin, and suffered for it in His own body on the tree so that sin might be atoned for, once and for all, by the sacrifice of himself. By His death upon the Cross our Lord made atonement for the sin of man, and those who believe in Him are delivered from evil and its consequences. The main point is that Jesus died for us, the just for the unjust. His atoning blood has a voice: *"See that ye refuse not him that speaketh."* The text says: See to it; look to it; make sure of it; be careful about it. Do not miss the salvation of your Lord through neglect; for he who dies by neglecting the healing medicine will as surely perish as he who stabs himself. Be in earnest to receive the Savior: I beseech you to do so, for I am afraid that many refuse Him that speaks, because they never think of Him, or of His sacrifice.

It seems to me that if I were a young man I would give this matter very early consideration. However deeply I might be engaged in business, I would feel that my first concern ought to be to set myself right with God. Other matters would be sure to drop into order if I could be right with the Lord of all. If I heard it said that salvation came by the blood of Christ, I think I would pull myself together and resolve to understand this singular statement. I would not let it go by me, but would endeavor to reach the bottom of it, and seek earnestly to understand it. I would meditate much upon teaching as wonderful as this—that the Son of God in man's stead honored the justice of God by death, and in doing so put away sin.

CONSIDER CAREFULLY

When I was a youth I had a great longing to begin life on right principles: I longed to find deliverance from sin. I would wake up with the sun in summer time to read my Bible, and such books as John Bunyan's *Grace Abounding*[92],

---

92. *Grace Abounding* by John Bunyan is available in the popular Pure Gold Classics line published by Bridge-Logos.

Richard Baxter's *Call to the Unconverted,* Joseph Alleine's *Alarm,* and Philip Doddridge's *Rise and Progress of Religion in the Soul.* In these books I tried to spell out the way of salvation; but the chief thing I longed to know was, "How can man be just with God? How can God be just with man and yet put away his sin?" Do you not think that these questions are of high importance? I beg you not to turn a cold shoulder to them. Give this question much due and deep consideration. I know that a great many things demand your attention nowadays; but I claim for this, which is the innermost revelation of God that it should have an early and earnest hearing. God incarnate in Christ Jesus bleeding and dying for human sin is a marvel of love too great to be passed over without thought.

I pray you, therefore, *"refuse not him that speaketh."* Do not say, "I pray you have me excused." I do not suppose that you will become an infidel or act as a blasphemer towards this grand truth. I will not accuse you of denying the fact of the atonement; but my great fear is that you might be indifferent to it. Moreover, because it is God's own Word that God himself has come to Earth to bleed and die to save guilty man, it is the greatest, gladdest news that ever came to our poor erring race, and every member of that race should receive it with hopeful attention.

When you resolve to study the doctrine, *do not approach it with prejudice through misapprehension.* Those that hate the Gospel of Christ are very busy mocking the doctrine of the atonement. They assert that we preach that God was not merciful by nature, but must be appeased by the blood of His own Son. They charge us with saying that Jesus, by His death, made God loving. We distinctly teach the very opposite of that statement. What we do say is this, that God is infinitely loving—that, in fact, God is love; but that love does not cause Him to be unjust or unholy; for in the long run *that* would not be love. God is the Judge of all the Earth and He must do right.

The Lord, as the great moral governor must execute that penalty if He makes a Law and threatens a penalty, or else His Law will lose its authority. If the threatened penalty is not executed, there is a tacit acknowledgment that it was threatened in error. Could you believe in a fallible God? The Lord has made a Law which is perfect, and just, and good. Would you rather be without Law? What reasonable person desires anarchy? He has backed up that Law with a threatening.

What is the use of a law if to break it involves no evil consequences? A government that never punishes offenders is no government at all. Therefore, God, as moral ruler, must be just, and must display His indignation against wrong and evil of every kind. It is written on the conscience of men that sin must be punished. Would you have it go unpunished? If you are a just man, you would not. Therefore, to meet the case, the Lord Jesus Christ, by himself bearing the penalty of death, has honored the divine Law. He has shown to all intelligences that God will not wink at sin and that even His infinite mercy must not diminish the way of His justice.

This is the doctrine: do not listen to those who twist and pervert it. It is the love of God that has provided the great atonement by which, in a judgment better than ours, the Law finds a glorious vindication, and the foundation of moral government is strengthened. Do consider this matter, and judge it fairly, with candid minds. We assure you from God's Word that apart from the atonement of our Lord Jesus you can never be saved either from the guilt or power of evil. You will find no peace for your conscience that is worth having, no thorough and deep peace, except by believing in this atoning sacrifice; neither will you meet with a motive strong enough to rescue you from the bonds of iniquity.

Therefore *"See that ye refuse not him that speaketh."* Hear, and your soul shall live. Object and quibble and ignore, and you will die in your sins.

Do not refuse the voice of the Lord Jesus by rejecting the principle of expiation. If God is content with this principle, it is not for us to raise objection. The Lord God is infinitely more concerned to fix matters on a right foundation than we ever can be, and if He feels that the sacrifice of Jesus meets the case at all points, why should we be dissatisfied with it? If there were a flaw in the proceedings His holy eyes would see it. He would not have delivered up His own Son to die unless that death would perfectly fulfill the design intended by it. God would never have perpetrated so expensive a mistake. Who are you to raise the question? If God is satisfied, surely you should be? To refuse the atonement because we are too wise to accept so simple a method of mercy is the utmost height of folly. What are you thinking! Will you refuse Him that speaks because the present phase of human madness dares to dispute the divine way of human redemption? I pray you will *not* do so.

Once more. *Do not refuse this voice of mercy by preferring your own way of salvation.* You have, no doubt, a way of salvation in your own mind, for few men have given up all hope. Perhaps your chosen hope is that you will be saved by doing your best. Alas! No man does his best; and the best acts of a rebel must be unaccepted of his king. However long he is a rebel his acts are those of a rebel, and will be of no esteem with his prince. Perhaps your hope lies in saying many prayers, and going to church, or attending chapel; or you are so unwise as to trust to a minister or priest. Now, we beseech you, hear the witness of God which He has given us in His holy Word, and learn that, *"For other foundation can no man lay than that which is laid, which is Jesus Christ"* [1 Corinthians 3:11]. There is one salvation, and there can be no other; all other hopes are lying vanities, and arrogant insults to Jesus. God has set forth Christ to be a propitiation for sin. There is no other propitiation, atonement, or way of acceptance; and if you reject this way, you must die in your sins.

I cannot help it if you do not like this teaching, although I shall be grieved if you refuse it. I can only tell you the truth, and leave it with your own hearts. Do not willfully refuse it. When I meet you face to face in that last day, to which we all must come, I will not be clear of your blood unless I tell you today what is assuredly the truth—that the precious blood of Christ is the only cleansing from sin, and the only acceptance with God. By believing in Jesus, as slain for you, you shall be saved. Therefore, do what you may, pray as you may, fast as you may, give alms as you may, you shall not enter Heaven by any other way. The way to glory is by the way of the Cross. *"Without shedding of blood there is no remission"* [Hebrews 9:22]. Look to Him whom you have pierced, and mourn for your sins. Look not to any other, for no other is needed, no other is provided, and no other can be accepted. Jesus is the sole messenger of the covenant of life and peace. *"See that ye refuse not him that speaketh."*

"See that ye refuse not." There is a choice about it. If you had never heard the Gospel, you could not have refused it; but now that you have heard the message, it lies within your power, and it is a very dangerous power to refuse Him that speaks. Oh, can you, will you, dare you refuse my bleeding Savior—refuse the Lord of love? I see Him now. The crown of thorns is around His brow. He is hanging on His Cross expiring in unutterable pangs! Can you refuse Him while He presents such a spectacle of sacrifice? His eyes are red with weeping; have you no tears for such sorrow? His cheeks are all stained with the spittle of the brutal soldier—have you

no love and homage for Him? His hands are fastened to the wood—His feet the same: and there He hangs to suffer in the sinner's stead.

Will you not yield yourselves to Him? I would joyfully bow before the foot of that Cross to kiss His dear feet stained with blood. What a holy yearning He brings forth in me to love, praise and glorify Him! And you—do you refuse Him? He is no mere man. It is God himself who hangs upon the Cross. His body is that of a man, but it is in union with the Godhead. He who died at Calvary is God over all, and this makes His death so effectual. He, whom you have offended, in order to be justly able to pardon you, hangs there and dies for you: and do you turn your back on Him?

O sirs, if you are wise you will come, as I said I would gladly come, and kiss those bleeding feet, and look up and say, "My Lord, I am reconciled to you—how could I be otherwise? My enmity is dead. How can I be an enemy to Him that died for me? In shame, and scorn, and misery, Jesus dies that I may live. O Lord Jesus you have wrought in me, not merely reconciliation, but full submission and hearty love. I joy to sink myself in you, and to be yours forever." See that you refuse not my Lord. May the sweet Spirit who loves the Cross, and hovers around it like a dove even now, descend upon you all who hear my message! May the Holy Ghost apply the blood of sprinkling to you; and may you feel that, instead of refusing him that speaks, you rejoice in His name!

When the text says, *"See that ye refuse not,"* it tacitly and pleadingly says, "See that you accept Him." Dear hearers, I trust you will receive my Lord into your hearts. When we read of refusing, or receiving, we perceive an action of the will. Jesus must be willingly received: He will not force himself upon any man. Whosoever accepts Jesus is accepted of Jesus. Never was there a heart willing to receive Him to whom Jesus denied himself. Never! But you must be willing and obedient. Grace works this in you; but in you this must be. Until the heart entertains Jesus gladly, nothing is done. All that is short of a willing hearing of Jesus, and a willing acceptance of His great atonement, is short of eternal life. Say now, will you have this Savior, or do you decline His love? Will you give Him a cold refusal? Oh, do not so; but, on the contrary, throw open the doors of your heart, and entreat your Lord and Savior to come in.

I do not wonder that the Israelites asked that they might no longer hear the voice of thunder from the top of Sinai; it was too terrible for human ears; but you have no such excuse if you refuse Him that speaks; for Jesus speaks in notes more sweet than music, more tender than a mother's sonnet to her babe. Let me remind you that He said in Matthew 11:28-30, *"come unto me, all ye that labor and are heavy laden, and I will give you rest. Take my yoke upon you, and learn of me; for I am meek and lowly in heart: and ye shall find rest unto your souls."* He declared that all manner of sin and blasphemy would be forgiven unto men. He stood and cried, on the last day of the feast, *"If any man thirst, let him come unto me, and drink"* [John 7:37]. I am telling you no fables; for Christ, who was born at Bethlehem and died on Calvary, by His own blood which He shed for many, assures you that there is forgiveness for every man and woman who, confessing their sin, will come and put their trust in Him.

"See that ye refuse not him that speaketh;" for though you hear only my poor feeble voice pleading with you, with an honest and loving heart, yet God the Holy Ghost is speaking, and Jesus Christ himself is speaking to you. Refuse me if you please, but do not refuse my Lord. The blood of Jesus says, "I was poured out for the guilty. I was shed to manifest divine love. I am sprinkled to cleanse from sin." Each drop as it falls creates peace of heart. Stand where that

blood is falling. Let it sprinkle you.

Thus the blood speaks. Will you not answer, "Lord, we come to you, for you have drawn us. Your wounds have wounded our hearts. Your death has killed our enmity. Sprinkle us unto yourself. Cover us with your blood. Let us be accepted in the Beloved?" Amen. So may God hear us!

PART THREE
THE BLOOD WASHED

Chapter 11
Walking in the Light and Washed in the Blood

A Sermon

Delivered on Sunday Morning, December 3, 1865,

by

Charles H. Spurgeon,

at The Metropolitan Tabernacle, Newington,
London, England.

*"But if we walk in the light, as He is in the light, we have
fellowship one with another and the blood of Jesus Christ,
His Son, cleanses us from all sin."*—1 John 1:7

Two Great Powers

There are two great powers in conflict in this world.
One is the power of good, of which God is the King and
the other is the power of evil, which is represented by the
Prince of the power of the air, Satan. The first principle is
set forth by the Apostle John under the figure of light. God
himself is essential Light; and everything which is good in
the world is an emanation from Him. *"Every good gift and
every perfect gift is from above, and comes down from the
Father of Lights, with whom is no variableness, neither
shadow of turning"* [James 1:17].

Light vs. Darkness

The light is the evident emblem of the Truth of God.
Darkness is the symbol of error. Light represents holiness.

Darkness is the appropriate figure for sin. Light represents knowledge, especially of spiritual things because light reveals. Darkness is the fit token of the ignorance under which the natural mind labors perpetually. By nature we are all born under the dominion of darkness—we grope our way like blind men and when we knew God by the light of His works, we glorified Him not as God, neither were we thankful, but became vain in our imaginations and our foolish hearts were darkened.

THE CARNAL MIND

In the natural, spiritual things are not discernible by man—they are spiritual and spiritually discerned and the carnal mind cannot perceive them—for it walks in darkness. [See 1 Corinthians 2:14.] The guilt of sin is a thing too high for the carnal mind to understand. The glory of the eternal sacrifice cannot be perceived by the carnal mind. The excellence of God, the faithfulness of His promises and the validity of His Covenant—all such things as these are swathed in mist—the carnal mind does not see them. However, as soon as the Grace of God comes into the heart, it makes as great a difference as did the eternal fiat[93] of Jehovah, when He said, *"Let there be light,"* and there was light. [See Genesis 1:3.]

As soon as God the Holy Spirit begins to work upon the soul of man to illuminate him, man perceives at once his own sinfulness. He abhors that sinfulness, he labors to escape from it and cries out for a remedy—he finds it in Christ. Therefore he no longer loves sin and he is not guided any longer by the darkness of policy, selfishness, and error but walks after the light of the Truth of God, of righteousness, holiness, and of true knowledge. God has brought him into the light—he sees now what he never saw before! He knows,

---

93. Command or legally binding decree.

feels, believes, and recognizes what he never had known anything of before—*he is in the light.*

Therefore, you constantly hear the Christian called a child of light, he is taught and now understands that he is of the light and of the day. He is told, "You are not of the night or of darkness. You were once of the darkness, but now you are light in the Lord: walk as children of light." [See 1 Thessalonians 5:5.] You perceive in the text, then, that the Christian is spoken of as a man who is in the light. But there is something more said of him than this. He is practically in the light, "if we walk in the light." It is of no use to pretend to have light in the mind—so as to comprehend all knowledge, or to be sound and orthodox in one's doctrinal opinions—this will be of no vital service as far as the great point of salvation is concerned. A man may think he has much light, but if it is only notional and doctrinal and not the light that enlightens his nature and develops itself in his practical walk then he lies when he talks of being in the light, for he is altogether in darkness. It is not truthful to pretend or profess that we have light within in the form of experience if we do not walk in it, for where the light is true, it is quite certain to show itself abroad.

LIGHT DISPELS DARKNESS

If there is a candle within the lantern, its light will stream forth into the surrounding darkness and those who have eyes will be able to see it. I have no right to say I have light unless I walk in it. The Apostle John is very peremptory with those who so speak. He says, *"He that says I know Him and keeps not His Commandments is a liar and the truth is not in him."* [See 1 John 2:4.] The Christian, then, is in the light and he is practically in it—his walk and conversation are regulated by the Truth of God, by holiness—and by that divine knowledge which God has been pleased to bestow upon him.

He now walks in the light of faith, in another path than that which is trod by men who have nothing but the light of sense. He sees Him who is invisible and the sight of the invisible God operates upon his soul. He looks into eternity, he marks the dread reward of sin and the blessed gift of God to those who trust in Jesus and eternal realities have an effect upon his whole manner and conversation—from now on he is a man in the light, walking in that light. There is a very strong description given here—"*If we walk in the light as He is in the light*" [1 John 1:7]. Beloved, the thought of that dazzles me! I have tried to look it in the face, but I cannot endure it. If we walk in the light as God is in the light! Can we ever attain to this? Will poor flesh and blood ever be able to walk as clearly in the light as He is whom we call "Our Father," of whom it is written, "God is light, and in Him is no darkness at all"? [1 John 1:5].

SEEK TO BE PERFECT

Let us say this much and then commend this wonderful expression to your meditations. Certainly this is the model which is set before us, for the Savior himself said, "*Be ye therefore perfect, even as your Father which is in Heaven is perfect*" [Matthew 5:48]. And if we take anything short of absolute perfection as our model of life we shall certainly, even if we attain to our ideal, fall short of the Glory of God! Beloved, when a schoolmaster writes the copy at the head of the page, he does not expect that the boy will come up to the copy—but then, if the copy is not a perfect one, it is not fit to be imitated by a child. Therefore, our God gives us himself as the pattern and copy, "Be you imitators of God as dear children," for nothing short of God he would be a worthy model. [See Ephesians 5:1, NKJV.]

Though we, as life sculptors, may feel that we can never rival the perfection of God, yet we are to seek after it and never to be satisfied until we attain it. The youthful artist, as he grasps his first pencil, can hardly hope to equal Raphael or Michelangelo! However, if he did not have a noble ideal before his mind, he would only attain to something very small and ordinary. Heavenly fingers point us to the Lord Jesus as the great Exemplar of His people and the Holy Spirit works in us a likeness to Him.

WALKING IN THE LIGHT IN QUALITY NOT EQUALITY

But what does it mean that the Christian is to walk in light as God is in the light? We conceive it to import likeness, but not degree. We are as truly in the light. We are as heartily in the light. We are as sincerely in the light, as honestly in the light, though we cannot be there in the same degree. I cannot dwell in the sun—it is too bright a place for my residence—unless I shall be transformed, like Uriel[94], Milton's angel who could dwell in the midst of the blaze of its excessive glory. But I can walk in the light of the sun though I cannot dwell in it. And so God is the Light, He is himself the Sun and I can walk in the light as He is

---

94. **Uriel,** in the Apocrypha, a leading angel, sometimes ranked as an archangel with Michael, Gabriel, and Raphael. Because his name in Hebrew means "fire of God," or "light of God," he has been variously identified in Jewish traditions as an angel of thunder and earthquake, as the wielder of the fiery sword in driving Adam and Eve from Eden, as the destroyer of the hosts of Sennacherib, as the figure who enlightens Ezra with visions, and, generally, as an angel of terror, prophecy, or mystery. John Milton in *Paradise Lost* described Uriel as "Regent of the Sun" and the "sharpest sighted spirit of all in Heaven"; but Christian tradition has generally paid little attention to Uriel.

in the light, though I cannot attain to the same degree of perfection and excellence and purity and truth in which the Lord, himself, resides. Trapp[95] is always giving us the Truth of God in a way in which we can remember it—so he says we are to be in the light as God is in the light for quality, but not for equality. We are to have the same light and as truly to have it and walk in it as God does, though as for equality with God in His holiness and perfection—that must be left until we cross the Jordan and enter into the perfection of the Most High.

THE FIRST PRIVILEGE: FELLOWSHIP WITH GOD

Having thus briefly sketched the character of the genuine Christian, observe beloved, that he is the possessor of two privileges. The first is fellowship with God. *"We have fellowship one with another."* And the second is complete cleansing from sin—*"and the blood of Jesus Christ, His Son, cleanses us from all sin."* [See 1 John 1:7.] The first privilege we will have but a word upon—it is fellowship with God. As you read this verse in our translation, it looks very much as if all that was meant was fellowship with your brother Christians. But this, according to able critics, would not convey the sense of the original. The Arabic version renders it, "God with us and we with Him," and several copies read, "We have fellowship with Him." Our version almost compels you to think of fellowship with other Believers, but such is not the intention of the Spirit. We have mutual fellowship—between God and our souls there is communion. This is the sense of the passage. God is Light—we walk in light—we agree. *"Can two walk together, unless they are agreed?"* [Amos 3:3]. It is clear we are agreed as to the

---

95. Joseph Trapp, English clergyman.

principles which we shall advance—God is the champion of truth, so are we. God is the promoter of holiness, so are we. God seeks that love may reign instead of selfishness, so does the Christian. God hates error and spares no arrows to destroy it. The Christian also contends earnestly for the faith once delivered to the saints.

God is pure, and *the pure in heart shall see God.* [See Matthew 5:8.] God is holiness and those who are holy are attracted to God from an affinity of nature, even as the needle is attracted to its pole. If the Lord has visited you and made you walk in light, you shall surely have fellowship with God your Father. He that is in darkness cannot have fellowship with God. Veiled in ignorance, guided by passion, controlled by error, led astray by falsehood—how can you aspire to speak with your God? Your prayer is but a chattering sound! Your song is the clang of a sounding brass, the noise of a tinkling cymbal! Your devotion bears you no further than the letter which kills!

But oh, if God should take you out of your darkness and make you to see yourself, to see Him and follow after truth and righteousness and holiness, why then your prayer would be heard in Heaven, your song would mingle with the sweet notes of celestial harps and even your groans and tears would reach your Father's heart, for you would enjoy fellowship with Him! If we walk with God as God is in the light, the secret of God is with us and our secret is with God. He opens His heart to us and we open our hearts to Him—we become friends! We are bound and knit together so that being made partakers of the Divine Nature, and having escaped the corruption which is in the world through lust, we live like Enoch having our conversation above the skies.

THE SECOND PRIVILEGE: COMPLETE CLEANSING FROM SIN

We intend to dwell on the second privilege. I have been driven to this text and yet I have been afraid of it. This text has been handled, regarding the latter part of it, very often out of its context. Yet it has had such a comforting influence on many souls that I have been half afraid to discourse upon it in its true context. And yet I have felt, "Well, if anything I say should take away any comfort from any seeking soul, I shall be very sorry, but I cannot help it." I do feel that it is essential to the Christian ministry not to pick passages out of God's Word and rend them away from the context, but to take them as they stand.

As this text stands, it does not seem to me to gleam with the particular ray of comfort that others see in it, but it has another beam of joy even more radiant! God's Word must be taken as God speaks it. We have no right to divide the divine truth, or to wrest it to make it mean other than it does. According to the text, special pardon of sin is the peculiar privilege of those who walk in the light as God is in the light and it is not the privilege of anyone else. Only those who have been brought by Divine Grace from a state of nature into a state of grace and walk in the light may claim the possession of perfect cleansing through the blood of Jesus Christ.

SEVEN CHOICE PEARLS

In dwelling upon this latter part of the verse, there seemed to me to be seven things in it which any thoughtful reader would be struck with. Considered as the privilege of every man who, however hesitatingly is walking in the light, this word, which tells of pardon bought with blood, is very precious—a crown set with jewels! I invite your loving gaze to the following seven choice pearls:

GREATNESS

1. The first thing that struck me was the greatness of everything in the text. In some places everything is little. You talk with some men—their thoughts, their ideas are all little. Almost everything is drawn to a scale and aspiring minds generally draw their matters to as great a scale as they can find, but that is necessarily a little one. See to what a magnificent scale everything is drawn in our text! Think, beloved, how great the sin of God's people is! Will you try and get that thought into your minds? How great is your own sin—your sin before conversion—think that over! Your sin of putting confidence in your own works while seeking the Lord and looking for excuses for your lies—turn them over in your mind.

Beloved, one sin towers up like an Alp! But we have many sins heaped upon each other, as in the old fable of the giants who piled Pelion upon Ossa[96], mountain upon mountain! O God, what an aggregate of sin there is in the life of one of your most pure and most sanctified children! Multiply this. All the sin of one child of God—multiply it by the number of those contained in that word "us." "Cleanses us from all sin!" How many are God's children? God's Word shall answer. *"A multitude that no man can number, out of all kindreds and peoples and tongues, stood before the Throne."* [See Revelation 7:9.] Can you imagine—deep as hell's bottomless pit! High as Heaven's own Glory—for sin sought to pluck even God out of His throne! Wide as the east is from the west! Long as eternity is this great mass of the guilt of the people for whom Christ shed His blood! And

---

96. Two mountains in Greece.

yet all this is taken away! "The blood of Jesus Christ, His Son, cleanses us from all sin."

Then observe the greatness of the Atonement offered. Will you inwardly digest those words, "the blood of Jesus Christ, His Son?" Blood is at all times precious, but this is no blood of a mere man—it is the blood of an innocent Man! Better still, it is the blood of Man in union with Deity—"His Son!" God's Son! Angels cast their crowns before Him! All the choral symphonies of Heaven surround His glorious Throne. "God over all, blessed forever. Amen." And yet He yields His blood! He takes upon himself the form of a servant and then is scourged and pierced, bruised and torn and at last slain—for nothing but the blood of Deity could make atonement for human sin!

The Atonement must not be by a mere man—He must be the God-Man Mediator, the Fellow of Jehovah, co-equal and co-eternal with Him—He must bear the pangs and bitterness of Divine wrath which was due to sin. Think of this—a sacrifice which no human mind can ever properly estimate in the infinity of its value! Here, indeed, we have greatness—great sin, but a great Atonement! Think again—we have here great love which provided such a Sacrifice. Oh, how He must have loved, to have descended from Heaven to Earth and from Earth to the grave! How He must have loved, to have chosen us, when we hated Him—when we were enemies! He has reconciled us unto God by His own death!

Dead in trespasses and sins corrupt and wrapped up in the cerements[97] of evil habits, hateful and hating one another, full of sin and every abomination—yet He loved us so much He yielded His soul unto death for us. We are dealing with great things here, indeed, and we must not forget the greatness of the influence which such an Atonement, the

---

97. Burial garments.

result of such love, must have upon the Christian's heart. Oh, the greatness of the peace which passes all understanding, which flows from this great Atonement! Oh, the greatness of the gratitude which must blaze forth from such a sacred fire as this! Oh, the greatness of the hatred of sin, of the revenge against iniquity which must spring from a sense of such love, when it is shed abroad in the heart!

You are citizens enjoying no small privilege; you are blood-bought citizens of a blood-bought city! God has loved you. You cannot, even though I would allot you a whole lifetime—you cannot get to the depth of that love God has loved you and to prove His love He has died in the Person of man for you. He loves you and has overcome the dread result of all your fearful sin! And now, by the love which God has manifested, we do pray you let your holiness, your truthfulness and your zeal prove that you understand the greatness of those things. If your heart can really conceive the greatness of the thing revealed here—the great sin, the great Savior offering himself out of great love that He might make you greatly privileged—I am sure your hearts will rejoice!

SOLITARINESS

2. The next thing which sparkles in the text is its simple solitariness—"We have fellowship one with another." And then it is added as a simple, gloriously simple statement, *"the blood of Jesus Christ, His Son, cleanses us from all sin."* Observe there is nothing said about rites and ceremonies. It does not begin by saying, "and the waters of Baptism, together with the blood of Jesus Christ, His Son, cleanses us." Not a word, whether it shall be the sprinkling in infancy, or immersion of Believers—nothing is said about it—it is the blood, the blood only, without a drop of baptismal water! Nothing is said about sacraments—what some call "the

blessed Eucharist," is not dragged in here—nothing about eating bread and drinking wine! It is the blood, nothing but the blood—"the blood of Jesus Christ, His Son." And if nothing is said of rites that God has given, then rites that man has invented are equally excluded. Not a syllable is uttered concerning celibacy or monasticism! Not a breath about vows of perpetual chastity and poverty! Not a hint about confession to a priest and human absolution! Not an allusion to penance or extreme unction! "The blood of Jesus Christ, His Son, cleanses us from all sin."

It was well done by a poor woman who, as she lay sick, heard for the first time the precious Gospel of her salvation. She was told that the blood alone cleansed from sin. She believed, and then, putting her hand into her bosom, she took out a little crucifix which she had always worn, hanging from a chain about her neck, and said to the preacher, "Then I don't want this, Sir." Ah, truly so! And so may we say of everything that man has devised as a consolation to a poor wounded spirit. "I have found Jesus and I do not want that, Sir." You who want it, keep it—but as for us, if we walk in the light as He is in the light—the blood of Jesus Christ, His Son, so completely purges us from all sin that we dare not look to anything else lest we come into the bondage of the beggarly elements of this world!

You will perceive, too, that nothing is said about Christian experience as a means of cleansing. "What?" says one. "Does not the first sentence of the verse imply that?" Assuredly not, for you perceive that the first sentence of the verse does not interfere, though it is linked, with the other. If I walk in the light as God is in the light, what then? Does my walking in the light take away my sins? Not at all! I am as much a sinner in the light as in the darkness if it were possible for me to be in the light without being washed in the blood.

Well, but we have fellowship with God, and does not

having fellowship with God take away sin? Beloved, do not misunderstand me! No man can have fellowship with God unless sin is taken away—but his fellowship with God and his walking in light, does not take away his sin—not at all. The whole process of the removal of sin is here, "And the blood of Jesus Christ, His Son, cleanses us from all sin." I beg to repeat it—the text does not say that our walking in the light cleanses us from sin! It does not say that our having fellowship with God cleanses us from sin—these are the result of cleansing, but they have no connection as cause—*it is the blood and the blood alone which purges us from sin!*

The dying thief looked to Christ and sin was taken away by the blood. And there is a brother in Christ here who has had such an experience of Christ's love for sixty years that his heart is now like a shock of corn, ripe for Heaven. He lives in his Master's presence; he spends the most of his time in his Master's service! But, beloved, there is not a single atom of difference between him and the dying thief so far as the cleansing away of sin is concerned! The blood cleansed the thief and the same blood washes this advanced and full-grown Christian, or otherwise he is still unclean.

Observe, yet again, that in the verse there is no hint given of any emotions, feelings, or attainments as co-operating with the blood to take away sin. Christ took the sins of His people and was punished for those sins as if He himself had been the sinner, and so sin is taken away from us. But in no sense, degree, shape or form is sin removed by attainments, emotions, feelings or experiences! The blood is the only Atonement—the blood, without any mixture of anything else, completes and finishes the work! *"For you are complete in Him."*

Now I could enlarge for a very long time on this point, but I do not think I shall. I will rather throw in a sentence or two and observe that there are some who urge you to look to your doctrinal intelligence as a ground of comfort. I beseech you beloved, look only to the blood! Whereas there are others who would set up a standard of Christian experience and urge that this is to be the channel of your consolation. I pray you, while you prize both doctrine and experience; rest not your soul's weight except in the precious blood! Some would lead you to high degrees of fellowship— follow them, but not when they would lead you away from the simple position of a sinner resting upon the blood! There are those who could teach you mysticism and would have you rejoice in the light within. Follow them as far as they have the warrant of God's Word, but never take your foot from that Rock of Ages in which the only safe standing can be found!

Certain of my brethren are very fond of preaching Christ in His Second Coming—I rejoice that they preach the truth concerning Christ Glorified, but, my beloved, I do beseech you do not place your hope on Christ Glorified, nor on Christ to come, but on "Christ Crucified." Remember that in the matter of taking away sin, the first thing is not the Throne, but the Cross—not the reigning Savior—but the bleeding Savior! Not the King in His Glory, but the Redeemer in His shame. Do not be studying dates of prophecies if you're burdened with sin, but seek your chief and best comfort in the blood of Jesus Christ which cleanses us from all sin—here is the pole star of your salvation—chart your course and sail by it and you shall reach the port of peace.

COMPLETENESS

3. A third brilliant flash in the light, viz., is the completeness of the cleansing. *"The blood of Jesus Christ, His Son, cleanses us from all sin"*—not from some sin, but *"from all sin."* Beloved, I cannot tell you the exceeding sweetness of this

Word, but I pray God the Holy Spirit to give you a taste of it. There is original sin, by which we fell in Adam before we were born, and there is inherited sin through which we were born in sin and *shapen in iniquity.* [See Psalm 51:5.] There is actual sin—the sin of my youth and my former transgressions, the sins of my riper years, the sins which defile the hoary head and make that which should be a crown of Glory to be a crown of grief—and all these sins, original and actual, are all gone! All gone!

Sins against the Law, though it is exceedingly broad so that it makes me a sinner in thought, word, deed, and heart—they are all gone! Sins against the Gospel when I kicked against the pricks, when I stifled conscience, when I resisted the Holy Spirit as my fathers did—when I hated the Truth of God and would not have it because my deeds were evil and I would not come to the light lest my deeds might be reproved. Sins when I would regard none of the sweet invitations of the Gospel—all cleansed away! Sins against Christ Jesus since my conversion when I have backslidden and my heart has been cold towards Him! Sins against the Holy Spirit when I have followed my own impulses instead of the indwelling Deity—all gone!

The Roman Catholic divides sin into venial sins and mortal sins. Be it so—the blood of Jesus Christ cleanses us from all sin, mortal or venial, deadly or pardonable. Sins of commission—here is a long catalogue—think it over! Sins of omission—that is still a larger list! The things which we have left undone which we ought to have done are probably more numerous than the things which we have done which we ought not to have done—all are gone! Some sins are greater than others. There is no doubt whatever that adultery, fornication, murder, blasphemy and such like are greater than the sins of daily life—but whether they are great sins or little sins—they are all gone! That same God who took away the plague of flies from Egypt also took away the plague of thunder and of lightning. All are gone—gone at once!

Pharaoh's chariot is drowned in the Red Sea and the lesser Egyptian is drowned in the same way. The depths have covered them. There is not one of them left. There are sins against God—how very many there are! Sins of breaking His Day and despising His Word—profaning His name, forgetting Him and not loving Him—but He blots out all! Sins against my friends and my enemies, against my neighbor, against my father, my child, my wife—sins in all relationships—yet all are gone! Then, too, remember there are sins of presumption and sins of ignorance—sins done willfully and unknown sins—the blood cleanses us from *ALL* sin!

Shall I go on? Surely I need not! But you see the purging is complete. Whether the bill is little or the bill is great, the same receipt can discharge one as the other. The blood of Jesus Christ is as blessed and Divine a payment for the sin of blaspheming Peter as it is for the sin of loving John! Our iniquity is gone, all gone at once and all gone forever. Blessed completeness! What a sweet theme to dwell upon!

PRESENTNESS

4. The next gem that studs the text is the thought of presentness. "Cleanses" says the text—not, "shall cleanse." There are multitudes who think that as a dying hope they may look forward to pardon, and perhaps within a few hours of their dissolution they may be able to say, "My sins are pardoned." Such can never have read God's Word, or, if they have read it, they have read it with unbelieving eyes. Beloved, I would not give the snap of my finger for the bare possibility of cleansing when I come to die!

Oh how infinitely better to have cleansing now! Some imagine that a sense of pardon is an attainment after many years of Christian experience. For a young Christian to say, "My sins are forgiven," seems to them to be an untimely fig, ripe too soon. But, beloved, it is not so. The moment a sinner trusts Jesus, that sinner is as fully forgiven as he will be when the light of the Glory of God shall shine upon his resurrection countenance. Beloved, forgiveness of sin is a present thing—a privilege for this day, a joy for this very hour! And whoever walks in the light as God is in the light has fellowship with God and has at this moment the perfect pardon of sin.

You perceive that it is written in the present tense as if to indicate continuance—it will always be so with you, Christian. It was so yesterday—it was "cleanses" yesterday, it is "cleanses" today—it will be "cleanses" tomorrow. It will be "cleanses" until you cross the river—every day you may come to this fountain for it "cleanses!" Every hour you may stand by its brim, for it "cleanses." I think there is sanctification here as well as justification. I am inclined to believe that this text has been too limited in its interpretation and that it signifies that the blood of Jesus is constantly operating upon the man who walks in the light so as to cleanse him from the indwelling power of sin. In addition, the Spirit of God applies the doctrine of the Atonement to the production of purity until the soul becomes completely pure from sin at the last. I desire to feel the constantly purifying effect of the sacrifice of my Lord and Master every day. Look at the foot of the Cross and I am sure you will feel that the precious drops cleanse from all sin.

CERTAINTY

5. Now in the fifth place, the text presents to us very blessedly the thought of certainty. It is not, "perhaps the blood of Jesus Christ cleanses from sin." The text speaks of it as a

fact not to be disputed—it does so. To the Believer this is a matter of certainty, for the Spirit of God bears witness with our spirits that we are born of God. [See Romans 8:16.] Our spirit becomes assured of its being cleansed by the joy and peace it receives through believing and then the Spirit of God comes in as a second Witness and bears witness with our spirit that we are born of God!

My being cleansed from all sin today is to me as much a matter of consciousness as my being better in health. I was conscious of pain when I lay on my sick bed and when I was living in sin I was conscious that guilt lay heavily upon me as soon as God gave me spiritual life. I am conscious now of pain removed and so I am equally conscious of sin removed—I do not hesitate to say it here, that my consciousness of pardoned sin is at this moment as clear and as distinct as my consciousness of removed pain while I look at Jesus Christ, my Lord, by faith.

This is often so with the Christian. It is frequently a matter of consciousness most positive and infallible with him that he is truly and really cleansed from all sin by the blood of Jesus Christ! It is not merely a matter of consciousness, but if you think of it, it is a matter of reasoning. If Jesus Christ did indeed take the sins of all who believe, then it necessarily follows that I, trusting in Christ, have no longer any sin—for if Christ took my sin—my sin cannot be in two places at once! If Christ bears it, then I do not bear it. Furthermore, if Christ was punished for it, then the punishment of my sin has been borne and suffered by Christ Jesus and I am no longer guilty of the sin, justice has been served and I cannot be punished. If Jesus Christ has paid the debt it is paid and—

> "Justice can demand no more,
> Christ has paid the dreadful score."[98]

---

98. Hymn titled "The Blood of Sprinkling" by J. Kent in 1803.

So the Christian's being cleansed from sin becomes to him a matter of spiritual argument—he can see it clearly and manifestly. In fact he is so certain of it that it begins to operate upon him in blessed effect. He is so sure that there is no sin laid to his door that he draws nearer to God than a sinner, defiled with sin, may do. He enters into that which is within the veil—he talks with God as his Father—he claims and enjoys familiar communion with the Most High God! Moreover, though God is so great that the Heaven of heavens cannot contain Him, the Christian believes and knows that same God lives in his heart as in a temple! Now this he could not feel if he did not know that sin is put away. Beloved, no man is capable of virtue in the highest sense of the term until it is a matter of certainty to him that his sin is cleansed.

You say, "That is a strong assertion," but I do assert it—all of you who are doing good works with the view to saving yourselves are missing the mark of pure virtue. "Why" you ask? Because the goodness of an action depends upon its motive. Your motive is to save yourselves—that is selfish— your action is selfish and the virtue of it has evaporated. But when the Christian performs good works he does not perform them with any view whatever of merit or self-salvation. "I am saved," he says—"perfectly saved. I have not a sin in God's Book against me—I am clean. Great and Holy God, before Your bar I am clean through Jesus Christ—"

"Loved of my God, for Him again
With love intense I burn."[99]

What can I do to prove to all mankind how much, and how truly I love my God? You now see and understand that this must be a matter of certainty or else it will never have its right effect upon you. I pray to God that you may

_____
99. Hymn by Augustus Toplady.

meditate on the certainty of this text and taste its sweetness to your own soul's inward contentment and be able to say, "Yes, without a doubt, the blood of Jesus Christ, His Son, cleanses us from all sin."

DIVINITY

6. I hope I shall not weary you, but a few words upon the sixth gem which adorns the text, namely, the divinity of it. "Where?" asks one. Does divinity not gleam in this text? Does it not strike you that the verse is written in a godlike style? The godlike style is very peculiar. You can tell the style of Milton from the style of Wordsworth, or the style of Byron. Read a verse and an educated person knows the author by the ring of the sentences. The godlike style is unique in its excellence. You need never put the name at the bottom when the writing is of the Lord. You know it by the very style of it. "Light be! Light was." Who speaks like that but Deity? Now there is a Divine ring about this sentence—"The blood of Jesus Christ, His Son, cleanses us from all sin." I can tell you that if man were talking of so great an Atonement he would have to fetch a compass! He would have to try to find a way to explain it in a condensed way but without success! We cannot afford to say such great things as these in a few words. We must adopt some form of speech that would allow us to extol the truth and indicate its beauties. God seems to put away His pearls as if they were but common pebbles. *"The blood of Jesus Christ, His Son, cleanses us from all sin"*—as if it were as much a matter of everyday work as for a man to wash his hands!

Notice the simplicity of the whole process. It does not take weeks or months—it is done at once! Slowly and by degrees is man's procedure to cleanse something—we must lay the thing to soak to get the color out of it, subject it to many processes and expose it to the wind and rain and frost and sun before it can be cleansed. But here God *speaks* and it is done! The blood comes into contact with the guilty conscience and it is all over for sin. As if it were but a handful that moves a mountain of sin, He takes up the isles as a very little thing. He counts great oceans of our sin as though they were but a drop in a bucket. Believing in Christ in a moment by the divine and majestic process which God has ordained, we get perfectly cleansed from sin.

WISDOM

7. In the last place, just a hint upon the wisdom of the text. What a wise way of cleansing from sin the text speaks of! Beloved, suppose God had devised a plan for pardoning sin which did not turn the sinner's face to God. Then you would have a very singular spectacle—you would have a sinner pardoned by a process that enabled him to do without his God—and it strikes me he would be worse off than he was before! But here, before the sinner can receive pardon he must say, *"I will arise and go unto my Father."* [See Luke 15:18.] And he must come closer into contact with God than he ever came before. He must see God in the flesh of Christ and must look to Him if he wants to be saved.

I do bless God that I do not have to turn my face to hell to get pardon, but I have to turn my face towards Heaven! That seems to me to be the wise way, for while it takes away the sin which was like a disease, it takes away the distance from God which was the true root of that disease. It turns the sinner's face in the direction of holiness and bliss. Observe the benefit of this plan of salvation in the fact that it makes the sinner feel the evil of sin. If we were pardoned in a way which did not involve pain to someone, we would say, "Oh, it is easy for God to forgive it." But when I see the streaming

271

veins of Jesus and mark the sweat of His blood fall to the ground and hear Him cry, "They have pierced my hands and my feet," then I understand that sin is a dreadful evil! If a man could be pardoned without being made to feel that sin is bitter, I do not know that he would be really any the better off—perhaps better unpardoned than pardoned—unless he is led to hate sin. Our gracious God has also chosen this plan of salvation with the wise design of making man glorify God. I cannot see sin pardoned by the substitutionary Atonement of the Lord Jesus without dedicating myself to the praise and glory of the great God of redeeming love. It would be a pity if man could be pardoned and afterwards lived a selfish, thankless life would it not? If God had devised a scheme by which sin could be pardoned and yet the sinner lives to himself, I do not know that the world or the man would be advantaged.

But here are many birds killed with one stone, as the Proverb puts it. Now therefore, at the foot of the Cross, the bands which bound our soul to Earth are loosened. We are strangers in the land and therefore, ". . . *God forbid that I* [we] *should glory, save in the cross of our Lord Jesus Christ, by whom the world is crucified unto me* [us] *and I* [we] *unto the world"* [Galatians 6:14].

I leave this text with the Believer, adding only, if any of you want it and would joy in it; you must walk in the light. I pray God the Holy Spirit will bring you to see the light of the Glory of God in the face of Jesus Christ! Then you will trust Him, have fellowship with Him, and by His blood you will be cleansed from all sin. God bless you for Jesus' sake. Amen.

CHAPTER 12
THE THREE WITNESSES

A SERMON

(No. 1187)

Delivered on Lord's-Day Morning, August 9th, 1874,

by

CHARLES H. SPURGEON,

at the Metropolitan Tabernacle, Newington,
London, England

*"And there are three that bear witness in earth, the Spirit,
and the water, and the blood: and these three agree in
one."—1 John 5:8*

CHRISTIANITY puts forth very lofty claims. She claims to be the true faith, and the only true one. She avows her teachings to be divine, and therefore infallible; while for her great Teacher, the Son of God, she demands divine worship, and the unreserved confidence and obedience of men. Her commands are issued to every creature, and though at present her authority is rejected by millions of mankind, she confidently looks forward to a time when truth shall obtain universal dominion, and Jesus the Lord shall take unto himself His great power and reign.

EVIDENCE

Now, to justify such high claims, the Gospel ought to produce strong evidence, and it does so. It does not lack for external evidences, these are abundant, and since many learned men have spent their lives in elaborating them, there is less need for me to attempt a summary of them. In these days hardly a stone is turned over among all the books written that does not proclaim the truth of the Word of God, and the further men look into history or nature, the more manifest the truth is of scriptural statements. The armory of external evidences is well-stored with weapons of proof. The Gospel also bears within itself its own evidence, it has a self-proving power. It is so pure, so holy, so altogether above the inventive capacity of fallen man, that it must be of God. The morning, however, we will not be dealing with these external or internal evidences. But I call your attention to the three witnesses which are spoken of in the text, three great witnesses still among us, whose evidence proves the truth of our religion, the divinity of our Lord, and the future supremacy of the faith. Our text speaks of three witnesses, the Spirit, the water, and the blood: may the Holy Ghost, who is our Interpreter, lead us into the full meaning of this very, remarkable passage.

OUR LORD HIMSELF WAS ATTESTED BY THESE THREE WITNESSES

I. If you will carefully read in the twenty-ninth chapter of the Book of Exodus, or the eighth chapter of the Book of Leviticus, you will see that when a priest was ordained (and a priest was a type of Christ) three things were always used: he was washed with water in every case, a sacrifice was brought, and the priest's ear, his thumb, and his toe were touched with blood, and then he was anointed with oil, in token of that unction of the Spirit with which the coming Christ Jesus, the High Priest of our profession would be anointed. Therefore, every priest came by the anointing Spirit, by water, and by blood, as a matter of type, and Jesus Christ who was indeed the High Priest to come, is known by these three signs.

Godly men in the olden times also understood well that

there was no putting away of sin except with these three things; in proof of which we will quote David's prayer, *"Purge me with hyssop"* [that is, the hyssop dipped in blood] *"and I shall be clean; wash me"* [there is the water] *"and I shall be whiter than snow."* And then, *"Restore unto me the joy of thy salvation, and uphold me with thy free Spirit."* [See Psalm 51:7, 51:12.] Thus the blood, the water, and the Spirit were recognized of old as necessary to cleanse from guilt, and if Jesus of Nazareth is indeed able to save His people from their sins, He must come with the triple gift of the Spirit, the water, and the blood. Now it was evidently so.

WITNESSED

Our Lord was attested by *the Spirit.* The Spirit of God bore witness to Christ in the types and prophecies, "Holy men of old spake as they were moved by the Holy Ghost" [2 Peter 1:21], and Jesus Christ answers to those prophecies as exactly as a well-made key answers to the wards of a lock. By the power of the Holy Spirit our Lord's humanity was fashioned and prepared for Him, for the angel said unto Mary, *"The Holy Ghost shall come upon thee, and the power of the Highest shall overshadow thee: therefore also that holy thing which shall be born of thee shall be called the Son of God"* [Luke 1:35].

When our Lord in due time commenced His public ministry, the Spirit of God descended upon Him like a dove, and rested upon Him, and a voice was heard from heaven saying, *". . . This is my beloved Son, in whom I am well pleased"* [Matthew 3:17]. This was indeed one of the surest seals of our Lord's Messiahship, for it had been given by the Spirit of prophecy unto John as a token *"upon whom thou shalt see the Spirit descending, and remaining on him, the same is he which baptizeth with the Holy Ghost"* [John 1:33].

The Spirit abode in our Lord without measure, throughout His whole public career, so that He is described as full of the Spirit and led of the Spirit.

Hence His life and ministry were full of power. How truthfully He said, *"The Spirit of the Lord is upon me, because he hath anointed me to preach the gospel to the poor, he hath sent me to heal the broken-hearted, to preach deliverance to the captives, and recovering of sight to the blind. . ."* [Luke 4:18]. The Apostle Peter said, *"How God anointed Jesus of Nazareth with the Holy Ghost and with power: who went about doing good, and healing all that were oppressed of the devil; for God was with him. . . ."* [Acts 10:38].

Mighty signs and miracles were the witness of the divine Spirit to the mission of the Lord Jesus. The Spirit abode with our Lord all His life, and to crown all, after He had died and risen again, the Holy Ghost gave the fullest witness by descending in full power upon the disciples at Pentecost. The Lord had promised to baptize His disciples with the Holy Ghost, and they tarried at Jerusalem in expectation of the gift and they were not disappointed, for all a sudden ". . . *they were all filled with the Holy Ghost, and began to speak with other tongues, as the Spirit gave them utterance"* [Acts 2:4].

Those cloven tongues of fire, and the *"rushing mighty wind,"* were sacred tokens that He who had ascended was Lord and God. [See Acts 2:2.] The apostles said, ". . . *And we are witnesses of these things; and so is also the Holy Ghost, whom God hath given to them that obey him"* [Acts 5:32]. The word of the apostles, through the Holy Spirit, convinced men *"of sin, of righteousness, and of judgment,"* [See John 16:8.], as the Master had foretold; and then the Spirit comforted the penitents, and they believed in the exalted Savior and were baptized the selfsame day. The Words of Jesus were abundantly fulfilled, *"But when the Comforter is come, whom I will send unto you from the Father, even the Spirit of truth, which proceedeth from the Father, he shall testify of me: . . ."* [John 15:26]. Thus from our Lord's birth, throughout His life, and after His ascension, the Holy Ghost bore conspicuous witness to Him.

THE WATER

It is also manifest that our Lord came with *water* too. I have shown you that every priest was washed with water; our Lord was not unclean, and therefore one would have thought He might dispense with this; but to *"fulfill all righteousness"* [See Exodus 29, Matthew 3:15.]. His first step was to be washed in Jordan by the hands of John the Baptist, coming thus to the door of His ministry by that baptism in water which indicates that by death, burial, and resurrection, He was about to save His people. As soon as that baptism had been accomplished, in fact even before that, you could see that He had come with water, for by water is signified that clean, pure, hallowed life which the outward washing was meant to typify. His first years of obscurity were years of holiness, and His after years of service were spotless.

"In him was no sin." [See 1 John 3:5.] Who ever brought forth a ministry as pure as His? Where else might we find such immaculate holiness? He came not by the water merely as a symbol, but by that which the water meant, by *unsullied purity of life.* His doctrine was as pure as His example. Point me to a single syllable of all His teaching which would create, foster, or excuse sin! He was the friend of sinners, but not the apologist for their sins. His tenderness to sinners was that of a physician whose aim is to remove the disease. His whole doctrine is fitly comparable to purifying and life-giving water, and it operated upon men's hearts in that manner. In this last sense especially He came by water.

It is very remarkable how John's Gospel is both the exposition and the text of John's First Epistle, for if you turn to it you find our Lord Jesus coming by water at the outset of His teaching. To Nicodemus He says a man must be *"born of water and of the Spirit"* [See John 3:5.], to the woman of Samaria He speaks at large of *"living water. . . ."* [See John 4:10.], and on the great day of the feast He vies, *"If any man thirst let him come unto me and drink."* [See John 7:37.] In His ministry He not only issued the invitation, but to all who believed on Him He gave of the water of the fountain of life freely. Thus our Lord came by water in the sense of communicating a new, pure, and purifying life to men. For the water is the emblem of the new life that springs up within the soul of believers, a life fresh and sparkling, leaping up from the eternal fountains of the divine existence. Life eternal which will flow on for ever, and widen and deepen like Ezekiel's river, and increase in fullness of power and joy until it unites with the ocean of immortal bliss. Jesus came to pour forth this living flood among the sons of men. Blessed be His name!

Our Lord closed His life by *"washing His disciples' feet"*, a fit conclusion to a life which had by its example been cleansing throughout, and still remains as the grandest corrective of the corrupt examples of the world. [See John 13:4-5.] Even after death our Lord retained the instructive symbol by giving forth from His pierced heart water as well as blood, which John evidently thought very significant; for when he wrote concerning it he said, *"He that saw it bare record, and his record is true: and he knoweth that he saith true, that ye might believe"* [John 19:35]. Therefore, from the Jordan to the Cross both the symbol and the substance were with our great Master, while His own personal purity and His gift of life to others, proved His mission to be from above.

THE BLOOD

With Jesus also was *the blood*. This distinguished Him from John the Baptist, who came by water, but Jesus came *". . . not by water only, but by water and blood. . . ."* [See 1 John 5:6.] We must not prefer any one of the three witnesses to another, but what a wonderful testimony to Christ was the blood! From the very first He came with blood, for John the Baptist cried, *"Behold the Lamb of God, which taketh away the sin of the world!"* [John 1:29]. Now, the lamb which takes away sin is a slaughtered lamb, a bleeding lamb; so that at the time when the baptismal waters were upon Him, John saw that He must bleed for human sin. In His ministry there was often a clear testimony to His future sufferings and shedding of blood, for to the assembled crowd He said, *"Except a man eat my flesh and drink my blood, there is no life in him:"* [See John 6:53.], while to His disciples He spoke of the decease which He would shortly accomplish at Jerusalem.

Then at the last, taking all our sins upon His shoulders, in the agony of Gethsemane, the blood bore witness that He was indeed the Lamb of God, and on yonder tree where He "Bore all incarnate God could bear, / With strength enough, but none to spare,"[100] disinterestedly dying for His enemies, unselfishly suffering an ignominious doom that He might redeem those who had rejected and scoffed at Him, His invincible love triumphed over death itself, and endured divine wrath without repining, as none but the Son of God could have done. Now Messiah was to be cut off, but not for himself; He was to make His soul an offering for sin, He was to make His grave with the wicked, and lie in the heart of the Earth. The blood of the covenant was to be shed, the paschal victim was to be slain, the Shepherd was

---

100. Hymn: "Come All Ye Chosen Saints of God" by Joseph Hart.

to be smitten, the Lamb was to be led to the slaughter, and therefore only by the shedding of His blood could Jesus prove himself to be the Messiah so long foretold.

However pure the life He led, had He never died He could not have been the Savior appointed to bear the iniquity of us all. The blood was needed to complete the witness. The blood must now with the water, show the suffering with the serving. The most pious example would not have proved Him to be the divine Shepherd, if He had not laid down His life for the sheep. Take away the atonement, and Jesus is no more than any other prophet, the essential point of His mission is gone. It is evident that He who was to come was to finish transgression, and to make reconciliation for iniquity. Now, this could not be done except by an expiation, and as Jesus has made such an expiation by His own blood, we know Him to be the Christ of God. His blood is the seal of His mission, the very life of His work. I have thus shown that our Lord himself was attested by these three sacred witnesses.

STANDING WITNESSES FOREVER

II. Now may God the Holy Spirit help me to show that these three remain as standing witnesses to Him for all time. First, *the Holy Spirit* is witness at this hour that the religion of Jesus is the truth, and that Jesus is the Son of God. I do not say that He bears such witness everywhere, for there are many that preach in the wisdom of men, and in carnal excellency of speech, and God the Holy Ghost does not work with them, because He has chosen other instruments. I do not say that He bears witness to the truth when it is defiled by a lukewarm ministry, and a prayerless church: but I do say this, that the Spirit of God, wherever Jesus is fully preached, is the great witness to the truth of His Word.

THE STANDING WITNESS
OF THE HOLY SPIRIT

What does He do? By His divine energy He convinces men of the truth of the Gospel: and these convinced men are not only persons who, through their education are likely to believe it, but men like Saul of Tarsus who abhors the whole thing. He pours His influences upon men, and infidelity melts away like the iceberg in the Gulf Stream; He touches the indifferent and careless, and they repent, believe, and obey the Savior. He makes proud men tremble, and wicked men quake for fear. The conversions which are wrought where Christ is truly preached are the miracles which attest the truth of the Gospel. He who can make the harlot to be chaste, the drunkard to be sober, the thief to be honest, the malicious to be forgiving, the covetous to be generous, and above all the self-righteous to be humble, is indeed the Christ of God, and when the Spirit does all this and more by the Gospel, He bears conclusive witness to the power of the Cross.

Then, too, the Spirit goes forth among believers, and by them He bears witness to our Lord and His gospel. Great is the variety of His operations, for which cause He is called the Seven Spirits of God; but in each one He witnesses to Jesus; whether He quickens, consoles, enlightens, refreshes, sanctifies, anoints, or inflames the soul, He does it always by taking the things of Christ and revealing them to us. How mightily does He comfort the saints! Have you not been consoled by Him in deep distress? Have you not endured the loss of dear ones without repining, because your heart has been sustained by the Comforter? Now, that wondrous influence which wrought peace in you through the gospel, must have confirmed you in the belief of the truth: and others who have seen your serenity under heavy trial, if they are not convinced, at least are led to inquire what strange thing is this which makes the

Christian suffer without repining. Therefore, the Spirit bears witness to Christ when He comforts the saints.

The Spirit does the same when He gives them guidance, enlightenment and elevation of soul. I will, however, for a moment, dwell upon *"utterance."* Some reject the idea, but for all that it is true that in the selfsame hour it is given to God's servants to speak in His name. Look at the martyrs! How wondrously feeble women like Anne Askew[101] baffled all their foes! How ignorant weavers stood up before bishops and doctors and confounded them! Even now, in answer to prayer, the Spirit comes upon chosen men who yield themselves to His influence and He bears them along with a whirlwind making them eloquent in the divine sense, speaking out of their hearts that which God gives them to deliver. Some of us know this; for we have cast ourselves upon that eternal Spirit, and thoughts have been given us, and we have opened our mouths and utterance has been given us also. By this also the Spirit bears witness to the truth of our faith.

I do not have the time to go into all the operations of the Spirit; only let me say that His sustaining and His consoling influences have been very especially seen in persecuting times. Men of God have been subjected to tortures which our mind finds it painful to dwell upon, yet they have not been vanquished by their foes; neither nakedness, nor peril, nor swords have separated them from the love of God.

Blandina[102] tossed in a net by a wild bull, and burned with hot plates of brass, wearies out her tormentors; and Lawrence[103], on his gridiron, finds joy enough for mirth. One cries aloud amid the flames, "None but Jesus" and another

---

101. A young Christian, imprisoned, tortured, and burned at the stake as a martyr in 1546 at Smithfield, England.

102. A young Christian woman, martyred during the reign of Marcus Aurelius.

103. Lawrence of Rome, one of seven deacons martyred.

claps his blazing hands and shouts victory as his soul leaves his body. The Spirit of God in the Church has preserved her amid furious persecutions and has long-continued filling the saints with a dauntless courage and a serene invincibility which has both amazed and alarmed their enemies. So mightily has this patience convinced the world, that it has passed into a proverb, "The blood of the martyrs is the seed of the church."

With equal power the Spirit of God bears witness to the gospel in great revivals of religion. How wondrously did the Spirit of God testify to Christ during the Reformation! Scarcely had Luther opened his mouth to proclaim the good news than straightway men received it eagerly; they sang psalms as they ploughed the field or threw the shuttle[104]; the precious Word was in all men's mouths. They said that angels carried Luther's writings all over the world: it was not so, but the ever-blessed Spirit makes the truth to fly like flames of fire. It was so in Whitfield's day, and in many revivals which we have read of, and some which we have seen. Sometimes men have been struck down and convulsed, and at other times, without outward violence, they have been renewed in their souls with equal power. What of those who have been at Edinburgh, and seen many hundreds of people rushing through the streets to one appointed meeting place, to fall on their knees and cry for mercy all at once, could doubt that the gospel must be true?

The Spirit of God, omnipotent in the realm of spirits, and able to guide the human will without violating it, has enlightened men's darkened minds and made them see that Jesus Christ is God and Savior. Overwhelmed by the love of Jesus, they have yielded at once to His commands. A formal church, with a minister to stand up and talk officially, and a people who come and go mechanically, bears no witness

---

104. A bobbin used in weaving.

to religion, but rather creates infidels. However, where we see what some have called "real Methodist fire," and others "the old Protestant enthusiasm," or where we see the Holy Ghost attended by marvelous conversions, deep repentance, singular illumination, and angelic and general love, we have indisputable evidence of the divinity of our faith.

THE STANDING WITNESS OF THE WATER

The next abiding witness in the church is *the water*—not the water of baptism, but the new life implanted in Christians, for that is the sense in which John's Master had used the word water: *"The water that I shall give him shall be in him a well of water springing up unto everlasting life."* [See John 4:14.] When the Spirit of God comes He creates in the man a new nature, pure, bright, fresh, vigorous, like a fountain, and the fact that this new nature does exist in multitudes of men is a standing evidence that the gospel is true, for no other religion makes men new creatures, no other religion even pretends to do it; they may propose to improve the old nature, but none of them can say, *"Behold, I make all things new."* [See Revelation 21:5.] This is the sole prerogative of Jesus our Lord.

The existence of the new life is matter of fact. We ourselves know many whose lives are pure and blameless; they have faults before God, but before the eyes of men they are perfect and upright, blameless and harmless. The godly lives of Christians are good evidence of the truth of the gospel. Did I hear someone object saying,"But many professors of Christianity are not holy." I grant you that, but then everybody knows that they are inconsistent with the religion which they profess. If I heard of a lustful Mahommedan I would not consider him inconsistent with Mahommedism; is he not allowed his harem? If I heard of a licentious Hindu, I would not consider him to be dishonoring his religion, for some of its sacred rites are disgusting and unmentionable. The same may be said of all the idolatries. But everybody knows that if a man professes to be a Christian and he is guilty of a gross fault, the world rings with the scandal, because it recognizes the inconsistency of his conduct with his profession.

Though some may at the first breath of a slander blaze it abroad and say, "This is your religion," the world knows it is not our religion, but the need of it. Why do they themselves make such a wonder of a fallen professor? Are adulterers so very scarce that such a noise would be made when a minister is, truly or falsely, charged with the crime? The world's conscience knows that the religion of Jesus Christ is the religion of purity, and if professed Christians fall into uncleanness the world knows that such a course of action does not arise out of the religion of Christ, but is diametrically opposite to it. The gospel is perfect, and if we would wholly yield to its sway, sin would be abhorred by us, and slain in us, and we would live our lives on Earth as the lives of the perfect ones above. Oh, I pray that God will produce in His Church more and more the witness of the new life, the testimony of holiness, love, meekness, temperance, godliness, and grace: these are the gospel's logic, its syllogisms and demonstrations, which none can refute.

THE STANDING WITNESS OF THE BLOOD

The third abiding witness is *the blood*. The blood of Christ is still on the Earth, for when Jesus bled it fell upon the ground and was never gathered up. O Earth, you are still spattered with the blood of the murdered Son of God, and if you reject Him this will curse you. But, O humanity, you are blessed with the drops of that precious blood, and believing in Him saves you. Now, does the blood really save from guilt, terror, and despair? Does it operate among men? Let us check our memory. Its answer is clear and full. I speak what I do know, and testify what I have seen. I have preached the blood of Jesus Christ and the love of the incarnate God, and I have seen proud, stout-hearted men shed tears in floods; the rock has wept when smitten with this wondrous rod of the Cross.

Men who could resist the thunders of Sinai have melted before the tender notes of Calvary. Yes, and on the other hand, I have seen the desponding, whose soul chose strangling rather than life, look up to that dear Cross, and their faces have been brightened, and a joy unspeakable has chased away despair. The blood has wrought miracle of consolation. We have seen men at war with God, and opposed to holiness, to whom the blood has spoken; they have seen a God reconciled to them, and they have been reconciled to Him themselves. We have seen them beneath the spell of the blood throw down their weapons and cry—

> "I yield, by Jesus' love subdued,
> Who can resist its charms?
> And throw myself to be reserved
> Into my Savior's arms." [105]

The blood of Jesus, after speaking peace to the conscience, inflames the heart with fervent love, and often fully leads men to high deeds of consecration, self-denial, and self-sacrifice, such as can scarce be understood until they are traced back to that amazing love which bled upon the tree. Well might the martyrs bleed for Him who was crucified for them; the

---

105. Hymn: "By Thy Victorious Hand Struck Down", compiled by Simon Browne in 1720.

blood is working mightily in men to will and to do for the glory of God. Yes, brethren, the blood has such a melting, converting, subduing, sanctifying, and such a joy-creating power to every conscience which hears its matchless voice, that it remains, with the Spirit and the water, a convincing witness to the Christ of God.

THE THREE WITNESSES IN BELIEVERS

The Holy Spirit

III. In the third place, let us observe that this triple yet united witness is peculiarly forcible within the believing hearts. John tells us, *"He that believeth on the Son of God hath the witness in himself"* [See 1 John 5:10.]. Now, brethren, these three witnesses bear testimony in our souls abidingly. I speak not of years ago, but of last night, when you bowed your knee in prayer and prayed, and were heard. Did not the Spirit help you to pray and bear witness that the gospel was no lie? Was not the answer to your prayer good evidence? And that Sabbath morning, when you prayed that you might gather up your thoughts and forget the week's cares, and you did so by the Spirit's aid, did not this sacred rest of your soul prove that Christ is indeed a Savior?

Sitting here this morning as your soul has burned within you, and your Master has been near you, has not that communion given you by the Spirit been a fresh witness to Christ? The other day, when you were so sad and the Holy Spirit comforted you, when you were so rebellious, and He made you quiet like a weaned child, did not this confirm your faith? The other day when you were so in the dark, and He enlightened you, when you were in such dilemmas and He guided you had you not then fresh evidence that there is a life, a power, and a divinity about the gospel? These sweet feelings of yours came to you by the Spirit of God revealing Jesus to you. He did not comfort you or elevate you by the law or by the flesh, but by the love of God shed abroad in your heart, [See Romans 5:5.], that precious love which comes streaming down from the Cross of Jesus Christ our Lord.

Ah, dear friends, I feel sick to death of the common talk about the healthiness of doubting and the beauty of *modern thought*. This talk is only the self-praise of a set of concealed infidels treacherously lurking in God's Church. There is a sure way to deal with skeptics which I commend to your use. Ask them "Do you know the Holy Ghost? Did you ever feel Him in your own souls?" If they say "No," we believe them; so let them believe us when we declare that we do feel the operations of the Holy Ghost. That makes an end of the controversy; if they are honest so are we, and we are witnesses to the divine working of the Holy Ghost in our own souls. If they never felt His power, their negative statements cannot in the least degree affect the truth of ours.

The Water

The next witness in us is *the water,* or the new and pure life. Do you feel the inner life, my brethren? I know you do. You feel the inner life fighting, struggling, contending, sometimes winning the mastery, and at other times captive and groaning. You often feel it aspiring, desiring, hungering, thirsting, yearning, sighing; and sometimes singing, and you feel it shouting, dancing, and leaping up to Heaven. You are conscious of the fact that you are not what you used to be; you are conscious of a new life within your soul which you never knew until the time of your conversion, and that new life within you is the living and incorruptible seed "*. . . which liveth and abideth for ever.*" [See 1 Peter 1:23.]

The fact that you know you are born of God forbids any doubt as to the truth by which you were begotten; the sense that you are forgiven forbids all skepticism as to the fact that Christ is come in the flesh, that He is the Son of God, and that His Gospel is the truth of God. To you all these things are clear.

The Blood

Witnessing within us is also *the blood.* Beloved, this is a witness which never fails, speaking in us better things than the blood of Abel. It gives us such peace that we can sweetly live and calmly die. It gives us such wondrous access to God that sometimes when we have felt its power we have been drawn so near to our Father that it is as if we had seen Him face to face. And oh, what safety the blood causes us to enjoy! We feel that we cannot perish while the crimson canopy of atonement by blood hangs over our head. What victory it gives us making us cry out, *"Thanks be unto God, who giveth us the victory, through our Lord Jesus Christ!"* [See 1 Corinthians 15:57.] These are mysterious sensations, not to be accounted for by fleshly enthusiasm, for they are strongest when we are calmest. They are not to be accounted for by any natural predilections to such emotions, for we are by nature as easily perturbed as others, and as apt to forget divine things. In times of trial we have looked to Jesus' flowing wounds and we have been comforted, we have found communion with Jesus to be so blessed that we would not envy Gabriel his angelhood.

Now, then, you young men, you need not read *Paley's Evidences,*[106] the evidence of the Spirit, the water, and the blood is better. You do not grant to study *Butler's Analogy,*[107] though you may if you please, but such books, excellent as

---

106. *Evidences of Christianity* written in 1794, by William Paley an English theologian.
107. Joseph Butler author of *Analogy of Religion, Natural and Revealed,* 1736.

they are, only prove the skin and shell of our religion for the vital matter is the kernel. If you come by simple prayer, and ask to have the blood of Jesus applied to your soul, and if the Spirit of God works mightily in your spirit so that you obtain a new inner principle, and lead a new life as the result, you will have the best evidence in the world. You will laugh at doubters, and make a fire of *Colenso's Objections*[108], and *Essays and Reviews*[109], Tyndall's[110] challenge, and Huxley's[111] dreams, and all that heap of worthless muck which has polluted the Church, and defiled the souls of men. O heavens, that we should ever live to see the day when ministers tell us that it is good to doubt, when poets almost deify that very skepticism of which the Apostle John says makes God a liar, and should be denounced as an insult to God, and the curse of the age. Go, fling your doubts away, you doting men and dreaming women, and bow like penitents at Jesus' feet, and you will find far more than all your fancied learning can bestow. But if you will not do this, then know that in vain you will arraign your Maker at your judgment bar, and in vain you will re-judge His judgment, and act as if you were the Gods of God! [See Romans 3:4.]

THE WITNESSES IN ORDER

Thus I have tried to show that these three witnesses testify in our souls; I beg you now to notice *their order*. These three bear witness in us thus, the Spirit, the water, and the blood; why in this order? Because this is the order in

---

108. Bishop Colenso author of *Colenso's Objections on the Veracity of the Pentateuch,* written in 1863.
109. Written in 1860 by Bishop Colenso.
110. John Tyndall, physicist, known for his study in 1850 on diamagnetism.
111. Thomas Henry Huxley, 1825, advocate of Charles Darwin's theory of evolution.

which they operate. The Spirit of God first enters the heart, perhaps long before the man knows that such is the case; the Spirit creates the new life, which repents and seeks the Savior, that is the water; and that new life flies to the blood of Jesus and obtains peace. The Spirit mightily working, the new life is secretly created, and then faith in the blood is begotten, and the triple witness is complete. We have also found this to be the order of our consolation. I have said to myself, Do I know that the Spirit of God is in me?" and I have been afraid that it is not; I have then turned to my inner life, the water, and have not always been certain concerning it, but when I have looked away to the blood, all has been clear enough! Jesus died; I throw myself once again into His arms. When I do not know whether I have the Spirit, and when I am in doubt as to whether I have the living water, I still know that I believe in the blood, and this brings perfect peace.

COMBINED WORK OF THE WITNESSES

Having observed their order, now note *their combination.* "These three agree in one," therefore every true believer should have the witness of each one, and if each one does not witness in due time, there is cause for grave suspicion. For instance, persons have arisen who have said the Spirit of God has led them to do this and that. We then ask them, "What are your lives? Does the water bear witness? Are you pardoned? Does the blood testify for you?" If these questions cannot be answered they may rave as they like about the Spirit of God, but the witness to their salvation is open to the gravest suspicion.

We have known some who will say, "Look at my life; I am very different from what I was. I am a sober, honest, excellent man." Yes, but do you test in the blood of Jesus? Practical evidence is good, but it must arise out of faith. If you do not believe in Jesus you do not have the essential witness, and your case is not proved. Many also say to us, "I believe that Jesus died for me," but we must ask them concerning their lives. Are you cleansed in your actions? Are you an altered man? For remember, unless the water speaks with the blood, you do not have the three-fold testimony. There may be some who say, "Well, we believe in Jesus, and our lives are changed": but remember, you may say that, but is it so? If so, the Spirit of God has changed you: if you have merely excited yourself into the belief that it is so, or if you were born by your own free will, you have not the witness, because the truly saved are born not of blood, nor of the will of man, but of the Spirit of God.

The three witnesses agree as one. He who believes in pardon by the blood believes also in sanctification by the water; he who rests in Jesus Christ's blood always honors the Spirit of God, and, on the other hand, he that believes in the Holy Ghost values both the inner life and the cleansing blood. God has joined these three together, and let no man put them asunder. The old theologians spoke of *baptismus flaminis*[112], *baptismus fluminis*[113], and *baptismus sanguinis*[114]. May we know all these, and rejoice in the Spirit, the [water] flood, and the blood.

THREE WITNESSES' CERTIFICATION OF VICTORY

IV. Lastly, these witnesses certify to us the ultimate triumph of our religion. Is *the Spirit* working through the

---

112. By the Spirit
113. By Water
114. By Blood

gospel? Then the gospel will win the day, because the Spirit of God is Almighty, and complete master over the realm of the mind. He has the power to illuminate the intellect, to win the affections, to curb the will, and change the entire nature of man, for He works all things after His own pleasure, [See Ephesians 1:5.] and, like the wind, He *bloweth where he listeth* [See John 3:8.]. When He puts forth His omnipotent energy none can stand against Him. He has converted three thousand in a day, and He could as readily convert three million, or three hundred million. He can do this, and He will. The wind at times blows so gently as scarcely to stir the wing of a butterfly, but at another time it rushes in a tornado, sweeping all before it. Do not judge from its soft breath what its full tempest could be, for nothing can stand against the wind when once it speeds forth with power. Let the Spirit of God blow across this land and it will at once drive away the miasma of superstition, and the clouds of ignorance.

The Holy Spirit is compared to fire. What can resist the energy of fire? There may be so little of it that a cowherd may carry it in his lantern, but beware for it easily sets a city ablaze. One match contains all the fire power needed to set a prairie on fire if it is flung into the dry grass, and the very heavens themselves are scorched with the exceeding heat. Is the Spirit of the Lord straitened[115]? Is anything too hard for the Lord? Behold, the universe was chaos once, and the Spirit brooded over it and this fair world came forth: let Him in like manner incubate over this chaos of sin, and a new Heaven, and a new Earth, wherein dwells righteousness shall rise. The gospel must conquer, because the Holy Ghost who works with it is almighty.

Next, the gospel must conquer, because of *the water,*

---

115. Restricted

which I have explained to be the new life of purity. What does the Apostle John say? *"Whatsoever is born of God overcometh the world."* [See 1 John 5:4.] It's impossible for the gospel to be vanquished so long as there remains one soul in the world that is born of God. Living and incorruptible seed abides for ever! Those who would destroy the Church only scatter her living seeds, and when Satan raises a hurricane it only bears those seeds further afield. Satan once sat down with his minions to scheme, he called in all the devils one by one to a conclave until pandemonium broke out, and what think you came of it all? The Papal Inquisition. They set that horrible machine to work to crush out what they called heresy. They said they would ride up to their saddle girths in the blood of Lutherans, and they almost redeemed their promise; but their cruelty did not avail, the living faith survived, and the martyrs murdered and the infernal cruelties of the murderers, stirred the world to a groan of sympathy, which helped the progress of the Gospel. They cannot destroy the Gospel. Do not talk about the Pope of Rome, or the ritualistic or infidel party destroying the Church and the Gospel, they might as well try to annihilate the Lord himself, because the inner life of Christians is a spark struck from the eternal sun of life, and can never be extinct while God lives.

Lastly, the Gospel must spread and conquer because of *the blood*. Has the blood got power? Oh, yes, I will tell you how. God, the everlasting Father, has promised to Jesus by covenant, of which the blood is the seal, that *". . . He shall see his seed, he shall prolong his days, and the pleasure of the Lord shall prosper in his hand"* [Isaiah 53:10]. As surely as Christ died on the Cross, He must sit on a universal throne. God cannot lie to His Son, cannot mock His wounds, or be deaf to His death cries, and, therefore, Christ must have what His Father has promised Him, and He has said, *"Ask of me, and I will give thee the heathen for thine inheritance, and the uttermost parts of the earth for thy possession"* [Psalm 2:8]. *"They that bow in the wilderness shall bow before Him, and His enemies shall lick the dust; for He must reign until he hath put all enemies under his feet"* [Psalm 72:9 and 1 Corinthians 15:25].

Brethren, the inference from all this is, if you are not on Christ's side it is not well with you, for you will surely be conquered in the battle: but, if you are on Christ's side, never speak hesitatingly or despondingly. When they bring out a new book to disprove Genesis, and another to evaporate the atonement, do not be afraid. As long as the Gospel is in the world the devil will find somebody to write books against it. Take no notice of them, they cannot stand against facts. A philosopher once wrote a book to prove that there is no such thing as matter, and a certain reader believed it until he chanced to knock his head against the bedpost, and then he abandoned the theory.

When a man feels the power of the Holy Spirit, or the power of the inner life, he does not care to argue; he has a homespun philosophy of facts which answers his purpose better. Though others may surround him and say, "You are not learned," he feels that one does not need learning to prove that which is a matter of personal consciousness, any more than we need proof that sugar is sweet when we have a piece in our mouths. Do you doubt the Gospel? Try it! The men who speak against the Bible as a rule have never read it; those who rail against Christ do not know Him; and those who deny the efficacy of prayer have never prayed. Nothing is more convincing than fact. Get out of the realm of word-spinning and windbag-filling into practical Christian life, proving personally that these things are so, and you will soon be convinced by the blessed witness of the Spirit, the water, and the blood.

CHAPTER 13
THE MEAT AND DRINK OF THE NEW NATURE

A SERMON
(No. 1460)
Delivered by
REVEREND CHARLES H. SPURGEON
At The Metropolitan Tabernacle,
Newington, London, England.

"For my flesh is meat, indeed, and my blood is drink, indeed."—John 6:55

W E KNOW THAT THE SAVIOR spoke of spiritual, not carnal things, and He spoke of himself not as being in any sense meat for our bodies—that could not be—but as being food for our souls. This statement is very plain to us, but those who heard it at the first, found it very difficult to understand. That should not make us wonder, for men of the schools who play with letters; words and phrases, frequently meet with difficulties where none exist. The Jews of our Lord's day had fallen into the foolish habit of dissecting words to pieces and dwelling upon the syllables and letters until they seemed to have lost all power of getting at the plain meaning which ordinary language was intended to convey. They blinded their own eyes with the pretense of superior wisdom; made puzzles and riddles out of plain words; raised a lot of dust; and sat down in it blinded to the end.

Our God has taught us more and helped us to understand more clearly, for His Holy Spirit has given us back the childlike spirit so that we are willing to see the natural sense that words were meant to reveal. Now we see great force and clear expressiveness in that very language which before seemed to conceal the Savior's meaning. It was a veil to the Jews and they saw not—it is an instructive parable to us, which, instead of hiding the Truth of God, shadows it out to us and softens the light for our weak eyes. Even now we see dimly, for our spiritual sight is not clear as yet, but we see, blessed be God for that, and we see Jesus and something of His loving meaning. We do more than see—we enjoy and understand in our spiritual life what it means to feed upon His flesh, which is meat, indeed, and to drink His blood, which is drink, indeed.

We cannot attempt to explain the deep mysteries of our text, but rather, as the swallow touches the brook with his wing and is away again, we will glance at these crystal waters of this sacred Truth of God and then up and away! The text teaches us:

> **First:** What Christ Must Be To Us
> **Second:** What Is Involved In This
> **Third:** What Reflections Naturally
>   Arise Out Of It

I. WHAT CHRIST MUST BE TO US

The answer from the text is, He must be our meat and drink. He must be everything to us—the one thing necessary, the indispensable, necessary all-sufficient supply. He must be the source of strength, the support of life and we must feel Him to be so. He must, to come back to the figure, be meat and drink to us. Our Lord, in speaking to the Jews, was doubtless thinking of the Paschal Lamb and of the time when Israel came out of Egypt—when they not only had the blood of the lamb sprinkled upon their houses for their security, but the lamb, itself, within them as their sustenance.

They sat down to feed upon it before they enjoyed the fullness of redemption by passing out of Egypt from under the bondage of Pharaoh. They did not understand that symbol and they little knew what our great Lord and Master meant when He employed it to set forth Himself and said, *"My flesh is meat, indeed, and my blood is drink, indeed."* Our Lord Jesus Christ must be to us, then, our spiritual meat and drink. What do we mean by that? First, that the doctrine of God Incarnate must be the food of our souls. Brothers and Sisters, we have no doubt as to the true and proper Deity of our Lord Jesus. We have long since passed out of the region of controversy about that, for He has been God to us in the work of salvation and in the new creation which we have experienced through His power.

DEITY AND HUMANITY IN ONE

We have, moreover, no doubt about His humanity, but we do not usually dwell enough upon it. We are bound to adore His Deity, but we must not forget that He is as truly Man as if He were not God, and as much a Brother to us as if He were not the Son of the Highest. Jesus is assuredly Man. Now feed on this. The man Christ Jesus heads up a new race—as the first Adam headed up the race of old and was our federal head to stand or fall for us, and we were to stand or fall in him—so is there now a new Head who brings us up from the ruin of the first Adam's fall and puts us into a new position before the living God. There is a Man who has redeemed us! There is a Man who has made all the men in Him well-pleasing to God. There is a Man who represents manhood in perfection in the Glory above. There is a Man in whom all Believers are—even as we read that Levi was in the loins of Abraham when Melchisidec met him!

HUMANITY IN DEITY

We are in Christ and we now stand before the eternal Throne in that blessed representative Man. Feed on this doctrine! Jesus is a real Man, though clothed with all power He is God and yet He is the mirror of tenderness! He rules all things and yet is touched with the feeling of our infirmities. [See Hebrews 4:15.] You must believe this and you must receive it—and you must rest upon it—otherwise you have no life in you. Some try to turn this fact into a myth, but, indeed, it is no parable or figure of speech, for the Christ who spoke these words was there before them—one whom they had often seen eat and drink! He spoke of himself with His own lips and was not a phantom or apparition, but a solid existence of flesh and blood. So, then, it is upon the historical Christ, whose existence is a matter of fact, that my soul must feed on, as I believe Him to be both Human and Divine.

CHRIST'S SUFFERING

But this is not all—the food to be fed upon is not merely God Incarnate, but Christ suffering. Notice that He puts it, *"My flesh is meat, indeed, and my blood is drink indeed"*— when the flesh and the blood are mentioned separately, death is implied. The two being divided and being named together in one connection are the token and emblem of our Savior's vicarious sacrifice. We also, (I am speaking of the Brothers and Sisters worshiping here), have long ago passed beyond the region of controversy as to the substitutionary sacrifice of Jesus Christ our Lord. If it is not so, then our preaching is in vain and our hope is also in vain and we are yet in our sins. We have no hope of eternal life save that which begins, centers and ends in the sacrifice of Jesus Christ! *"But this man, after he had offered one sacrifice for sins for ever, sat down on the right hand of God*"—that is our sole hope [Hebrews 10:12].

> He has made expiation for sin—
> "He bore, that we might never bear,
> His Father's righteous ire."[116]

FEED UPON . . .

We are now to build up our souls by feeding upon the suffering, crucified, dead, and buried Christ, as having stood as our Representative and as having endured death in our place. You cannot obtain comfort apart from this if you have felt the weight of sin! And you cannot continue happy apart from this great historical fact if you are conscious of sin. Fly, my hearers, into the wounds of Jesus and, like doves, you shall find shelter in that Rock! And with eager wings you may glide over the waste of human thought without finding a rest for the soles of your weary feet until you light upon the Truth of God of the great Substitution.

"The Word was made flesh and dwelt among us," [John 1:14] is the first bell of Heaven's marriage peal—and the second has an equally sweet note of its own—"Christ died for our sins" [1 Corinthians 15:3]. Ring them both often! Listen to them as they sound forth, "God with us, Christ for us." Incarnation, Substitution—was there ever better meat and drink for a hungry soul? This surely satisfies the desire of the most hungry spirit—". . . The blood of Jesus Christ his Son cleanses us from all sin" [1 John 1:7]. I have, as it were, in those few words set out the viands[117] of the feast.

---

116. Hymn by Augustus Toplady.
117. Choice food.

SOCINIAN BELIEF

But now I would have you note that our Lord must be to us meat and drink—and meat is not intended to look at, but to feed on. I heard the other day that in a certain Socinian[118] place of worship they have gone to the trouble of setting the bread and wine on the table for the people to look at, but they believe that it is quite unnecessary that they should actually eat and drink it. It is fittingly done by them—that is consistent with their creed. They have no Christ to feed upon! There is nothing in their belief which could feed the soul of a mouse, if a mouse had a soul! Why should they attempt to feed the people in figure when really they have no Incarnate God or atoning Savior? If it is, indeed, true that in one of their places of worship they have exhibited the bread and wine instead of handing it out to be eaten, it is remarkably typical of their bloodless, lifeless gospel! Their Christ who is no Deity! Their Jesus who is no sacrifice for sin!

How can the soul find food there? But we must beware lest we, ourselves, should ever rest content with merely glancing at Christ and not partaking of Him. What is to be done with food, with meat and drink? It is to be received! Food on the table does not nourish! It must be taken into the hand. The cup on the board will never cheer—it must be lifted—it must be appropriated. I know that many of you have, by a humble but brave faith, appropriated Christ as He is set before you in the Gospel. He has bid you come and eat and you have come pressed by a sore famine that was in your soul. You have come and you have said, "He is mine," and you have taken Him to yourselves by simple childlike confidence in Him. You have done well—continue to do the same.

"As you have received Christ Jesus the Lord, so walk you

---

118. One who rejects the divinity of Christ, the Trinity, etc.

in him" [Colossians 2:6]. Go on receiving Him. *"To whom coming,"* says the Apostle, *"as unto a living stone"* [1 Peter 2:4]. Regard Him not as one to whom you have come by one act and then are done with Him, but as one to whom you come continually! *"Of his fullness have all we received, and grace for grace,"* [John 1:16], but we are going on receiving by continuing to believe in Him! Hold on to this. Having begun in the spirit, do not hope to be perfected by the flesh! [See Galatians 3:3.] Do not think that you are to be fed, afterwards, on something other than Christ, but go on receiving, appropriating and taking home the great truths concerning your Lord. Here, my brethren, is the life of your faith.

But even appropriating is not enough to constitute feeding. After taking the morsel, it is put into the mouth and received inwardly—the draught of wine is poured into the throat and it disappears. Receive the Truth of God not only as a matter of creed, but drink it in deeply as the ox sucks in the water when he stands up to his knees in the water. Take Christ into your very soul—into your heart's belief as well as into your mind's belief! Mental beliefs shift and change, but the inward soul's belief never alters. I believe that we know nothing rightly until we have absorbed it and made it part and parcel of ourselves. The vital truths with regard to our Lord Jesus must go down into the inward parts of the soul, as the food descends into the secret parts of the belly to feed the entire man.

And you know what becomes of the food. It is taken into the stomach and goes through the various processes and ultimately becomes the lifeblood out of which is built up nerve, muscle, sinew, bone, flesh, and heart etc. It brings life to all parts of the body. Now, you must believe in Jesus so that it is no longer a matter of question with you whether you will retain Him or not, for if you have inwardly received Him, you cannot lose Him. Oh that blessed *"Quis separabit"*—*"Who shall separate us from the love of God . . . which is in Christ Jesus our Lord?"* [Romans 8:35, 39]. It is difficult to deprive a person of facts he has learned in childhood for they are remembered even to old age.

THE ETERNAL WORD

No one can compel someone to forget, yet without such compulsion the memory might relax its hold through lapse of years—the mind might part with that which it has received, but no known power can take away from a man that which he has eaten and assimilated! A person may very readily pick my pocket of my wallet, but what I ate yesterday he cannot steal! That is mine—it is joined to me and has built me up. I do not know what portion of my flesh comes of my morning meal, or of my midday repast, but there it is and there it must be. It has entered into me and never can be taken away from me. So when the soul takes in Christ's Word with that simple childlike faith which is the mouth, the truth goes into the soul and is meditated on, trusted in, delighted in, and becomes part and parcel of the inner consciousness and of the new nature of the man. Therefore, it would be utterly impossible to tear away that truth from him!

Pound a true Christian in a mortar and every single atom would say, "I belong to Christ." Grind him finer than the smallest dust of the threshing floor and every minute particle would still say, *"Christ is in me."* [See Colossians 1:27.] When Christ enters man, He permeates his nature, becomes his very life and now the man says, *"I live, yet not I, but Christ lives in me"* [Galatians 2:20]. Now is the text fulfilled in us, *"For ye are dead, and your life is hid with Christ in God"* [Colossians 3:3]. "When Christ, who is our life, shall appear, then shall ye also appear with Him in

Glory" [Colossians 3:4]. *"Abide in me . . ."* said our Lord and He gave His own promise to be with us for ever. [John 15:4]. This is the wondrous result of spiritually eating and drinking in Christ Jesus—this we must do! *"Then Jesus said unto them, Verily, verily, I say unto you, Except ye eat the flesh of the Son of man, and drink his blood, ye have no life in you. Whoso eateth my flesh, and drinketh my blood, hath eternal life; and I will raise him up at the last day. For my flesh is meat indeed, and my blood is drink indeed.* [John 6:53-55]

Beloved, I have thus explained the matter as well as I can, but as old Rollock[119] says, "The only way to understand feeding upon Christ is to feed upon Christ." This is a practical, personal, experimental business. In learning certain acts you must become a practical scholar, the master cannot teach by merely setting the copy—the scholar must imitate it line by line with his own hand—here I can teach little by words only, you must practice what is spoken. Now feed on the Lord Jesus! Let each one of you do it. I know what some will do—they will not feed on Christ, but they will pick over the heavenly bread like dainty folks who have no stomach for their meat. This bit of Christ they would have, but the other does not suit their taste—Justification by Faith they would have, but not Sanctification—they do not like that.

You and I must have *ALL* of Christ—we must have every part of His teaching, character, work, offices. We must receive Him into ourselves without division, rejoicing to take Him just as He is. We must especially receive the spirit of Christ, for, *". . . if any man have not the spirit of Christ, he is none of his"* [Romans 8:9]. We must partake of the loving spirit, the self-denying spirit, the generous spirit which lives not

---

119. Robert Rollock, 1849, English clergyman, and author of biblical commentaries, etc.

within itself, but goes forth in forgiveness of injuries and in seeking to benefit all mankind. We must have Jesus *in us,* delighting to take *in all* of Him, for He says farther on in this very chapter, *"He that eateth me"*—that is even more comprehensive than His, *"flesh and His blood"*—*". . . He that eateth me, even he shall live by me"* [John 6:57]. The entirety of Christ must be taken into the soul to build up the inner man.

II. What Is Involved in This

Now here we will take you back to the context. Notice first that there is for this eating the flesh and drinking the blood of Christ an essential necessity that he who has not so eaten and drank has no spiritual life at all. It is a strong word, *"Except you eat the flesh of the Son of Man and drink His blood, you have no life in you."* He does not mean that they have no natural life—He is speaking about spiritual things.

Some that are as foolish as Judaizers in the matter of sticking to the letter tell us that this means existence and that no man's eternal existence is certain except that of a believer in Christ. That dogma is certainly not taught here. Our Lord is not speaking of existence—He is speaking of a far higher thing than existence, namely, life. Have you ever learned the difference between death and non-existence and between life and existence? If you have not, you are babes in understanding and you will often be blundering and losing your way in the midst of texts of Scripture. A man may exist in everlasting death, as, alas, all who die unbelievers must do. But blessed is he who lives! Blessed is he who shall live for ever! Let me repeat the word, "lives"—I did not say "exists."

Living in Christ

What a glorious thing living in Christ is! Yet, if I had to

explain what that life is to you, I might find it far easier by
some action of my own to show that I lived than to tell you
exactly what that life is. He, however, who eats Christ has
life. He who has not done so has not life. Do you understand
this—that unless you have received Christ by faith into
your souls you have no life? You can work, you can walk,
you can speak—you have all sorts of natural life—but you
do not have life everlasting of which Jesus speaks! The life
of God is not in you! You are dead and what a frightful
condition that is—and to what greater horror does it lead!
For wherever there is death, the dead thing will go a stage
farther on. And what is that stage? Corruption!

CORRUPTION

Leave a corpse alone long enough and it will corrupt. Flesh
corrupts necessarily. There are already signs of corruption
about every ungodly man—outward sin and especially the
inward sin of rejecting Christ are grievous corruptions. Their
worm has begun to devour and that worm never dies. Then
will be reached another stage, for corruption must be cast
into the fire. For utter rottenness, the end must be burning!
O Sinner, your fire has begun to burn—the fire that will never
be quenched—for sin is the kindling of hell! It is an awful
thing to abide in death and yet he that believes not on Christ
is condemned already, because he has not believed on the Son
of God! It is enough to make you spring from your seats.
Alas, O you that are unbelievers, to think that you are not
waiting to be tried—you are condemned already! This is not
a state of probation, as I often hear it said. Your probation
is past! You are condemned already because you have not
believed on the Son of God—and death is now upon you.
The sentence has already begun to take effect and it will go
on to the consummation of corruption until, at last, the Lord

shall say, ". . . *bury my dead out of my sight.*" [See Genesis 23:4.] and you must be driven from the presence of the Lord and from the glory of His power. There is no life in you unless you have received Christ! Will you think about this, you thinkers? Only think of your being dead! Will you think of this, you ceremonialists to whom the outward Baptism and the outward Lord's Supper and the church attendance and the chapel going are everything? Unless you have fed on Christ there is no life in you!

Next comes the further truth of God, namely, that all who have received Jesus Christ as their meat and drink have eternal life. "*Whoso eateth my flesh and drinketh my blood, hath eternal life*" [John 6:54]. I do not know how our brethren who doubt the final perseverance of the saints manage to escape from the plain teaching of the text. There are always ways of getting over everything—you can drive a coach and six, they say, through any form of human language. But it does seem to me that if I have eternal life I must eternally live and cannot possibly die! If I have eternal life—if words mean anything—I am an eternally saved man! If I have received Jesus Christ into my soul, I have the life in me which will no more die than the life of God, for God's own life is eternal life and if I have received such life as His, how can I perish?

I shall not be slain by sin—the life in me cannot sin because it is born of God! The life in me will throw off the darts of temptation if it is eternal life. There remains nothing for it but to shake off the death which often surrounds it by reason of the old man and to mount up like a bird set free from its cage, singing because of its escape, singing in the joy of life and winging its happy way upward to the throne of God! Rejoice then, dear friends, for if you have received Christ, you have eternal life in actual possession at this moment! "Sometimes I don't feel it," you say. Do not try to live by feeling! It is the most uncertain thing in the world.

You might as well try to live by the barometer. Feeling goes up and down, up and down and changes more often than the moon. It is hard, uncomfortable living. Live by faith, for it is written, *"the just shall live by faith"* [Habakkuk 2:4]. Your life is a life of trust. Keep to it.

"Ah, but I see so much about me that grieves me." Thank God it grieves you! If you see sin and it does not grieve you, it is a token of death! But if it grieves you, there is life in you, no matter how much death surrounds it. You may have seen a spark in the midst of a heap of autumn leaves which are all damp and will not burn, but only smolder and smoke. Yet that spark continues to live and the very smoke from the heap proves it is so. There is One who will not quench the smoking flax but will fan it until it rises to a flame, and then it will devour the leaves which covered it and dry up the dampness which sought to destroy it! [See Matthew 12:20.]

Furthermore, if you believe in Jesus and have received Him, you have gathered a life in which Christ gives us the victory, even through His name—life which will rise and rise and rise and conquer all sin. The Believer's inner life must come to absolute perfection and tread every sin beneath its feet. This is very different from the doctrine that a man who is a child of God may sin as he pleases and yet be saved! That doctrine is of the devil! But this is quite another doctrine and ministers to holiness. The quickened man will not willingly and habitually sin, for His Seed remains in him and he cannot sin because he is born of God. The tone and tenor and bearing of his life will be towards holiness and not towards sin—*and the Lord who is able to keep him from falling will preserve him to His eternal kingdom and glory* and *He that has begun a good work in him will perfect it unto the day of Christ.* [See Jude 1:24 and Philippians 1:6.]

Our Lord, having thus given us the negative and the positive in our text, tells us that His flesh and blood, or himself, received into the soul are most efficient nourishment—in it is satisfaction. *"My flesh is meat indeed."* The Greek word is "truly," or, some say, "true meat." Now that which we eat for the body is not true meat. As George Herbert[120] says, "When you are at your meat, eat a bit and then say, 'Earth to earth I commit.'" It is a deadly business. It is burying earth in earth and that living grave of earth will be buried in earth, by-and-by. The eating of material meat is the poor building up of a fabric that must ultimately crumble into nothingness. The meat we eat has all the elements of dissolution about it before we receive it and it only feeds for a short time and, therefore, it is not meat, indeed.

In the matter of mental food, bread can never satisfy the mind. There is nothing in the world that can fill a soul to the fullest, except Jesus. Perhaps I may be addressing some thinker who has been trying to satisfy his soul by sniffing up the east wind of speculative philosophy. Ah, well, if you swallow a dose of Kant[121], or Hegel[122], Schleiermacher[123], or any one of those gentlemen—if you do not feel as if you had been eating bubbles and bladders, your mental constitution and mine greatly differ! There is nothing in them but gas, or a less substantial vapor. Why, a man may take down their books—a whole dozen of them—and devour their contents and then say, "What is it? Is it not much ado about nothing? These thoughts are dreams, vacuums, and airy nothings!" All the philosophies that ever were invented could not satisfy a soul!

The worst of it is that many do not want to be satisfied. "We," they say, "would sooner be seekers after truth than finders of it." They differ somewhat from men of practical

---

120. English poet, orator, and priest—1593-1633.
121. Immanuel Kant, German philosopher.
122. Georg Wilhelm Friedrich Hegel, German philosopher.
123. Friedrich Schleiermacher, German theologian and philosopher.

common sense who, ordinarily, would rather have money than earn it and would rather eat their dinners than hunt for them. Still, that is their way and if they like it, I suppose they must have it. Every creature after its own order! But if you want to be fed, dear friends, depend upon it, nothing will feed you but Christ! There was a man of great appetite who lived many years ago and he began to feast ravenously. He drank copiously, so much that I may say of him that he drank up Jordan at a draught and he was a ravenous eater, so much so that if you heard the story of what was brought to his table, you would be like the Queen of Sheba, utterly astonished, and say that the half was not told you!

His name was Solomon and he fed his soul with all the arts and sciences and with all the poetries and luxuries of the age. He did not refrain from laughter and wantonness. There was not a cup he did not drain, or a dainty from any land, or a fruit from any tree of which he did not eat. Yet, when he rose up from that abundant banquet, all he had to say was, *"Vanity of vanities; all is vanity!"* [See Ecclesiastes 1:2.] I have seen a poor soul feed on Christ in a very humble cottage, upon a bed in a little room where she has lain alone almost all day and all night long, year after year, with many aches and pains and scarcely able to lift her hand to her head—with little but dry bread and a cup of water. Yet, I have seen in that bedridden woman's pain-worn face a fullness of satisfaction! I have heard her speak like one that had not a wish ungratified, nor a grief worth mentioning. I have beheld her when, in her sufferings she could scarcely speak, and yet her every word was essential poetry when she spoke of Him, her best Beloved, who had filled her soul even to overflowing!

There is no food indeed, no drink indeed, for soul and spirit, but that which you find in the Incarnate God and in the sacrifice of Christ! O you, who are hungry, come here and eat that which is good and let your soul delight itself in fatness! O you who are thirsty, come here, for behold the waters are flowing freely and the wines on the lees are ready for you in Christ Jesus! That is what is involved in feeding upon Jesus! There is satisfaction in Him!

INDWELLING

There is involved one other matter, namely, indwelling. I will mention the same Scripture again. The Lord Jesus says, *"He that eats my flesh and drinks my blood, dwells in me and I in him."* When you have eaten bread, it dwells in you and you in it—it goes into you and it is in you—it becomes part of you and you live by it and in its strength. It is a part of the fabric in which you dwell. Even so, he that believes in Christ lives in Christ. He does not merely go to Christ, but he enters into Christ. I delight to remember that I am not merely under the shadow of my Lord, but, as David in the caverns of Engedi, my soul hides herself right away in Jesus. We dwell in Him and are at home!

Moreover, He enters into us by our feeding upon Him so that He becomes our life, the spring of our being, the object of our desire, the motivating force of our service! We are woven together—Christ warp and ourselves woof—woven together in a living loom and so conjoined that it were hard to tell where He ends who has no end and where we begin who are lost in Him! We are less than the least of all saints and yet members of His body who is Lord of All! We must leave the mystery remarking that if we have fed on Christ for ourselves, we have proof of what good meat it is we have fed on and we shall always pray, *"Lord, evermore give us this bread"* [John 6:34].

III. What Reflections
Naturally Out of it

Let's consider these reflections. I will simply throw them out for you to turn over in your mind for yourselves. They occurred to me when I was hearing a Brother preach on a kindred subject and they took hold of my soul! May they prove useful to you.

First Reflection

If I have a life that feeds on Christ, what a wonderful life it must be. My bodily life is wonderful, yet it only feeds on the fruits of the earth. My mental life is a marvel, but I know that I can build it up with literature and thought. Above all these I have a life which cannot feed on anything but the flesh and blood of the Son of God! What a life that must be!

What a wonderful being a man is when God is in him! I almost reverence the least of the saints when I think of this, for he bears about with him not a Kohinoor[124], but a gem of life, compared with which the queenly diamond pales into a glittering vanity! O Love Divine, do you tabernacle in the sons of men? I have been speaking of mysteries, but I ask you to explain which is the greater mystery, the Incarnation of God in Christ or the indwelling of the Holy Spirit in Believers? They are two wondrous gifts of Deity which can only be likened to each other, being each one without parallel. The spiritual life given to the regenerate must be a life of inconceivable excellence and heavenliness since it can only feed on Christ himself.

Second Reflection

The next thought is, if we have the life that feeds on such meat as this, how strong it must be. They say of such-and-

---

124. Diamond

such men that they may well be strong, seeing what good food they have. Yes, but see what food we have—how strong we must be! Do we know our own strength? I do not mean our natural strength, for that is weakness, but I mean the strength which lies in the new Nature when it has fed on Christ! O Brothers and Sisters, we are strong to do! We are strong to be! We are strong to suffer! And to take an easy illustration of this—the one that occurs to me first—look at how the saints have suffered. Take down *Foxe's Book of Martyrs*. Read of Marcus, Bishop of Arethusa[125], stung to death by wasps without a sigh!

Think of Blandina[126] tossed on the horns of bulls, exposed in a red-hot iron chair and yet never flinching! Give up Christ? They never dreamed of such a thing! Think of Lawrence[127] on the gridiron and other innumerable heroes who were made strong because Christ was in them! Yes, and turn to humble men and women in Smithfield[128] who could clap their hands while every finger burned like a candle and could shout, "None but Christ! None but Christ!" Why, because they fed on the flesh and blood of Christ and that made them mighty! They were tortured on the rack like Anne Askew[129] and yet they scorned to yield. Brave woman! The priests and the friars could not vanquish her! Neither could all the Bishop Bonners in the world burn Christ out of poor Tomkins[130]! When Bonner held the poor man's finger over the candle and said, "How will you like that in every single limb of your body?" Tomkins smiled at the bishop and said that he forgave him the cruelty that he

---

125. Christian Martyr
126. Christian Martyr
127. Martyr
128. Martyrdom of Christians
129. Christian Martyr
130. Martyred in 1555.

was doing him. Christ in a man makes him a partaker of Divine strength.

Do you not think, my Brothers and Sisters, that as you are not called to suffer, or that you ought to lay out your strength in the line of doing, giving, self-denial and serving Christ by holy living? Certainly you should try to do so and your strength will be found equal to it! You do not know how strong you are, but Paul shall tell you—*"I can do all things through Christ which strengtheneth me"* [Philippians 4:13].Well may you do all things if you have fed on Him who is All and in all!

Third Reflection

If we have a life that feeds on Him, then it is immortal. We have a text to prove that and we have given it to you already—"He that believes on Him has everlasting life." When a man has nothing but bad food, you do not wonder why he dies. It is easy to understand why millions died in India and China when you consider how little nourishment they had during the famine. But if you and I eat Christ, eat the Incarnate God and drink His blood, how can we die? We cannot, man cannot be killed even with only a particle of Christ in him? The devil cannot do it—he knows his Master! And what does Christ say? *"I give unto my sheep eternal life and they shall never perish, neither shall any man pluck them out of my hand"* [John 10:28].

Oh, blessed Truth of God! We live, not only because our life is itself eternal, but because it feeds on eternal meat! We keep on receiving Christ day by day, for we live upon Him. Eating is not a work that we finished 25 years ago, but we continue to feed upon Jesus and, therefore, we live. Feeding upon Christ does not mean being converted and then saying, "I am safe and have no more need to care." Ah, no! It means beginning to receive Him in conversion and continuing to feed upon Him forevermore! And they who do this may be sure that their life is immortal!

Fourth Reflection

The next thought that struck me was this—how well that life develops in us because we feed on Christ. I do not quite see in myself and, I may say that I do not see in some Believers, the full result I would like to see yet, but we are still developing.

What about this man, has he been eating the Divine food of Christ? Listen to what he says, "My leanness, my leanness, woe unto me!" He is doing Christ's work spasmodically, feebly, sleepily. He does his work without joy, and is soon weary. Is this all he is going to do? Is this all he is going to be? Oh no, Brothers and Sisters, ". . . *It doth not yet appear what we shall be: . . .*" [1 John 3:2]. We shall grow! We shall grow! When I hear a man talk about being perfect in the flesh, I hope for the best and trust that he is not willfully lying. At any rate, I do not believe him! I would like to see his perfection rather than to hear him talk about it! I have generally found that when a cart needs a bell, it is a dust cart. I never knew the people of the Bank of England to ring a bell when they were going through the streets with bullion and I do not think it is likely that a man who has much grace will boast of it!

However, I do believe that we can be developed into something very wonderful. A man may grow in grace and in the knowledge of the Lord until his conversation is in Heaven and he becomes wholly consecrated to the Lord—hating sin and living like Enoch who walked with God. There have been such men and there are such men and women still among us whose lives glow with the light of God—why should not we be like they are? They are stars in God's firmament and they shine in the Glory of the Most High! The Lord grant us that feeding on the Divine Christ we may develop until the image of Christ Jesus is perfected in us!

FIFTH REFLECTION

And, lastly dear friends, he who feeds on Christ keeps blessed company! *"He that eateth my flesh and drinketh my blood, dwells in me,"* says Christ, *"and I in him"* [John 6:56]. What heavenly company this is! He goes home at night to his poor family, and perhaps there is nothing great about his house that you can see—but if your eyes are opened you will see that it is a king's palace. If you are one of the Lord's and can step inside, you will see that He has come *"To the general assembly and church of the firstborn, which are written in heaven and to God the Judge of all, and unto the spirits of just men made perfect,"* [Hebrews 12:23], because he that has Christ in him has Heaven around him!

All good things are attracted to the one who has Christ in him. Put down a little honey and see how wasps and flies and bees come all around it! What is the sweetest honey in the universe? It is Christ—and if you have Christ in you, *His name is as ointment poured forth, therefore do the virgins love Him and they will come where He is.* [See Song of Solomon 1:3.] I will tell you—Christ is never without God and he that has Christ has the company of the Father! And Christ is never without the Spirit of God, for the Spirit of God is upon Him and he that has Christ is never without the Spirit! What Divine society this is! Our Lord Jesus is never unattended by a retinue of sublime intelligences and so if Christ is in you, *"He will give His angels charge over you to keep you in all your ways! They shall bear you up in their hands lest you dash your foot against a stone"* [Psalm 91:11-12].

O child of God, you are a prince of the blood royal of Heaven! You are a peer of God's Kingdom, and you are more nearly related to the King of kings than the peers of the realm can be to the Queen, for are you not married to the Prince Imperial? Is He not coming to receive you to himself, that where He is, you may be, also? [See John 17:24.]. If you are feeding on Him, your union with Him is complete! If He is your food; if He is your raiment; if He is your dwelling place; if He is your All in All, I think I may compare you to that angel of whom Milton[131] sang, even Uriel[132], who dwelt in the center of the sun! It is there we live—in the very substance and essence of all things and all things move around us like satellites around a central globe, *for we are a chosen generation, a royal priesthood, a peculiar people* inasmuch as we have fed on Christ—and Christ dwells in us and we in Him! [See 1 Peter 2:9.]

THE UNCONVERTED

I have not said anything to the unconverted and yet I have meant it all for them. When you spread a dainty feast, in practicality, you are inviting the family to come and dine. It is the very best way of enticing them. If they are hungry, the foods on the table will make their mouths water and they will long to partake. Oh, my Hearers, whoever you may be, if your mouths water after Christ, come and have Him for He is free to every soul that hungers and thirsts after Him! May the Lord give Him to you at once, for Jesus' sake. Amen.

A Letter from Mr. Spurgeon to the Congregation at the Metropolitan Tabernacle

---

131. John Milton's *Paradise Lost.*
132. One of the four angels mentioned in the Talmud.

Beloved Friends. By the time that this note is printed, the Special Services at the Tabernacle will be drawing to a close and it will be good to harrow in the seed with renewed supplication. Shall so much effort be in vain? It cannot be and yet everything depends upon the mighty working of the Spirit of God, and therefore, we must seek His face if we would see large results! I suggest that every sermon reader should spend a special time in prayer, next Lord's Day, in pleading for the revival of Evangelical religion.

The Times pronounced the funeral oration of the Evangelical party, but it is not dead, even, within the Established Church and certainly not among Dissenters! Let us, however, pray that it may exhibit more vigorous life. There is need of such supplication, but it must be presented in faith and with holy importunity. So let it be. For myself, one word only. I am recovering and rest is restoring mind and heart. Pray for me.

Yours to serve always,
C H. Spurgeon, Mentone,
February 20, 1879.

CHAPTER 14
DEPTHS AND HEIGHTS INTENDED FOR READING

A SERMON
On Lord's-Day, August 13th, 1899
Delivered by
REVEREND CHARLES H. SPURGEON,
at The Metropolitan Tabernacle, Newington, London,
England, on Lord's-Day Evening, May 21st, 1882.

*"God, who at sundry times and in divers manners spake
in time past unto the fathers by the prophets Hath in
these last days spoken unto us by his Son, whom he hath
appointed heir of all things, by whom also he made the
worlds Who being the brightness of his glory, and the
express image of his person, and upholding all things by
the word of his power, when he had by himself purged
our sins, sat down on the right hand of the
Majesty on high."—Hebrews 1:1-3*

I HAVE NOTHING TO DO TONIGHT but to preach
Jesus Christ. This was the old subject of the first
Christian ministers: ". . . *Daily in the temple, and
in every house, they ceased not to teach and preach Jesus
Christ*" [Acts 5:42]. When Philip went down to the city
of Samaria, he *"preached Christ unto them"* [Acts 8:5].
When he sat with the Ethiopian eunuch in his chariot, he
"preached unto him Jesus" [Acts 8:35]. As soon as Paul was
converted, *"straightway he preached Christ in the synagogues"*
[Acts 9:20].

For once, we count the venerableness of our subject well worthy of mentioning. We shall not be ashamed to preach what the apostles preached, and what martyrs and confessors preached. We hope to proclaim this glorious gospel of the blessed God as long as we live; and we hope that, when this generation of preachers shall have passed away, unless the Lord shall come, there will be ever found a succession of men who will determine to preach nothing *"save Jesus Christ and Him crucified"* [1 Corinthians 2:2].

This is the subject that men need to hear more than all other needs. They may have cravings after other things, but nothing can satisfy the deep and real need of their nature except Jesus Christ and salvation by His precious blood. *He is the Bread of life which came down from heaven; he is the Water of life whereof, if a man drink, he shall never thirst again.* [See John 6:35.]

Hence, it behooves us to be often dwelling upon this theme, for it is most necessary to the sons of men. This is the subject that God the Holy Ghost delights to bless. All things being equal, I am sure that He honors preaching in proportion to the savor of Christ that is in it. I may preach a great deal about the Church, but the Holy Spirit does not take of the things of Christ to glorify the Church. I may preach doctrine or practice apart from Christ;—that would be giving the husk without the kernel;—but where Jesus Christ sweetens all, and savors all, there will the Holy Spirit delight to rest upon the ministry, and make it quick and, powerful to the conversion of men.

And I am sure, dear friends, that the preaching of Christ is ever sweet in the ears of His own people. *"Because of the savor of thy good ointments thy name is as ointment poured forth, therefore do the virgins love thee"* [Song of Solomon 1:3]. And this theme is most pleasing to God the Father, who loves to hear His Son extolled and exalted. He delights in

His Son, and those that delight in Him are friends of God. When Jesus Christ is lifted up, it is as God the Father would have it, it is as the Holy Ghost would have it; and, where this is the case, we may expect to have seals to our ministry, and souls for our hire.

I want, at this time, to let Jesus Christ speak for himself. I cannot speak for Him as well as He can speak for himself. Shall I hold my candle to the sun, as if it needed it in order to reveal its light? No, certainly not; and, therefore, I shall, with studied plainness, try to set the text itself before you, and to speak of it not so much that you may remember what I have said of it as well as you remember the subject itself. My theme is to be the Savior, the only Savior,—the Savior who must save you, or else you must perish, *"for there is none other name under heaven given among men, whereby we must be saved"* [Acts 4:12]. I am about to speak of Him, and I think that all who are aware of the necessity of being saved will only want to hear about Him, and to know how they may get to Him, and how He may be made their Savior; and if they can be told this, they will be only too glad to listen.

First, I shall speak of *who the Savior is.* Let me read the text to you again: *"His Son,"*—God's Son,—*"whom he hath appointed heir of all things, by whom also he made the worlds; who being the brightness of his glory, and the express image of his person, and upholding all things by the word of his power."* That is who Jesus is.

Second, I shall speak of *what Jesus did:* *"when he had by himself purged our sins"* [Hebrews 1:3b].

Third, I want to tell you *what He enjoys.* After He had finished His great work of salvation, He *"sat down on the right hand of the Majesty on high"* [Hebrews 1:3c].

1. WHO JESUS IS

It is not possible for any language to fully express who Jesus is; yet, by the Holy Spirit's gracious teaching, I must tell you what I know of Him.

First and most importantly of all, *Jesus is God's own Son.* What do I know about that wondrous truth? If I was to try to explain it, and to talk about the eternal filiations[133], I should but conduct you where I would soon be entirely out of my depth, and very likely I would drown all that I could tell you in floods of words. Deity is not to be explained, but to be adored; and the Sonship of Christ is to be accepted as a truth of revelation, to be apprehended by faith, though it cannot be comprehended by the understanding. There have been many attempts made by the fathers of the Church to explain the relationship between the two Divine Persons, the Father and the Son; but the explanations would have been better never given, for the figures used are liable to lead into mistake. Suffice it for us to say that, in the most appropriate language of the Nicene Creed, Christ is "God of God, Light of Light, and very God of very God." He is co-equal with the Father; though how that is, we know not. He stands in the nearest possible relationship to the Father,—a relationship of intense love and delight, so that the Father says of Him, *"This is my beloved Son"* [Matthew 3:17]. Yes, He is one with the Father, so that there is no separating them, as He himself said, in reply to Philip's request, *"Show us the Father,"* [John 14:8]. *"Believe me that I am in the Father, and the Father in me"* [John 14:10].

Let me just pause here, and say to everyone who is seeking salvation,—what a comfort it should be to you that He, who is come to save men, is Divine! Therefore, nothing can be impossible to Him. No, I do not say merely that

---

133. lineages

He is Divine; I will go further, and say that He is the Deity itself; Christ Jesus is God, and being God, there can be no impossibilities or even difficulties with Him. He is able to save you, whoever you may be. Though you have gone to the very verge of eternal ruin, you cannot have gone beyond the range of omnipotence; and omnipotence is inherent in the Godhead. O dear friends, do rejoice in this wondrous truth, He that was a babe at Bethlehem, was God incarnate! Being weary, He that sat on the well at Sychar was God incarnate. He that had not where to lay His head was God incarnate. And it is He who has undertaken the stupendous labor of the salvation of men; and, therefore, men may hope and trust in Him. We need not wonder that, when angels heard of Christ's coming to Earth, they sang, *"Glory to God in the highest, and on earth peace, good will toward men,"* [Luke 2:14], for God had taken upon himself human flesh that He might save the sons of men. So, the first words in our text—"His Son"—are full of good cheer.

Now notice next that Jesus Christ is the *"Heir of all things."* Of which nature of Christ does the apostle speak in this sentence, *"whom he hath appointed heir of all things"?* I do not think that Paul is separating the two natures here by speaking with absolute reference to either one or the other; but he speaks of the person of Christ, and in that person there is God, and in that same person there is most surely and most truly man. But we must take this description of Jesus Christ as appointed *"Heir of all things"* in His person as man, and as God and man combined; for, as God alone, Christ is necessarily *"Heir of all things"* without any appointment; but in His complex person as God and man conjoined, the Father has appointed Him to be *"Heir of all things."*

Now this means that Christ possesses all things as an heir possesses his inheritance. Christ is Lord of all things and as an heir becomes lord and ruler among his brethren. This appointment is to be fully carried into effect by-and-by; for, *"now we see not yet all things put under him"* [Hebrews 2:8]. Christ is Lord of all the angels; not a seraph spreads his wing except at the bidding of the *"Heir of all things."* There are no bright spirits, unknown to us, that are beyond the control of the God-man, Christ Jesus; and the fallen angels, too, are obliged to bow before His omnipotence. As for all things here below, material substances, men regenerate or unregenerate, God has given Him power over all flesh that He should give eternal life to as many as His Father has given Him. He has put all things under His feet, *"and the government shall be upon his shoulder"* [Isaiah 9:6].

He is Heir, or Master, and Possessor of all things;—let me say, of all sorts of blessings, and all forms of grace, for *"it pleased the Father that in him should all fullness dwell;"* [Colossians 1:19], and as surely as time revolves, and you mark the fleeting minutes upon the dial's face, the hour is coming when Christ shall be universally acknowledged as King of kings and Lord of lords. Even now I seem to hear the shouts go up from every part of the habitable globe, and from all Heaven and all space, *"Alleluia! For the Lord God, omnipotent reigneth"* [Revelation 19:6]. All must willingly, or else unwillingly, submit to His way, for His *"Father hath appointed him Heir of all things."*

To my mind, this is another wondrous encouragement to anyone who is seeking salvation. Christ has everything in His hand that is needed in order to save you, poor sinner. Sometimes, when a physician has a sick man before him, for example suppose it is on board ship, he may have to say to him, "I think I could cure your disease if I could get such-and-such a medicine; but, unfortunately, that medicine is not on board this ship." Or the doctor might have to say to the sufferer, "I believe an operation would effect a cure, but I do not have the necessary instrument on board for that operation." Never will the great Physician of souls have to speak like that, for the Father has committed all things into His hand. Oh, brethren, have we not beheld Him as the glory of the Father, full of grace and truth? You great sinner, Christ is not lacking in power to save you; and if you come, and trust yourself in His hands, He will never have to search to find the balm for your wounds, or the ointments or liniments to bind up those putrefying sores of yours! No, He is *"Heir of all things."* So again I say, "Hallelujah!" as I preach Him to you as the blessed Savior of sinners, the Son of God, the "Heir of all things."

Notice, next, that *Jesus Christ is the Creator:* "by Him the worlds were made." However many worlds there are, we know not. It may be true that all those majestic orbs that stud the midnight sky are worlds filled with intelligent beings; it is much easier to believe that they are rather than they are not, for surely, God has not built all those magnificent mansions and left them untenanted. It would be irrational to conceive of those myriads of stupendous worlds; vastly bigger than this poor little speck called Earth in God's great universe were all left without inhabitants. But it matters not how many worlds there are; God made them all by Jesus Christ: *"All things were made by him; and without him was not any thing made that was made"* [John 1:3].

I see Him standing, as it were, at the anvil of omnipotence, hammering out the worlds that fly off like sparks on every side at each stroke of His majestic arm. It was Christ who was there,—*"the wisdom of God and the power of God"* [1 Corinthians 1:24] as Paul calls Him,—creating all things. I love to think that He who created all things is also our Savior, for then He can *"create in me a clean heart, and renew a right spirit within me"* [Psalm 51:10], and if I need a complete new creation—as I certainly do—He is equal to the task.

Man cannot create the tiniest midge that ever danced in the summer evening's ray; man cannot create even a single grain of dust; but Christ created all worlds, so He can make us new creatures by the wondrous power of His grace. O sinners, see what a mighty Savior has been provided for you, and never say that you cannot trust Him! I agree with good Mr. Hyatt[134] who, when he was asked on his death-bed, "Can you trust Christ with your soul?" answered, "If I had a million souls, I could trust them all with Him." And so may you; if you had as many souls as God has ever created, and if you had heaped upon you all the sins that men have ever committed, you might still trust in Him who is the Son of God, *whom he hath appointed Heir of all things, by whom also he made the worlds.*

Now go a little further and see that Christ is called: *the brightness of His Father's glory.* Shade your eyes, for you cannot look upon this wondrous sight without being dazzled by it. The Revised Version [*The Darby Translation of the Bible*] renders it, "the effulgence of his glory;" but I do not see much more in that expression than in the word "brightness." Some commentators say—and it is not an incorrect explanation, yet we must not push any explanation too far,—that, as light is to the sun, so is Jesus to the glory of God. He is the brightness of that glory; however, that does not mean there is no glory in God—it means when God the Ever-glorious is most glorious that greatest glory is also in Christ. Oh, this wondrous Word of God,—the very climax of the Godhead,—the gathering up of every blessed attribute in all its infinity of glory! You shall find all this in the person of the God-man, Christ Jesus. There is a whole sermon in those words, *the brightness of his glory;* but I cannot preach it tonight because I would not get through the rest of my text.

---

134. John Hyatt, English clergyman 1767-1826.

So let us pass on to the next clause: *"and the express image of his person."* I said, a few minutes ago, "Shade your eyes;" but I might now say, "Shut them," as I think of the excessive brilliance described by these words: *"the express image of his person."* Whatever God is, Christ is; the very likeness of God, the very Godhead of Godhead, the very Deity of Deity, is in Christ Jesus: *"the express image of his person."* Dr. John Owen[135], who loves to explain the spiritual meaning in the Epistle to the Hebrews by the types in the Old Testament, which is evidently what Paul was doing under the guidance of the Holy Spirit,—explains the brightness of the Father's glory by a reference to the Shekinah glory over the mercy seat. An extraordinary brightness is said to have shone from between the cherubim which was the only visible token of the presence of God there.

Now, however, Christ is God manifesting himself in His brightness. But, the high priests in the Old Testament wore a golden plate on their foreheads which was deeply engraved, in Hebrew letters, the inscription, "Holiness to [or of] Jehovah." Dr. Owen thinks there is a reference, in this "express image of his person,"—this cut-out inscription of God—to that which was on the forehead of the high priest that represented the glorious wholeness or holiness of Jehovah, which is His great glory. Well, whether the apostle referred to this or not, it is for you and me to take our shoes from our feet in the presence of Christ, *"the brightness of his Father's glory, and the express image of his person."* To me, these words are like the burning bush in which God dwelt, yet the bush was not consumed, they are all on fire; what more shall I say of them? [See Exodus 3: 2-6.].

Now, Christ being all this that Paul describes, who will dare to turn his back on Him? If He is the Shepherd who has

---

135. John Owen, English theologian, 1616-1683.

come to seek the lost sheep,—O poor lost sheep, will you not be found of Him? If this is God's Ambassador, who comes clothed in the crimson robe of His own blood, to redeem the sons of men, who will refuse the peace He brings?

Note once again what Christ is, as I mention the sixth point in the apostle's description: *"upholding all things by the word of his power."* Just think of it, this great world of ours is upheld by Christ's Word! If He did not speak it into continued existence it would go back into the nothingness from whence it sprang. There is not a being who exists who is independent of the Mediator, save only the ever-blessed Father and the Holy Spirit. *"By him all things consist,"* that is, continue to hold together. Just as these pillars uphold these galleries, or as the foundations uphold a house, so does Jesus Christ *"uphold all things by the word of his power."*

Only think of it; those innumerable worlds of light that make illimitable space to look as though it were sprinkled over with golden dust would all die out like so many expiring sparks, and cease to be if the Christ who died on Calvary did not will that they should continue to exist. I cannot bring out of my text all the wondrous truths that it contains, I only wish I could; but, surely, if Christ upholds all things, He can uphold me. If the Word of His power upholds Earth and Heaven, surely, that same Word can uphold you, poor trembling heart, if you will trust Him. There need be no fear about that matter; come and prove it for yourself. May His blessed Spirit enable you to do so even now!

Where there is so much more to say, I might well tarry, but I must hasten on to the next point.

2. WHAT JESUS DID

Follow me with all your ears and hearts while I speak

to you about He who is all that I have tried to describe and what He did.

First, *He effectually purged our sins: "when he had by himself purged our sins."* Listen to those wondrous words. There was never such a task as that since time began. The old fable speaks of the Augean stable, foul enough to have poisoned a nation, which Hercules cleansed; but our sins were fouler than that.[136] Dunghills are sweet compared with these abominations; what a degrading task it seems for Christ to undertake,—the purging of our sins! The sweepers of the streets, the scullions of the kitchen, the cleansers of the sewers, have honorable work compared with this of purging sin. Yet the holy Christ, incapable of sin, stooped to purge our sins. I want you to meditate upon that wondrous work; and to remember that He did it before He went back to Heaven. Is it not a wonderful thing that Christ purged our sins even before we had committed them? There they stood, before the sight of God, as already existent in all their hideousness; but Christ came, and purged them, surely this ought to make us sing the song of songs. Before I sinned, He purged my sins away; singular and strange as it is, yet it is so.

Then, further, the apostle says that *Christ purged our sins by himself;* that is, by offering himself as our Substitute. There was no purging away of sin possible, except by Christ bearing the burden of it, and He did bear it. He bore all that was due to guilty man on account of his violation of the Law of God, and God accepted His sacrifice as a full equivalent, and so He purged our sins. He did not come to do something by which our sins might be purged, *but He purged them effectually, actually, really, completely.* How did He do it? By His preaching? By His doctrine? By His Spirit? No "By himself." Oh, that is a blessed word! The Revised

---

136. Greek mythology.

Version has left it out, but the doctrine is taught in the Bible over and over again.

Who his own self bare our sins in his own body on the tree. [1 Peter 2:24]. By his own blood he entered in once into the holy place, having obtained eternal redemption for us. For if the blood of bulls and of goats, and the ashes of a heifer sprinkling the unclean, sanctifies to the purifying of the flesh: how much more shall the blood of Christ, who through the eternal Spirit offered himself without spot to God, purge your conscience from dead works to serve the living God? [Hebrews 9:12-14].

He gave himself for us; not only His blood, but all that constituted himself, His Godhead, and His manhood. All that He had, and all that He was, He gave as the ransom price for us; can any of you estimate the value of that price? The acts of one, Divine as He is, are Divine actions; and there is a weight and force about them that there could not be about the deeds of the best of men or even of all the holy angels: *"he by himself purged our sins."*

Now, let every believer who wants to see his sins stand on tiptoe and look up; will he see them there? No. If he looks down, will he see them there? No. If he looks around, will he see them there? No. If he looks within, will he see them there? No. Where shall he look then? Wherever he likes, for he will never see them again, according to the ancient promise.

In those days, and in that time, saith the Lord, the iniquity of Israel shall be sought for, and there shall be none; and the sins of Judah, and they shall not be found: for I will pardon them whom I reserve. [Jeremiah 50:20]

Shall I tell you where your sins are? Christ purged them, and God said, "I will cast all their sins behind my back." [See Isaiah 38:17.] Where is that? All things are before God. I do not know where behind God's back can be. It is nowhere, for God is everywhere present, seeing everything. So that is where my sins have gone; I speak with the utmost reverence when I say that they have gone where Jehovah himself can never see them. Christ has so purged them that they have ceased to be. The Messiah came to finish transgression and to make an end of sin—and He has done it.

O believer, if He has made an end of it, then there is an end to it, and what more can there be of it? Here is a blessed text for you; I love to meditate on it often when I am alone: *"As far as the east is from the west, so far hath he removed our transgressions from us"* [Psalm 103:12]. This He did on Calvary's Cross; there effectually, finally, totally, completely, eternally, He purged all His people from their sin by taking it upon himself, bearing all its dreadful consequences, canceling and blotting it out, casting it into the depths of the sea, and putting it away for ever: and all this He did "by himself" It was indeed amazing love that made Him stoop to this purgation, this expiation, this atonement for sin; but, because He was who and what He was, He did it thoroughly, perfectly. He said, *"It is finished,"* and I believe Him [John 19:30]. I do not—I cannot—for a moment admit that there is anything to be done by us to complete that work, or anything required of us to make the annihilation of our sins complete. Those for whom Christ died are cleansed from all their guilt and they may go their way in peace. He was made a curse for us, and there is nothing but blessing left for us to enjoy.

3. WHAT CHRIST NOW ENJOYS

"When he had by himself purged our sins, he sat down on the right hand of the majesty on high" [Hebrews 1:3]. Here again I shall have to say that I am quite out of my depth; I have waters to swim in, but I am not a good swimmer in such blessed deeps as these.

There is an allusion here, no doubt, to the high priest

who, on the great Day of Atonement, when the sacrifice had been offered, presents himself before God. Now Christ, our great High Priest, having, once for all, offered himself as the sacrifice for sin, has now gone into the most holy place, and there He sits on the right hand of the Majesty on high.

Notice, first, that *this implies rest*. When the high priest went within the veil, he did not sit down. He stood, with holy trembling, bearing the sacrificial blood, before the blazing mercy seat; but our Savior now sits at His Father's right hand. The high priest of old had not finished his work; the next year, another atoning sacrifice would be needed; but our Lord has completed His atonement, and now, *"there remaineth no more sacrifice for sin,"* for there remains no more sin to be purged [Hebrews 10:26].

"But this man, after he had offered one sacrifice for sins for ever, sat down on the right hand of God; from henceforth expecting till his enemies be made his footstool. For by one offering he hath perfected for ever them that are sanctified. [Hebrews 10:12-14]

There He sits, and I am sure He would not be sitting if He had not finished the salvation of His people. Isaiah had been inspired to record in Isaiah 62:1 what the Messiah would say long before He said it.

For Zion's sake will I not hold my peace, and for Jerusalem's sake I will not rest, until the righteousness thereof go forth as brightness, and the salvation thereof as a lamp that burneth.

But Christ is resting now; my eye, by faith, can see him sitting there, so I know that—

> Love's redeeming work is done;
> Fought the fight, the battle won.[137]

---

137. Hymn titled, "Christ the Lord Is Risen Today", written by Charles Wesley in 1739.

Notice, next, that *Christ sits in the place of honor:* "on the right hand of the Majesty on high." Of course, we are talking figuratively now, and you must not interpret this literally. Jesus sits on [or at] the right hand of His Father, and He dwells in the highest conceivable honor and dignity. All the angels worship Him, and all the blood-washed host adore Him day without night. The Father delights to honor Him.

The highest place that heaven affords Is his, is his by right, The King of kings, and Lord of lords, And heaven's eternal light.[138]

Not only does Jesus sit in the place of honor, but He *occupies the place of safety.* None can hurt Him now; none can stay His purposes, or defeat His will. He is at the powerful right hand of God. In Heaven above, and on the Earth beneath, and in the waters under the Earth, and on every star, He is supreme Lord and Master; and they that will not yield to Him *shall be broken with a rod of iron, He shall dash them in pieces like a potter's vessel.* [See Psalm 2:9.] So His cause is safe; His kingdom is secure, for He is at the right hand of power.

And, last of all, Christ at the right hand of God signifies *the eternal certainty of His reward.* It is not possible that He would be robbed of the purchase of His blood. I tremble when I hear some people talk about the disappointed Christ,— or about His having died at a peradventure, to accomplish He knew not what,—dying for something which the will of man might give Him if it would, but it might possibly be denied Him. I buy nothing on such terms as that; I expect to have what I purchase; and Christ will have what He bought with His own blood; especially as He lives again to claim His purchase. He shall never be a defeated and

---

138. Hymn titles, "The Head That Once Was Crowned" By Thorns, written by Thomas Kelly, 1769-1854.

disappointed Savior. He loved the church, and *"gave himself for it."* [See Ephesians 5:25.] He has redeemed His loved ones from among men; and He shall have all those whom He has purchased. *"He shall see of the travail of his soul, and shall be satisfied"* [Isaiah 53:11]. Therefore, let us again say, "Hallelujah!" and fall down and worship Him.

It does seem to me that there is no proof of men's natural blindness that is as conclusive as this—that men will not go and trust in Jesus. O sinners, if sin had left you sane in heart, you would come at once, and fall down at His feet! There is all power laid up in Jesus, and there is all the Father's love concentrated in Jesus; so come and trust Him. If you will but trust Him, you will prove that He has given himself for you. That simple trust is the secret mark that distinguishes His people from all others. *"My sheep hear my voice, and I know them, and they follow me"* [John 10:27]. To those who rejected him when He was upon the Earth, our Lord said, *"Ye believe not, because ye are not of my sheep, as I said unto you"* [John 10:26]. O poor souls, do you mean for ever to wear the damning mark of unbelief? If you die with that brand upon your soul, you will be lost for ever. Oh, may you instead have that blessed mark of faith which is the token of the Lord's people! May you even now hang out the scarlet line as Rahab hung it out of her window,—the scarlet line of confidence in the crimson blood of Jesus! And while Jericho falls,—while all the Earth shall crumble in one common ruin,—your house, though built upon the wall, shall stand securely, and not one who is within its shelter shall be touched by the devouring sword, for all who are in Christ are in everlasting safety. [See Joshua 2:1-24.] How can they be otherwise, since He has purged their sins? God give to every one of you to have a part and lot among this blessed company, for His dear name's sake! Amen.

CHAPTER 15
TRULY EATING THE FLESH OF JESUS

A SERMON
(No. 1288)

A Sermon Delivered on Lord's Day Morning, April 9, 1876

by

REVEREND CHARLES H. SPURGEON,

At The Metropolitan Tabernacle, Newington,
London, England

*"Then Jesus said unto them, Verily, verily, I say unto you,
Except you eat the flesh of the Son of Man and drink His
blood, you have no life in you. Whoever eats My flesh
and drinks My blood has eternal life, and I will raise him
up at the last day. For My flesh is meat, indeed, and My
blood is drink indeed. He that eats My flesh, and drinks
My blood, dwells in Me, and I in him."—John 6:53-56*

OUR LORD JESUS did not, in this passage, allude to
the Lord's Supper, as some, desiring to maintain
their sacramental superstitions, have dared to
affirm! I will not dwell upon the argument that there was
no Lord's Supper at the time to allude to, though there is
certainly some force in it, but I will rather remind you that
with such an interpretation this passage would not be true. It
must be confessed, even by the most ardent advocate of the
sacramental meaning, that the expressions used by our Lord
are not universally and, without exception, true if used in that
sense, for it is not true that those who have never eaten the
Lord's Supper have no life in them, since it is confessed on
all hands that hundreds and thousands of children dying in

childhood are, undoubtedly saved, and yet they have never eaten the flesh of Christ nor drank His blood, if the Lord's Supper is meant here.

There have also been many others in bygone times that, by their conduct, proved that the life of God was in their souls, and yet they were not able to eat bread at the sacramental table, because of sickness, banishment, imprisonment and other causes. Surely there are some others, though I would not excuse them, who have neglected to come to that blessed commemorative ordinance, and yet, nevertheless, for all that, they are truly children of God. Would the highest of high churchmen send every Quaker, however holy and devout, down to the bottomless pit? If this should refer to the Lord's Supper, then it is certain that the dying thief could not have entered Heaven, for he never sat down at the communion table, but was converted on the Cross—and without either Baptism or the Lord's Supper—went straight away with his Master into Paradise!

It can never be proved, indeed, is utterly false that no one has eternal life if he has not received the bread and wine of the communion table. But on the other hand, it is certainly equally untrue that whoever eats Christ's flesh has eternal life, if by that is meant everyone who partakes of the Eucharist, for there are unworthy receivers, not here and there, but to be found by the hundreds. Alas, there are apostates who leave the Lord's Table for the table of devils and who profane the holy name they once professed to love! There are also many who have received the sacramental bread and wine and yet live in sin—who increase their sin by daring to come to the table and who, alas, we fear, will die in their sins as many others have done.

Unregenerate persons are very apt to make much of the sacrament and nothing of Christ. They think a great deal of the bread and wine of the (so-called) "altar," but they have never known what it is to eat the flesh and drink the blood of Christ. These eat and drink unworthily—carnally eating bread, but not spiritually eating the Redeemer's flesh—to them the ordinance is a curse rather than a blessing. Our Lord did not refer to the feast of His supper, for the language will not bear such an interpretation. It is evident that the Jews misunderstood the Savior and thought that He referred to the literal eating of His flesh. It is no wonder that they strove among themselves over such a saying, for, understood literally, it is horrible and revolting to the last degree!

But far greater is the wonder that there are millions of people who accept so monstrous an error as actual truth and believe in literally feeding upon the body of the Lord Jesus! This is probably the highest point of profane absurdity to which superstition has yet reached—to believe that such an act of cannibalism as could be implied in the literal eating of the flesh of Christ could convey Grace to the person guilty of such a horror!

While we wonder that the Jews so misunderstood the Savior, we wonder a thousand times more that there should remain upon the face of the Earth men in their senses not yet committed to a lunatic asylum who endeavor to defend such a dreadful error from Holy Scripture and, instead of being staggered, as the Jews were, by so fearful a statement, actually consider it to be a vital doctrine of their faith—that they are literally to eat the flesh of Christ and to drink His blood!

Brothers and Sisters, if it were possible that our Lord required us to believe such a dogma, it would certainly need the most stupendous effort of credulity on the part of a reasonable man—and the laying aside of all the decencies of nature. In fact, it would appear to be necessary, before you could be a Christian, that you should altogether divest yourself of your reason and your humanity! It would be a gospel certainly more fitted for savages and madmen than for persons in the possession of their senses and in the least degree removed from absolute barbarism! I greatly question whether the creed of the king of Dahomey[139] contains a more unnatural doctrine.

We are not required, however, to believe anything so impossible, so degrading, so blasphemous, and so horrifying to all the decencies of life! No man ever did eat the flesh of Christ or drink His blood in a literal and corporeal sense. A deed so beastlike, no, so devilish, was never yet perpetrated, or could be. No, Brethren, the Jews were under an error—they made the mistake of taking literally what Christ meant spiritually. Judicially blinded as the result of unbelief, they stumbled at noonday as in the night and refused to see what was plainly set forth. The veil was on their hearts. Ah, how prone is man to pervert the Words of the Lord!

I believe that if Christ had meant this word literally, they would have spirited it away, but such is the perversity of the human mind, that when He intended it spiritually then straightway they interpreted it in a grossly carnal manner. Let us not fall into their error, but may Divine Grace lead us to see that our Lord's Words are spirit and life. Let us not be held in bondage by the letter which kills, but follow the spirit which quickens. The spiritual meaning is clear enough to spiritual men, for to them belong spiritual discernment. But as for the unregenerate, these things are spoken unto them in parables, that seeing they might not see, and perceiving they might not understand. [See Luke 8:10.]

Our first point will be what is meant by eating the flesh and drinking the blood of Christ?

And our second point of enquiry shall be what are the virtues of this act?

---

139. Dahomey was an African kingdom from the 1600's to the 1900's. It was a center of slave trade, etc.

1. What Is Meant by Eating the Flesh and Drinking the Blood of Christ?

First of all, it is a very beautiful and simple metaphor when understood to refer spiritually to the Person of our Lord. The act of eating and drinking is transferred from the body to the soul and the soul is represented as feeding—feeding upon Jesus as the Bread of Life. Eating is the taking into yourself of something which exists externally, which you receive into yourself and which becomes a part of yourself and helps to build you up and sustain you. That something supplies a great need of your nature and when you receive it, it nourishes your life. That is the essence of the metaphor and it well describes the act and the result of faith.

To eat the flesh and drink the blood of Christ, we must first believe in the reality of Christ—we must not regard Him as a myth, an imaginary personage, an invention of genius, or a conception of the Oriental mind, but we must believe that such a Person actually and in very deed lived and still lives. We must believe that He was God and yet condescended to be Incarnate on Earth and here lived, died, was buried and rose again. "Except a man eat My flesh and drink My blood." It is a mode of expressing the actual existence and true materialism of our Lord's body and the sureness and truthfulness of His existence in human nature. You cannot be saved unless you believe in a historical Christ, a real Person—

> "A Man there was, a real Man,
> Who once on Calvary died,
> And streams of blood and water ran
> Down from His wounded side."[140]

---

140. Poem by English clergyman, Joseph Hart.

That same actual Person has, in His own proper personality, ascended to the skies. He is now sitting at the right hand of the Father and is ordained to descend, before long, to be the Judge of the quick and the dead. We should not use the terms, flesh and blood, unless we meant to indicate an actual Person—such language could not describe the creation of a dream, a phantom, or a symbol. Before all things, if you want to be saved, you must believe in Jesus Christ, the Son of God, as having been really manifested in human nature among the sons of men. "The Word was made flesh and tabernacled among us," and the Apostles declare that they *"beheld His glory, the glory as of the only begotten of the Father, full of grace and truth"* [John 1:14].

We must believe not only in the reality of the Savior, but in the reality of His Incarnation, acknowledging that while He was divine, He was human. Also, that He did not assume human nature in outward appearance, as certain heretics have said, but that Jesus came in the flesh and, as such, was heard, seen, touched and handled. He was in an actual body, really nailed to a tree, and was really laid in the grave. Thomas did put his finger into the print of the nails and thrust his hand into His side. We must also believe that He did assuredly and in very deed rise again from the dead and that in His own real body, He ascended into Heaven. There must be no doubts about these foundational facts. If we would feed upon Christ He must be real to us, for a man does not eat and drink shadows and fancies.

We must also truly believe in the death of the Incarnate Son of God. The mention of His flesh as eaten, apart from His blood which is drunk, indicates death. The blood is in the flesh while there is life. His death is more than hinted at in the 51st verse of John 6, where our Lord says, *"And the bread that I will give him is My flesh, which I will give for the life of the world."* Brothers and Sisters, we must believe in our Lord's death as it accomplishes the expiation of sin, for faith feeds on His body as given for the life of the world.

There are some who profess to believe in Christ's life and they hold Him forth as a great example who will save us from selfishness and other evils if we follow Him. Such is not the teaching of the text—the blessing of eternal life is not promised for following Christ's example, but for eating and drinking His flesh and blood, or, in other words, taking Christ into oneself! And the promise is not made for receiving His example or His doctrine, but His Person, His flesh, His blood—His flesh and blood as separated and, therefore, himself as dead for us and made a sacrifice for us. Just as in the peace-offerings the offerer sat down and feasted with the priest upon the victim which he had presented. In the same way, Jesus Christ, our Passover, is sacrificed for us and we are to feed upon Him as the Lamb of God, receiving Him in His sacrificial and propitiatory Character, into our souls.

It is vain for us to hope for salvation apart from this! The Father sets Him forth as propitiation through faith in His blood. If we refuse Him in this Character, Christ has become of no use to us. Christ the Exemplar cannot save you if you reject Him as the Christ who bowed His head to death, even the death of the Cross, suffering in His people's place. Christ as a King cannot save you unless you believe in Christ as a victim. This is absolutely necessary to saving faith—unless you eat His flesh and drink His blood, that is, accept Him in His real personality, offered as a sacrifice for sin, you have no life in you!

This is what is to be believed. But in order to eat, a man not only believes that there is bread before him and accepts that bread as being proper food for his body, but the next thing he does is to appropriate it. This is a great part of the act of feeding upon Christ. As a man, in eating, takes the morsels to himself and says, "This is bread which I believe nourishes the body and it shall now nourish me, I take it to be my bread," this is the way we must do with Christ.

Dear Brothers and Sisters, we must say, "Jesus Christ is set forth as a propitiation for sin, and I accept Him as the propitiation for my sin. God gives Him to be the foundation upon which sinners' hopes are to be built. I take Him to be the foundation of my hopes. He has opened a fountain for sin and for uncleanness. I come to Him and desire to wash away my sin and my uncleanness in the fountain of His blood.

You cannot eat unless you make the food your own. In fact, nothing is more especially a man's own than what he has eaten—his possession of it cannot be denied, nor can it be taken away from him. So you must take Christ to be as much your own as the bread you eat or the water you drink—He must, beyond question, be yours personally and inwardly. Looking up to Him upon the Cross, you have to say, "Savior of sinners, those who trust in You are redeemed. I also trust You as my Savior and I am, therefore, assuredly redeemed by Your most precious blood." Eating lies, in part, in appropriating food and so, unless you appropriate the flesh and blood of Christ to be your own personal hope and confidence, you cannot be saved.

I have laid stress upon a personal appropriation, for each man eats for himself, not for anyone else. You cannot eat for anybody but yourself. And so, in taking Christ, you take Him for yourself. Faith is your own act and deed—nobody can believe for you, nor can your believing save someone else— each must believe for themselves. I say it with reverence— the Holy Spirit, himself, cannot believe for us, although He can, and does, lead us to believe. And, indeed, if the Divine Spirit did believe for us, we would not obtain the promise, since it is not made to proxy faith, but solely and alone to personal believing. We are not passive in believing—we must be active and perform the personal act of appropriating the

Lord Jesus to be our soul's meat and drink.

This believing in Jesus and appropriating Him go far to explain what is meant by eating His flesh and drinking His blood. Eating and drinking also consist principally in receiving. What a man eats and drinks, he appropriates to himself and that not by laying it on one side in a treasury or casket, but by receiving it into himself. You appropriate money and you put it in your pocket—you may lose it. You secure a piece of land and you put your hedge about it, but that hedge may be broken down. But when you receive, by eating and drinking, you have placed the good things where you will never be robbed of them! You have received them in the truest and surest sense, for you have real possession and enjoyment in your own person.

Now, to say, "Christ is mine," is a blessed thing. But to really take Christ into you by the act of faith is the vitality and the pleasure of faith! In eating and drinking, a man is not a producer, but a consumer—he is not a doer or a giver, for he simply takes in. If a queen should eat, if an empress should eat, she would become as completely a receiver as the pauper in the workhouse. Eating is an act of reception in every case. So it is with faith—you have not to do, to be, or to feel, but only to receive! The saving point is not a something which comes forth of you, but the reception of a something imparted to you. Faith is an act which the poorest sinner, the vilest sinner, the weakest sinner, the most condemned sinner may perform because it is not an act requiring power on his part, nor the going forth of anything from him, but simply the receiving into himself!

An empty vessel can receive and receive all the better because it is empty. Oh Soul, are you willing to receive Jesus Christ as the free gift of Divine mercy? Do you, this day, say, "I have so received Him"? Well then, you have eaten His flesh and drunk His blood! If you have received the Incarnate

God in your soul, so that you now trust in Him and in Him alone, then you have eaten His flesh and drunk His blood!

The process of eating involves another matter which I can hardly call part of it, but yet it is indissolubly connected with it, namely, that of assimilation. What is received, in eating, descends into the inward parts and is there digested and taken up into the body. Even so, faith takes up and absorbs into the man the heavenly Bread, Christ Crucified. *"The word preached,"* we read in one place, *"did not profit them, not being mixed with faith in them that heard it"* [Hebrews 4:2]. Now, in the original, there is the idea of food taken into the body, but never getting mixed with the gastric juices and, consequently, remaining undigested, unassimilated, unprofitable and even injurious. Faith is to the soul what the gastric juices are to the body—as soon as Christ is received into the man; faith begins to act upon Him—to extract nutriment from His Person, work and offices. And so Christ becomes taken up into the understanding and the heart, builds up the entire system of manhood and becomes part and parcel of the renewed man.

Just as bread, when it is eaten, becomes dissolved and absorbed and afterwards is turned into blood and flows through all the veins and goes to make up the body, even so is Christ the soul. He becomes our life and enters mysteriously into vital union with us. As the piece of bread that we ate yesterday could not now be taken away from us, because it is a part of ourselves, even so does Jesus become one with us. You ate the bread yesterday and whereabouts it is now no philosopher can tell. Part of it may have gone to form brain and other portions to make bone, sinew and muscle. But its substance is taken up into your substance, so that the bread dwells in you now and you in it, since it makes up your bodily house.

This is to feed upon Jesus Christ—to take Him in so

that your life is hid with Him, until you grow to be like He is—until your very life is Christ and the great fact that Jesus lived and died becomes the mightiest Truth of God under Heaven to your mind—swaying your whole soul, subduing it to itself and then elevating it to the highest degree.

"For the love of Christ constrains us; because we thus judge that if one died for all, then were all dead: and that He died for all, that they which live should not, from now on, live unto themselves, but unto Him which died for them, and rose again."
—[2 Corinthians 5:14-15]

Even as flowers drink in the sunlight until they are tinted with rainbow hues, so do we receive the Lord Jesus until we become comely with His comeliness and He lives, again, in us! This it is to eat His flesh and drink His blood.

But now I will make a series of remarks, somewhat out of order, with the view of setting forth this mysterious eating and drinking in a clearer manner. Observe that Christ is as necessary to the soul as bread is to the body. Meat and drink are absolutely requisite—and so you must have Christ, or you cannot live in the true sense of that word. Take away food from the body, it must die—deny Christ to a man and he is dead while he lives! There is in us a natural desire after meat and drink, an appetite which springs out of our necessity and reminds us of it—we must labor to feel just such an appetite after Christ! Your wisdom lies in your knowing that you must have Jesus to be your personal Savior and in acknowledging that you will perish if you do not receive Him! And it is well with you when this knowledge makes you crave and pine and pant for Him. Hunger after Him! Thirst after Him! Blessed are they that hunger and thirst after Him, for He will fill them.

Meat and drink really do satisfy. When a man gets bread

and water, having eaten enough, he has what his nature requires. The need is real and so is the supply. When you get Christ, your heart will obtain exactly what it needs. You do not fully know what the needs of your soul are, but rest assured that known or unknown, your necessities will all be supplied in the Person of Jesus Christ. And if you receive Him, as surely as meat and drink stop hunger and thirst, so surely will He satisfy the cravings of your soul. Dream no longer of any satisfaction apart from Him and ask for nothing beyond or beside Him. Christ is All and more than all! He is meat and drink, too. Be content with Him and with nothing short of Him. Hunger after Him more and more, but never leave Him to spend your money for that which is not bread and your labor for that which satisfies not.

Beloved, a hungry man never gets rid of his hunger by talking about feeding, but by actually eating. Therefore do not talk so much about receiving Christ as actually doing it—receive Christ now. Look not on supplies of food and say, "Yes, these will satisfy me—oh, if only I had them," but eat them at once. The Lord beckons you to the banquet, not to look on, but to sit down and feast! Sit down at once! Ask not for a second invitation, but sit down and feed on what is freely presented to you in the Person of our Lord Jesus Christ. You need Him to be formed in you, the hope of Heaven—but this can never be unless you receive Him into your inmost soul.

In healthy eating there is a pleasure. No healthy person needs to be flogged to make him eat, for the palate is conscious of pleasure while we are feeding—and truly, in feeding upon Jesus there is a delicious sweetness pervading the whole soul. Rightly royal are His dainties! Nothing can more delight immortal banqueters than Jesus delights Believers! He satiates the soul. A thousand heavens are tasted in the Savior's body and blood. If ever you lose your relish for Christ, rest assured that you are not healthy. There can be no surer sign of a sad state of heart than not to delight in the Lord Jesus Christ. But when He is very sweet to your taste—when even a word about Him, like a drop from the honeycomb, falls sweetly upon your tongue—then there is not much the matter with you—your heart is sound at the core. Even though you might feel faint, it is a faintness of Nature, and not a failure of Grace! And if you feel sick, if it is sickness after Him whom your soul loves, it is a disease that would be well to die of!

Eating times as to our bodies come several times a day—so take care that you partake of the flesh and blood of Jesus very often. Do not be satisfied with yesterday's receiving of Jesus, but receive Him again today. Do not live upon old fellowships and experiences, but go to Jesus hourly and be not content until He fills you again and again with His love. I wish that we could become spiritually like certain animals that I know of that stand in the stall and eat all day long and halfway through the night, too. Here I would gladly possess the appetite of the horse-leech and never feel that I must pause! Happy is that Christian who can eat abundantly of heavenly meat, as the Spouse bids him, and never cease eating while Christ is near, but feed on and on until far into the night—and then awake with the dawn to feed on the Bread of Heaven!

It is well to have set times for eating. People are not likely to flourish who pick up their food just as they can and have no regular meals. It is well to have settled times when you can sit down to the table and take your food properly. Assuredly, it is wise to have appointed periods for communing with Christ, for meditating upon Him, for considering His work and for receiving His Grace. You know with children it is, "little and often," and so with us, let it be line upon line, and precept upon precept, here a little and there a little. A bit between regular meals often comes very sweet to a laboring man and so, though you have special seasons for getting alone with Christ, do not deny yourself a snatch by the way. Get a wafer made with honey between meals, and lay it on your tongue to sweeten your mouth—a choice thought, a Scripture text, or a precious promise about Jesus.

I am sure there is one thing I can say about this feeding upon Christ that never was a man guilty of gluttony in feeding upon Christ's flesh and blood. The more you eat of Christ, the more you will be able to eat of Him. We readily weary of any other food, but never of this Bread of Life! We are often in a sickly condition in reference to our Lord because we have not had enough of Him, but we can *never* have too much. When we receive Him to the full, we still find that He enlarges our capacity and we are all the more able to enjoy His preciousness.

Observe that the text tells us that the Believer is to eat His flesh and drink His blood, for Christ is both meat and drink, He is All in All, and All in One. A man must not only eat Christ, but he must drink Christ—that is to say, he must not receive Christ one way only, but in all ways—not a part of Christ, but all of Christ—not merely Christ's flesh as Incarnate, but Christ's blood as the slaughtered Sacrifice and bleeding Lamb. You must have a whole Christ and not a divided Christ! You have not truly received Christ if you have only said I select this and that virtue in Him. You must open the door and let a full Christ come in to take possession of your soul.

You must receive not merely His work, His offices, and His graces, you must receive Him totally, His whole self for *Christ Is God's Everything For You.*[141] Those receive no Grace at all who reject the blood of Christ, for that has special

141. By Harold J. Chadwick, and published by Bridge-Logos, Inc.

mention. Oh, what hard stings I have heard said, even lately, about those that preach the blood of Christ! Let them say on if they will, it is at their peril! But as for me, my Brothers and Sisters, I hope I shall deserve their censures more and more and preach the blood of Christ even more abundantly. Nothing, absolutely nothing can give satisfaction to the soul and quench that fierce, strong thirst that is aroused within our nature, except the blood of Jesus as of a Lamb slain from before the foundation of the world!

Beloved, it is one sweet thought that the flesh and blood of Christ is food suitable for all conditions. This suits babes in Grace and is equally suitable for old men. This suits sick Christians—they cannot have a daintier morsel—and this suits Christians in the full vigor of their strength. This is meat for morning and meat for night and meat for midday! This is meat to live by and meat to die by—yet, he that eats it shall never see death! This is meat for feast days and this is meat for days when we mourn and sorrow. This is meat for the wilderness and meat for the royal gardens—meat, I was about to say, for Heaven itself—for what better food shall our souls find, even there, than His flesh and blood? And remember all the Lord's people are free to eat it—yes, and every soul that hungers for it is welcome! No one needs to ask whether he may have it. It is set forth to be food for all believing souls, whatever their previous character may have been. Come and welcome, come and welcome, hungering, thirsting souls! Come eat His flesh and drink His blood!

Thus I have tried to stress the importance of and to explain what it means to eat Christ's flesh and drink His blood. It is to take a whole Christ into you by trusting yourself entirely to Him as a man trusts his life to the bread he eats and the water he drinks. How do you know bread will feed you? How do you know water will sustain you? Well, you know by experience—you have tried them—you have found that bread and water are good for you. Why do you not take plaster of Paris[142]? Why do you not drink vitriol[143]? *You know better!*

You know you can trust bread to build you up and water to refresh you, and by experience you have learned not to take in priest craft[144] and false doctrines, but you can trust and take in the blessed Person and work of Jesus Christ in His life and in His sacrificial death. You take these in, for you feel that you can feed upon them—these are the dainty provisions that your soul loves!

2. WHAT ARE THE VIRTUES OF THIS EATING AND DRINKING OF CHRIST?

Turn, now, to your Bibles, and in the 53rd verse [John 6:53] you find that this act is essential. *"Verily, verily, I say unto you, except you eat the flesh of the Son of Man, and drink His blood, you have no life in you."* It is essential, for if you have no life in you, you have nothing that is good. "No life in you."

You know the modern theory that there are germs of life in all men which only need developing. Universal Fatherhood spies some good in all of us and what he has to do is to educate it and bring it out. This is the philosophical notion, but it is not Christ's way of putting it! He says, *"Except you eat the flesh of the Son of Man and drink His blood, you have no life in you."* No, not an atom of true life! There is no life to be educated. The sinner is dead and in him there is no good thing whatever. If ever there is to be any good thing it will have to come into him—it must be

---

142. Gypsum cement.
143. Sulfuric Acid.
144. A derogatory reference to priests who use their influence to control secular or political affairs.

an importation—and it can never come into him except in connection with his eating the flesh and drinking the blood of Christ!

But suppose a man has many convictions of sin? He begins to see the evil of sin and he dreads the wrath to come. This is hopeful, but I solemnly remind any of you who are in this state, that unless you eat the flesh of the Son of Man you have no life. Until you have believed in Christ, you have no life. Until you have washed in His precious blood, you are still dead in sin. Oh, do not be satisfied because you feel some legal convictions! Do not sit down in thankfulness because you are somewhat disturbed in mind! You never must be satisfied until you have received Christ! You have NO LIFE in you until you have received Christ!

But perhaps you have attended some ceremonies. You may have been baptized and taken the sacrament. Yes, but if you have never eaten Christ, taken Him into you, you have no life in you! You are dead while you live! Now, here is a proof in our text that life does not mean existence, as people now say, who, when they read that, "the sinner dies," say that means that he goes out of existence. Ungodly men have an existence in them, but that is a very different thing, indeed, from eternal life—and you must never confuse existence with life or death, with non-existence—they are very many leagues apart from one another!

The unconverted man, not having Christ, has no life in him at all. You members of the Church, do you have life in you—real life? You have not if you have not eaten the flesh of Christ! You may have been professing yourselves as Christians for many years, but did you ever eat Christ and drink Christ? If not, you have NO life in you! You may be excellent moral people. Your characters may be fine patterns to others. There may be everything that is beautiful about you. But if Christ is not in your heart, you are the child of Nature, finely dressed, but dead. You are not the living child of Grace—you are the statue beautifully chiseled, but like the cold marble, there is no life in you! Nothing but Christ can be life to the soul and the highest excellencies to which human nature can reach apart from Him fall short of salvation. You MUST have Jesus, or death abides in you and you abide in death! That is the first virtue of feeding upon Christ; it is absolutely essential.

Now, in the second place it is vital. Read the next verse—"*Whoever eats My flesh, and drinks My blood, has eternal life; and I will raise him up at the last day.*" That is to say, he has been quickened by receiving into himself a whole Christ—he is, therefore, alive! Though sometimes he may be led to doubt it by his state of heart, yet if he has really received Christ, he has been quickened from the dead and is alive! Furthermore, he shall always be alive, for he "has eternal life." Now, a life that can possibly die out is evidently not eternal life and the life which the Arminian gets as the result of his faith, according to his own statement, is not eternal life because it may come to an end.

Good soul, I know if he has really believed in Jesus, he will sweetly find out his mistake and his life will go on living under temptation and trial, for it shall be in him, "*a well of water springing up unto everlasting life.*" [See John 4:14.]. It shall be, "*a living and incorruptible seed which lives and abides forever.*" [See 1 Peter 1:23.] Oh, let us believe the precious doctrine of the Final Perseverance of the Saints! "*He that eats my flesh and drinks my blood HAS eternal life.*" [John 6:54,NKJV, Emphasis by author.] He has it now! It is a life that shall last as long as God, himself—eternal as Jehovah's Throne!

And then, as to the body, that will die, will it not? Yes, but such is the power of the life, which Christ puts into us that the body itself shall rise again! We have our

Lord's pledge for it—*"I will raise him up at the last day."* As yet the body is dead because of sin, though the spirit is life because of righteousness—but there is a redemption coming for this poor frame—and for this material world in which we dwell. When Christ shall come the creation shall be delivered from the bondage it was placed under, and our material bodies, with the rest of creation, shall be emancipated! The bodies of the saints will be delivered from all imperfection, corruption and defilement! We shall live again, in the glorious image of Christ and the Lord shall fulfill His gracious Word, *"I am the resurrection and the life; he that believes in Me, though he were dead, yet shall he live"* [John 11:25, NKJV]. Therefore, this eating and drinking of Christ is vital!

In the third place it is substantial, "for My flesh is meat, indeed, and My blood is drink, indeed." This is opposed to the unsubstantial character of symbols. The Jewish feasting was a mere shadow. "But," says Jesus, *"My flesh is meat, indeed."* This is also said in contradistinction[145] from carnal food. Carnal food, being eaten, only builds the body and then disappears, but it cannot touch the soul. But feeding upon Christ, the soul is fed and fed unto life eternal, so that Jesus claims to be, "meat indeed."

Do you ever attend a ministry where the preacher preaches anything and everything but Christ? Do you get fed? Well, if you are of a windy sort, you may get blown up with the east wind as wild donkeys are when they snuff it up. But I know, if you are a child of God, it does not matter who preaches, or how poor his language—if he preaches Christ you always feel as if you were fed—your soul is satisfied with marrow and fatness when Christ is the subject! There is no such meat for the soul as Christ—and the sweetest refreshment

---

145. A distinction drawn on the basis of contrast.

is from the weakest parts of Christ—for God's strength is perfect in His weakness!

You say to me "What do you mean?" Well, our Lord in the text says, *"My flesh is meat, indeed,"* not, "my Godhead." *"My blood is drink indeed,"* not my Resurrection and Ascension. Not, "my Second Advent," but my weakness as a Man, My death as a Man, My sufferings, My griefs, My groans—these are the best food for Believers. Do you not find it so? O I rejoice to hear of Christ as coming a second time, but there are times when that doctrine does not yield me an atom of comfort! The brightest stars that charm the day for a poor benighted pilgrim are those that burn around the Cross! Strange that we should turn to that spot where sorrow culminated to find our purest comfort, but it is so—"My flesh is meat, indeed"—Christ in His weakness! *"My blood is drink, indeed"*—Christ pouring out His soul unto death! This is the truest and best food of the heart!

Now, Brethren, if you want to grow in grace, feed on Christ! If you want to become strong in the Lord, feed on Christ! If you want something that will build you up in all parts permanently and well, feed on Christ, for other things are meat and drink, but His flesh is meat, indeed, and His blood is drink, indeed! This is substantial fare!

And, lastly, another virtue of this feeding is that it produces union. Notice the next verse—*"He that eats My flesh, and drinks My blood, dwells in Me, and I in him."* How wonderful is that word—*"dwells in Me."* By taking Christ into you as a whole Christ, you get to live in Christ and Christ in you!

There is this difference between the two privileges—to live in Christ is the peace of Justification. You believe in Him, you trust yourself with Him, you feel that you died with Him and that you rose with Him—that you have gone to Heaven with Him—and, therefore, you are accepted in Him and so you live in Him! For Him to live in you is another thing, namely, the peace of Sanctification, for when you have fed on Jesus, He enters into you and abides in you, living, again, in you. He speaks through your lips, loves with your heart, looks through your eyes, works with your hands and witnesses among the sons of men by your tongue—He lives in you! Oh, wondrous union! Blessed union!

The next verse makes it still more wonderful, for it says *"As the living Father has sent Me, and I live by the Father: so he that eats Me, even he shall live by Me"* [John 6:57, NKJV]. Three living things—the living Father, the living Son and, then, the living Believer. There is the Father with life in himself as God. Then there is the Son as Mediator, God-Man, deriving life from the Father. And then the Believer, taking the life which came from God through Jesus Christ. O blessed union this is, not merely with Jesus, but through Jesus with the Father! So that Christ says, *"I live, and because I live, you shall live also"* [John 14:19, NKJV]. He lives by the Father and we live by Him—and all this because we receive Him and feed upon Him!

Oh, my Brothers and Sisters, I charge you, open your mouth wide after Christ and take Him into your very self! Give Him a lodging in your heart, yes, let Him dwell forever in the best pavilion of your nature, in the rarest place of your soul! Hunger after Him! Feed on Him every day and when you have done so, and He dwells in you and you in Him, then tell others about Him and spread His dear name abroad, that hungry, perishing sinners may know that there is corn in Egypt and bread to be had in Jesus! And may many come and eat and drink of Him as you have done. I charge you, Brothers and Sisters, remember this, and the Lord bless you, for His name's sake. Amen.

CHAPTER 16
THE DOUBLE
FORGET-ME-NOT

A SERMON
(No. 3099)
A Sermon Published on Thursday, July 2, 1908
Delivered by
REVEREND CHARLES H. SPURGEON,
At The Metropolitan Tabernacle, Newington,
on the Lord's-Day Evening, July 5, 1874

"This do in remembrance of me."—*1 Corinthians 11:24*

THERE ARE SOME PERSONS who do not consider the Lord's Supper to be a divine ordinance. They say that they cannot see where it is commanded in Scripture. I have long ago given up trying to understand other people's understandings, for some of them are constructed upon such peculiar principles that I believe they would understand just the opposite of a Truth of God that the Holy Spirit teaches in the Word of God!

Now to me, Christ's command to observe the Lord's Supper seems to be so plain and positive that it would take greater ingenuity than I possess to be able to justify myself as a Christian if I lived in neglect of the Communion! I know a good deal of what has been invented by others, but I cannot invent any syllogism, argument, or reason by which I could set aside such a plain divine precept as that which is recorded in 1 Corinthians 11:23-25:

> The Lord Jesus, the same night in which he was
> betrayed, took bread: and when he had given thanks,

he brake it, and said, "Take, eat: this is my body, which is broken for you: this do in remembrance of Me." After the same manner also He took the cup, when He had supped, saying, "This cup is the new testament in my blood: this do ye, as oft as ye drink it, in remembrance of me."

If Christ did not mean that we were to do this, and to do it in remembrance of Him, what did He mean? It seems to me to be very plain and positive that this is what He did mean, and because of that the precept comes to Christians with very great force for it is issued upon the highest possible authority! It is not the Apostle Paul who tells us to do this in remembrance of Christ, but the Master himself, who says, *This do in remembrance of me.* The utmost solemnity appertains to the Ten Commandments because they were issued by God himself on Mount Sinai—and there is no less weight attached to the command before us, since it was issued by the Son of God, himself, who could truly say, *"I and my Father are one"* [John 10:30].

It also seems to me that this command derives singular solemnity from the occasion upon which it was given. If the issuing of the Law of God was especially solemn because *"Mount Sinai was altogether on a smoke, because the Lord descended upon it in fire"* [Exodus 19:18a]. I venture to say that the giving of this plain, positive command, *"This do in remembrance of me,"* is none the less solemn because it was given by *"the Lord Jesus the same night in which He was betrayed"* [1 Corinthians 11:23]. What other night, in the world's history, can be more august and more solemn to Him and to us as Believers in Him, than that night when He went, with His disciples for the last time to Gethsemane? My Lord, as this command was given by you at such a special time, how dare I neglect it if I am indeed your disciple? Let none of us who believe in Jesus, live in habitual disobedience to this command of His!

Let me make just one other introductory observation, namely, that this commandment was evidently not issued for one occasion only, for it is quoted by the Apostle Paul in writing to the Corinthians—and he adds these significant words, *"For as often as ye eat this bread, and drink this cup, ye do show the Lord's death till he come"* [1 Corinthians 11:26]. The command, therefore, remains in force until the Second Advent—and until Christ, himself, shall again appear upon this Earth—these memorials of His passion are to be constantly before us!

I. "THIS DO IN REMEMBRANCE OF ME"

I am going to remind you, first, of the need of such commemoration of Christ. The need exists:

First, because of our forgetful memories. Memory, in common with every other faculty, has been injured by the Fall. It is more retentive of that which is evil than of that which is good and, as you all know, far more easily recollects injuries than benefits. But it certainly does show the deep depravity of the human heart that we should ever be likely to forget our Lord. Have we not often sung—

> "Gethsemane, can I forget?
> Or there Thy conflict see, Thine agony, and bloody sweat, And not remember Thee?"[146]

Yet we have practically forgotten Gethsemane and have

---

146. Hymn titled "According To Thy Gracious Word", words by Christian psalmist, James Montgomery in 1825 and music by Hugh Wilson in 1800.

omitted to act towards our Lord as we would have acted had Gethsemane been perpetually painted on our memories. Yes, we are apt to forget our truest Friend, our best Beloved Jesus, in whom our souls delight! We do forget Him, and it ought to humble us when we remember that Christ knew what forgetful lovers we would be and, therefore, gave us this love-token, this double forget-me-not.

Second, does there not also exist a need for this command due to our condition as children? We are not, my dear Brothers and Sisters in Christ, "what we shall yet be" [See 1John 3:2.]. We are, to a great extent, still underage. We are children of God and *"heirs and joint-heirs"* of the Kingdom of God, but at present we are under tutors and governors. [See Romans 8:17.] Now in a child's book there should be pictures. We are not altogether little children—we have grown somewhat—and some Christians think we have grown so big that we do not need pictures, but Jesus knew that we would be, in many respects, little children or big children, so He has put two pictures in the Book which He has given to us because He wants us to remember that we are not yet men, and we have not yet come to our full growth. The two word pictures[147] are Believers' Baptism[148] and the

---

147. Graphic or vivid verbal descriptions.

148. Believers' Baptism: Water baptism is clearly a Figure or Type of something which already took place in the heart of the believer the moment he or she was saved (1 Peter 3:21). Water baptism is the ordinance representing the identification of the Christian with the death, burial, and resurrection of Jesus Christ. You are "crucified" (standing upright in water), you are "buried" (immersed into the water), and you are "resurrected into life" (raised out of the water). Water baptism then, is a picture of spiritual baptism as defined in Romans 6:3-5 and 1 Corinthians 12:13. It is the outward testimony of the believer's inward faith. A sinner is saved the moment he places his faith in the Lord Jesus Christ. Baptism is a visible testimony to that faith.

Lord's Supper[149]. Because I am a child, therefore, I must still have emblems and tokens, for these are more powerful to my mind than mere words would be. No doubt, also, the two ordinances were left, and especially this one, because we are yet in the body. We are still linked with materialism. We are not yet purely spiritual and it is no use for us to pretend that we are. Some good people sit still until they are moved, which would be an admirable form of worship if we did not have bodies. But, as long as we have bodies, there must be some kind of linking of the spiritual with the material, let the links be as few as they may. Christ has made two—they are enough, but they are none too many, for let it be remembered that there is a time coming when the material itself is to be lifted up and re-united with the spiritual! *"The creature itself also shall be delivered from the bondage of corruption into the glorious liberty of the children of God"* [Romans 8:21].

And as if to teach us not to despise the material, not to consider everything that can be touched and seen as therefore foul and beneath the consideration of spiritual minds, our Lord has given us water in which we can wash, and bread and wine, the products of the Earth, that, being yet earthy, we may anticipate the time when the Earth shall shake off the slough which came upon her at the Fall and, as a new Earth, with her new Heaven of pure blue over her, shall become the New Jerusalem, the tabernacle of the living God! [See Revelation 21:1-2.]

I have often grieved over the fact that these two ordinances, Baptism and the Lord's Supper, have become nests in which the foul bird of superstition has laid her eggs. But the Lord foresaw that when He instituted them— yet I have often rejoiced that we are able through these

---

149. See Matthew 26:26-29.

material symbols, to get nearer to Him whose body was material and is material, whose blood was real blood, who was born into this world of a virgin of real flesh and blood, was often weary and was a Man such as we are. A real Man, who died on Calvary—no phantom, no myth, no dream of history, but One who could have gripped my hand, as I, my Brother or Sister, can grip yours, and One who felt the nails that went through His hands as you and I would feel it if nails were driven through our hands! Therefore, we come to no shallow feast, but to a real one of bread and wine to make us feel that it was a real Christ who died for us and that this poor body, which is so real to us, is yet, after all, to be cleansed and purified by that great Sacrifice of His upon the Cross of Calvary!

I hope I shall not be thought uncharitable if I suggest that the Lord's Supper was given to us for other reasons. Some have said, "We do not need this memorial, for we can think of Christ through hearing about Him from ministers in the pulpit." Yes, you can hear the ministers, but what can you hear from some of them? In many a case, you will hear what will do you little good, for the one thing that is absent from many a ministry, nowadays, is the clear proclamation of the great central Truth of God of the substitutionary Sacrifice of Jesus Christ. Earthly ministries are not to be relied upon, for almost all of them by degrees fall back from the faithfulness, seriousness, and earnestness with which they commenced. There is scarcely an instance in history in which human ministries have fully preserved their pristine purity, yet, wherever Christians have been able to meet together to observe this ordinance as a memorial of Christ's death, they have always kept up a living testimony to Christ's death! If ministries were silenced, or if ministers had lost their zeal, there was always this memorial ministry—the breaking of bread and the pouring out of wine in remembrance of Christ!

Somebody probably says, "But, surely, the Church would always keep Christ in memory." Alas, alas, that which ought to be the very Glory of the earth-organized Christianity has often fully become one of the main agents of evil in the Earth! And therefore I bless God for an ordinance which is not a Church ordinance, or a minister's ordinance. I hope none of you are under the impression that at the close of the present service, I am going to administer the Lord's Supper. God forbid that I should ever venture to do such a thing as that! No, it is you, or we, who come to the Lord's Table to break bread and to drink of the cup—and we come together, not as a Church holding certain views, but we come simply as Christians to, *"do this in remembrance"* of the Savior who died for us! You may break bread wherever you will, wherever two or three Christians can meet together and if you truly love your Lord, the oftener you do this, the better. *"This do you, as often as you drink it,"* is no command addressed to an ecclesiastical organization concerning an ordinance to be administered by men who have the impertinence or impudence to call themselves priests, but a command to all Christians everywhere. It can be on any day of the week, and in any place—beneath the blue sky of Heaven, or in a barn, or in a tavern if they happen to be tarrying there—to break a piece of bread in memory of their Lord's broken body, and to drink of the cup in mutual loving memory of His precious blood poured out for them!

And remember if it should ever come to this, if ministries fail, I mean what we usually consider to be ordained earthly ministries. And if churches fail, there will still be found faithful followers of Christ—hunted and harried, they may be—to the very ends of the Earth! And they will break the bread and drink the wine in remembrance of Christ until the trumpet sounds to announce His return. It shall be remembered that Jesus was Incarnate and that Jesus died, and that through Him we have access to the Father.

Thus I have tried to show you why a commemoration feast is needed, but I do not pretend to know all the reasons for its institution. Jesus said, *"This do you in remembrance of me"*—and that is all the reason that any truly obedient child of God will ever need!

II. THE SUITABILITY OF THIS COMMEMORATION FOR THE PURPOSE INTENDED

Dear Brothers and Sisters in Christ, let me try to show you that this ordinance is in itself a very suitable commemoration of the death of Christ. A crucifix might have been suggested as a means of keeping the death of Christ before us, but I need not remind you how that has become the very emblem of idolatry. I do not know of any memorial of Christ that could have been so suggestive and as admirable as the one which Christ has ordained. In itself it is admirable, for here is bread, the very staff of life—a fit token of that flesh of Christ which is, spiritually, "meat, indeed." The fact of His Incarnation is most nourishing food to our hearts. We believe in Him as God, veiled in human flesh, and that great Truth of God, that wondrous fact is as much food for our souls as bread is for our bodies. Furthermore, in this memorial we have the bread broken, indicating Christ's sufferings and the breaking that He endured on our behalf. The bread is, in itself, a most appropriate memorial of suffering. Was it not wheat that was sown in a furrow in the field and there buried?

Did it not spring up to be bitten by frosts, to be blown about by rough winds, to suffer all the extremities of climate, to be drenched by the rain and scorched by the sun, to be cut down by the sharp sickle, to be threshed, to be ground, to be kneaded, to be put into the oven, to be passed through I know not how many processes, any one of which might be a sufficient type of suffering?

The suffering body of the Incarnate God is the spiritual food for our souls, but we must partake of it if it is to nourish us. This emblematic bread must not only be broken, but eaten—a significant type of our receiving Jesus by faith and depending upon Him, taking Him to be the nutriment of our new spiritual life. What can be more instructive than all this?

Then there is the wine, "the fruit of the vine." There are two tokens because the two represent death. The blood *in the body* is life, the blood *out of the body* is death, so the two emblems are separate, the wine in the cup and the bread—these together indicate death. Water was not used, for water had been applied in the other ordinance of Believers' Baptism, and water would have been a pale, faint memorial of Him whose rich living blood could far better be set forth by the blood of the grape, trodden under foot of man and made to flow forth from the winepress. The wine is an admirable token of the blood of the atoning Sacrifice. Men need drink as well as food— therefore both are put upon the Communion Table to show a whole Christ as the true food of the soul. You do not go to Christ for spiritual food and go somewhere else for spiritual drink, but all you need you can find in Jesus, and find it in Jesus crucified, in Jesus sacrificed and put to death in your place. Surely the emblems themselves are most significant and suitable reminders of Christ's death.

And the whole ordinance is a most suitable memorial of Christ's death because the Lord's Supper can be celebrated anywhere. There is no climate where we cannot have bread and wine. There are no persons so poor that, among them, they cannot furnish the table with these simple emblems. It may be decorous to have a silver cup and plate, but it certainly is not necessary—any cup and plate will do. They talk of the "chalice" and "water" in the strange ecclesiastical jargon that so-called "priests" use, but I say, "cup" and "plate." They may be of any material, and the table of any sort. A cloth of "fair white linen" is decorous, but not necessary. Let there be but a table and bread and wine, and that is all that is required. And if half a dozen godly peasants, women in homespun and men in smock frocks, are gathered together in a cave, or under a wide-spreading beech tree, they can show forth Christ's death *"till He come."* [See 1 Corinthians 11:26.]

But as for that man-millinery show over yonder, and that "altar" of theirs, and that bell and the people bowing down to worship Jack-in-the-Box—for I will give it no better name—all that is sheer idolatry! It is no memorial of Christ! It may be a memorial of the devil, and of the way in which he turns Christianity into Popery, and puts Christ off the throne and sets a man up who calls himself infallible! But wherever the bread is broken and the wine is poured out by true believers in memory of Christ, there His command is obeyed.

The Lord's Supper is also a suitable memorial because it can be frequently celebrated. You may break this bread and drink of this cup as often as you please. A costly rite could only be performed now and then, but this ordinance can be observed in the morning and in the evening and every day of the week if you will—and very little expense will need to be incurred. To the end of this dispensation, there will be enough bread and wine and sufficient gracious men and women to come to the table of their Lord and thus keep the remembrance of Jesus Christ, the Son of God who died on Calvary's Cross, *"the Just for the unjust, that He might bring us to God."* [See 1 Peter 3:18.]

I devoutly thank my Lord and Master for giving me such an easy, inexpensive, unostentatious, significant, and symbolic way of celebrating the memorial of the death He died for me and for all His people!

III. THE PERSONS TO WHOM THIS CELEBRATION WAS ENTRUSTED

Now, let me speak very briefly on this point and start with a question. Who are they who are to *"do this in remembrance"* of Christ? Well, if you look at the connection of our text, you will find that they are persons who discern the Lord's body. Meaning, the persons who rightly come to this communion table understanding that the bread and the wine are types or emblems of Christ's broken body and shed blood. They are also persons who have the spiritual perception to discern that the Christ Incarnate, the Christ who died upon the Cross is very precious to them. I trust there will be many who will come to this table, each one of whom will be able to say, "Ah, I know what a precious Christ He is! He is my joy, my hope, my delight, my All in All." Come and welcome, all of you who can thus discern the Lord's body. I know that you can do so, by the joy which this Communion gives you, by the sweetness it leaves upon your spiritual palate when you feed upon it. You may certainly come, for you have the spiritual life that possesses the spiritual senses, by which you discern the Lord's body. Yes, you may come—even more, you must come, for your Lord and Master said, *"This do in remembrance of me."*

We are told that those should come who have fellowship with Christ. The cup of blessing which we bless, is it not the communion of the blood of Christ? The bread which we break, is it not the communion of the body of Christ? Therefore, none may come to the Lord's table but those who are prepared to acknowledge that they are in fellowship with the Lord. Is God your God? Is Christ your Savior? Do you avow yourself to be a disciple of Jesus and a child of God? If so, come and welcome to this table! But if not, stand back, for you have no right to come here! If you do, you will bring upon yourself a curse, and not a blessing. But as for all of you who are trusting in the blood of Jesus, all to whom Christ is all your salvation and desire—all who call Jehovah your Father through faith in Jesus, and all who are reconciled to God by the death of His Son—come to this table and have fellowship with the God of Heaven and Earth and the God and Father of our Lord and Savior Jesus Christ!

NONE EXCEPT BELIEVERS

But let no one else come. I am always sorry when persons are urged to come to the Communion Table as though they would receive some benefit from it although they are not converted, for by no possibility can there be any benefit to any who come to the Lord's Table unless they are Believers in Jesus! God might bless the ordinance to their conversion, but in the nature of things it is highly improbable, for they would be acting in direct disobedience to His command! They have no right there and they will be far more likely to be blessed if they humbly stay away until they have believed in Jesus—and then they will have the right to come, the right given by His love.

IV. LET US CARRY OUT THE DESIGN OF THIS ORDINANCE

The Lord's Supper is intended to remind us of Jesus. I am not going to preach now. I want you who can, to carry out the text—"*This do in remembrance of me.*" Many of you are coming to the Communion Table—remember your Lord and Savior now. Remember who He is and who He was. Remember Him, let Him stand before your mind's eye now as the "*Man of Sorrows, and acquainted with grief*" [Isaiah 53:3]. I do not appeal to your imagination, I appeal to your memory. You know—

"The old, old story,
Of Jesus and His love."[150]

Recall it now. Remember that He died, for that is what you are especially told to remember here. I have met with one, who was, I hope, a Christian, who said to me, "My confidence is in a glorified Savior." But I could not help saying to him, "My confidence is in a Crucified Savior." Christ Crucified is the foundation of all our hopes, for Christ could not have risen from the dead if He had not first died. Of what use would His plea be if He had not His blood to offer? Do not be led astray even by ideas about the Second Advent if they depreciate the death of Christ! Rejoice in Christ's Second Coming and look and long for it, but remember that the basis of our hope lies in Christ Crucified. "We preach Christ Crucified" and as we have preached so have you believed, so let no one turn you away from your confidence in Christ Jesus suffering in the sinner's place, and—

---

150. Hymn titled "Tell Me the Old, Old Story" by A. Katherine Hankey in 1866, music by W. Howard Doane in 1867.

"Bearing, that we might never bear,
His Father's righteous ire."

"Look unto me, and be ye saved, all the ends of the earth," is a call from Christ upon the Cross [Isaiah 45:22]. Remember that all your hope hangs upon Him who hung upon the Cross and died there. Remember that when He died, you died in Him, for *"if one died for all, then all were dead"* [2 Corinthians 5:14]. And now you must *"reckon ye also yourselves to be dead indeed unto sin, but alive unto God through Jesus Christ our Lord"* [Romans 6:11].

Remember Him, I pray you, until your hearts grow warm and your love burns within you.

Remember Him, until you resolve to serve Him, and until you go from this Table of Communion determined to die for Him if necessary.

Remember Him until you also remember all His people, for it is not to one that He says, "This do you," but, *"This do in remembrance of me,"* is said to all His people, and it needs at least a little company to do this.

Remember Him until all the Church militant, and the Church triumphant, too, seems gathered around your heart and you commune with the whole Church of Christ in Heaven and on Earth!

Remember Jesus until you feel that He is with you.

Remember Jesus until His joy gets into your soul and your joy is full.

Remember Him until you begin to forget yourself and forget your temptations and your cares.

Remember Him until you begin to think of the time when He will remember you and come in His Glory for you.

Remember Him until you begin to be like He is.

Gaze upon Him until when you go down from this mount into the wicked world again, your face will glow with the glory of having seen your Lord! I long to get to this Communion Table again, though I have not been away from it any Sabbath for many a long day. It has been my constant habit, wherever I have been, to get a few Christian friends together to break bread in remembrance of Christ. When I am with you, you know that I would never be absent on the first day of the week, from my Master's Table unless there was something that absolutely prevented it and I trust you may come with as keen an appetite as I have now, and then you shall lack no stores for this feast! And may the Lord feed us with himself to the full!

How sorry I am that there are many here who must not come to this Table of Communion, for they have never trusted in Christ! If it seems nothing to you now not to love and trust the Lord Jesus Christ, remember that if you die in that state, a day will come when it will seem to you to have been the most horrible thing that ever happened that you should have lived and died without love to Him and trust in Him! God save you! Believe in Jesus now and you shall be saved now. Cast yourselves upon Him and He will not cast you away. So may He bless you, for His dear name's sake! Amen and Amen.

[**Note:** The following exposition by C. H. Spurgeon on Mark 15:1-39 was at the end of this sermon. It may have been read prior to receiving the Lord's Supper.]

"Let us read again what we have often read before, that saddest of all stories which, nevertheless, is the fountain of the highest gladness—the story of our Savior's death, as recorded by Mark."

Mark 15:1. *And straightway in the morning the chief priests held a consultation with the elders and scribes and the whole council, and bound Jesus, and carried Him away, and delivered Him to Pilate.*

Exposition: "The whole council" could be there, so early in the morning, for such an evil purpose! Wicked men are very diligent in carrying out their sinful schemes, so, when Christ was to be murdered, His enemies were there, as Luke tells us, "as soon as it was day." How much more diligent ought the followers of Christ to be to give Him their devoted service! It is a good thing to begin the day with united prayer and holy converse with His people. Let these wicked men who were so early in the morning seeking to secure the death of Christ make us ashamed that we are not more diligent in His blessed service.

Mark 15:2-3. *And Pilate asked Him, "Art thou the King of the Jews?" And He answering said unto him, "Thou sayest it." And the chief priest accused Him of many things: but He answered nothing.*

Exposition: Silence was the best answer, the most eloquent reply that He could give to each accuser—they deserved no other answer. Moreover, by His silence, He was fulfilling the prophecy, *"As a sheep before her shearers is dumb, so He opens not His mouth"* [See Acts 8:32.].

Mark 15:4-5. *And Pilate asked Him again, saying, "Answerest thou nothing? Behold how many things they witness against thee." But Jesus yet answered nothing; so that Pilate marvelled.*

Exposition: You will often find that your highest wisdom, when you are slandered, will lie in the imitation of your Lord and Master. Live a blameless life and it shall be the best reply to the false charges of the wicked.

Mark 15:6-10. *Now at that feast He released unto them one prisoner, whomsoever they desired. And there was one* *named Barabbas, which lay bound with them that had made insurrection with him, who had committed murder in the insurrection. And the multitude crying aloud began to desire him to do as he had always done unto these. But Pilate answered them, saying, "Will ye that I release unto you the King of the Jews?" For he knew that the chief priest has delivered him for envy.*

Exposition: And he therefore hoped that the people, who were not moved by the same envy, would have chosen to have Jesus set at liberty.

Mark15:11-13. But the chief priests moved the people, that he should rather release Barabbas unto them. And Pilate answered and said again unto them, *"What will ye then that I shall do unto him whom ye call the King of the Jews?"* And they cried out again, "Crucify him."

Exposition: This was the very best reply to the charge of high treason, for if Jesus had really set himself up as a king in the place of Caesar, the people, when they were thus publicly appealed to, would not have cried out, "Crucify him." If there had been any truth in the allegation that He was the ringleader of a sedition, the Jews would not have said again and again, "Crucify Him." Thus Christ gave Pilate a much more effectual answer than if He had himself spoken.

Mark15:14-15. Then Pilate said unto them, *"Why, what evil hath he done?"* And they cried out the more exceedingly, "Crucify him." And so Pilate, willing to content the people, released Barabbas unto them, and delivered Jesus, when he had scourged him, to be crucified.

Mark 15:16-18. *And the soldiers led Him away into the hall, called Praetorium. And they called together the whole band. And they clothed him with purple. . . .*

And they platted a crown of thorns, and put it about his head, and began to salute him, Hail, King of the Jews!

Exposition: The uniform of the Roman soldiers was purple, as if to indicate that they belonged to an imperial master. So when these soldiers, in mockery, put on our Lord the old cloak of one of their comrades, it sufficed to clothe Him with the royal purple to which, as King, He was fully entitled.

Mark 15:19. *And they smote him on the head with a reed, and did spit upon him, and bowing their knees worshipped Him.*

Exposition: All this homage was paid to him in mockery, yet what stern reality there was in that mockery! That band of soldiers really preached to Christ such homage as a whole world could give Him.

Mark 15:20. *And when they had mocked him, they took off the purple from him, and put his own clothes on him, and led him out to crucify him.*

Exposition: They *"led Him out to crucify him."* It seems as if Christ had to lean upon those who led Him. The word almost signifies as much as that. At least it might be the word employed concerning anyone leading a child or a sick man who needed support, for the Savior's weakness must have been very apparent by that time. After the agony and bloody sweat in Gethsemane and the night and morning trials, the scourging, mockery, and the awful strain upon His mind and heart in being made a sacrifice for sin, it was no wonder that He was weak! Besides, He was not like the rough, brutal criminals that are often condemned to die for their crimes. He was a man of gentle mold and more delicate sensibilities than they were, and He suffered much more than any ordinary man would have done in similar circumstances.

Mark15:21. *And they compel one Simon, a Cyrenian, who passed by, coming out of the country, the father of*

Alexander and Rufus, to bear his cross.

Exposition: Christ could not bear it himself. The soldiers saw that He was faint and weary, so they laid the Cross, or at least one end of it, on Simon's shoulders.

Mark 15:22. *And they bring him . . .*

Exposition: Here the word almost implies that they lifted Him and carried Him, for His faintness had increased. They *"led him out to crucify him,"* but now they bear Him. . . . *Unto the place Golgotha, which is, being interpreted, The place of a skull.*

Exposition: We sometimes speak of it as Mount Calvary, but it was not so—it was a little rising ground, the common place of execution, the Tyburn or Old Bailey of Jerusalem.

Mark 15:23. *And they gave him to drink wine mingled with myrrh: but he received it not.*

Exposition: He did not wish to have His sufferings abated, but to bear them to the bitter end. Christ forbids not that pain should be alleviated in the case of others, wherever that is possible. But in His own case, it was not fit that it should be so relieved, since He was to bear the full brunt of the storm of vengeance that was due on account of sin.

Mark 15:24. *And when they had crucified him, they parted his garments, casting lots upon them, what every man should take.*

Exposition: Christ's garments must go to His executioners in order to carry out the full shame associated with His death as well as to fulfill the prophecy, *"They parted my garments among them, and cast lots upon my vesture."* [Psalm 22:18].

Mark 15:25-27. *And it was the third hour, and they crucified him. And the superscription of his accusation was written over, The King Of The Jews. And with him they crucify two thieves; the one on his right hand, and the other* *on his left*

Exposition: As if, in carrying out that ordinary etiquette which gives the central place to the chief criminal, they gave to Christ the place of greatest contempt and scorn.

Mark 15:28. *And the Scripture was fulfilled, which saith, And He was numbered with the transgressors* [Isaiah 53:12].

Exposition: You could not count the "transgressors" on those crosses without counting Him. There were three, and the One in the middle could not be passed by as you counted the others.

Mark 15:29-32. *And they that passed by railed on him, wagging their heads, and saying, Ah, thou that destroy the temple, and buildest it in three days, Save thyself, and come down from the cross. Likewise also the chief priests mocking said among themselves with the scribes, he saved others; himself he cannot save. Let Christ the King of Israel descend now from the cross, that we may see and believe.* That is the world's way—*"that we may see and believe."*

Exposition: But Christ's way is, *"Believe and you shall see."* [See John 20:29.] Christ off the Cross is admired by worldlings, but Christ on the Cross is our hope and stay, especially as we know that this same Christ is now on the throne waiting for the time when He shall return to claim as His own all who have trusted in the crucified. *And they that were crucified with him reviled him.*

Exposition: Out of their black hearts and mouths came words of ridicule and scorn even then.

Mark 15:33-34. *And when the sixth hour was come . . .* when the sun had reached the zenith, at high noon . . . *there was darkness over the whole land until the ninth hour. And at the ninth hour Jesus cried with a loud voice, saying, Eloi, Eloi, lama Sabachthani? which is, being interpreted, My God, My God, why hast thou forsaken me?*

Mark 15:35-37. *And some of them that stood by, when they heard it, said, Behold, he calleth Elias. And one ran and filled a spunge full of vinegar, and put it on a reed, and gave him to drink, saying, Let alone; let us see whether Elias will come to take him down. And Jesus cried with a loud voice, and gave up the ghost.*

Mark 15:38-39. *And the veil of the temple was rent in twain from the top to the bottom. And when the centurion, which stood over against him, saw that He so cried out, and gave up the ghost, he said, Truly this man was the Son of God!*

Amen

Study Guide

1. What Scripture reference did Charles Spurgeon use as the foundation for his ministry, and the countless sermons and many books he wrote?

   _____

   _____

   List the three points Spurgeon chose to discuss in his text on the Doctrine of Substitution in Chapter 1.

   _____

   _____

   _____

   _____

2. Why is Jesus referred to the Paschal Lamb in Chapter 2?

   _____

   _____

3. Explain the difference between the priesthood work of Aaron and other priests in the Old Testament and the priesthood work of Christ in the New Testament.

   _____

   _____

4. Romans 3:23 states: "For all have sinned, and come short of the glory of God;" therefore why does man need Hebrews 9:22?

   _____

   _____

5. In Chapter 7 the Scripture reference says: "*The blood of sprinkling, that speaketh better things than that of Abel.*" Fill in the blanks:
   - The blood of Abel speaks r_____e. The blood of Christ speaks m_____.
   - Life is in the _____. Leviticus 17:11

- Spurgeon speaks on three areas in Chapter 9 that the blood of sprinkling signified. Fill in the blanks: C_____n, P_____n, and S_____f_____n.

6. In Chapter 11 what are the first and second privileges we have as Christians?

   _____

   _____

7. 10. Name the three witnesses spoken of in Chapter 12.

   _____

   _____

8. 11. In Chapter 13 Spurgeon's text involves three areas: List those areas.

   _____

   _____

9. 12. In Chapter 15 Spurgeon explains the meaning of eating the flesh and drinking the blood of Christ in two powerful, but concise sentences. Read them, meditate on them and then write them in your own words.

   _____

   _____

   _____

   _____

10. In *The Double Forget-Me-Not,* Chapter 16, Spurgeon teaches on two very special ordinances Christ has given us. List those and use the remaining lines to jot down any personal notes that the blood of Jesus Christ means to you.

    _____

    _____

    _____

    _____

    _____

Pure Gold Classics
Timeless Truth in a Distinctive, Best-Selling Collection

An Expanding Collection of the Best-Loved Christian Classics of All Time.
AVAILABLE AT FINE BOOKSTORES.
FOR MORE INFORMATION, VISIT WWW.BRIDGELOGOS.COM

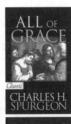

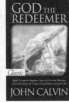

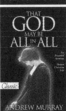

THE GREATEST THING IN THE WORLD
Classic
HENRY DRUMMOND

R. A. TORREY
Classic
THE HOLY SPIRIT
WHO HE IS and WHAT HE DOES

THE HOLY SPIRIT POWER
10 Faith to Timeless Messages
Classic
JOHN WESLEY

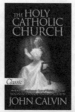
THE HOLY CATHOLIC CHURCH
Classic
JOHN CALVIN

HUMILITY
Classic
ANDREW MURRAY

THE IMITATION OF CHRIST
Classic
THOMAS à KEMPIS

IN HIS STEPS
Millions of copies sold in over #1 overtten
Classic
CHARLES M. SHELDON

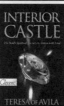
INTERIOR CASTLE
The Soul's Spiritual Journey by Union with God
Classic
TERESA OF AVILA

JEWELS FROM E.M. BOUNDS
Classic
E.M. BOUNDS

THE KNEELING CHRISTIAN
Classic
AN UNKNOWN CHRISTIAN

MADAME JEANNE GUYON
EXPERIENCING UNION WITH GOD THROUGH INNER PRAYER
Classic

MORNING BY MORNING
Classic
CHARLES H. SPURGEON

OBTAINING THE GRACE OF CHRIST
Classic
JOHN CALVIN

THE OVERCOMING LIFE
Classic
D.L. MOODY

THE PILGRIM'S PROGRESS
IN MODERN ENGLISH
Classic
JOHN BUNYAN

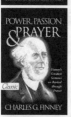
POWER, PASSION & PRAYER
Classic
CHARLES G. FINNEY

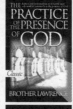
THE PRACTICE OF THE PRESENCE OF GOD
Classic
BROTHER LAWRENCE

SECRET POWER
Classic
D.L. MOODY

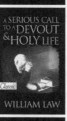
A SERIOUS CALL TO A DEVOUT & HOLY LIFE
Classic
WILLIAM LAW

THE SERMON ON THE MOUNT
Classic
JOHN WESLEY

SINNERS IN THE HANDS OF AN ANGRY GOD
Classic
JONATHAN EDWARDS

THE SOVEREIGNTY OF GOD
Classic
A.W. PINK

SPURGEON ON CHRIST
Classic
CHARLES H. SPURGEON

SPURGEON ON GOD
Classic
CHARLES SPURGEON

SPURGEON ON THE HOLY SPIRIT
Classic
CHARLES H. SPURGEON

SPURGEON ON PRAYER
HOW TO CONVERSE WITH GOD
Classic
CHARLES H. SPURGEON

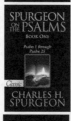
SPURGEON ON THE PSALMS
BOOK ONE
Psalm 1 through Psalm 25
Classic
CHARLES H. SPURGEON

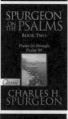
SPURGEON ON THE PSALMS
BOOK TWO
Psalm 26 through Psalm 90
Classic
CHARLES H. SPURGEON

TABLE TALK
MARTIN LUTHER
Classic

TORREY ON PRAYER
Classic
THE POWER OF PRAYER & THE PRAYER OF POWER

TOZER
Classic
FELLOWSHIP OF THE BURNING HEART

TOZER: MYSTERY OF THE HOLY SPIRIT
Classic
A.W. TOZER

WALKING WITH GOD
Classic
THE ANDREW MURRAY TRILOGY ON SANCTIFICATION

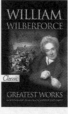
WILLIAM WILBERFORCE
Classic
GREATEST WORKS

WITH CHRIST IN THE SCHOOL OF PRAYER
Classic
ANDREW MURRAY